STUDIES IN CHINESE-WESTERN COMPARATIVE DRAMA

STUDIES IN CHINESE-WESTERN

COMPARATIVE
DRAMA

EDITED BY YUN-TONG LUK

The Chinese University Press

ISBN 962–201–451–8

THE CHINESE UNIVERSITY PRESS
The Chinese University of Hong Kong
SHATIN, N. T., HONG KONG

Printed in Hong Kong by Turbo Printing Co., Ltd.

Contents

Chinese-Western Comparative Drama in Perspective

Yun-tong Luk

The map for Chinese-Western comparative drama study can be charted out from the area pertaining to Chinese-Western comparative literature study. In other words, it may generally be assumed that methods and practices apropos the former study may not be dissimilar to those apropos the latter. Bearing in mind theatre's mediumistic exigencies, which call for special treatment and investigation, one could perhaps propose that Chinese-Western comparative study, as dramatic literature study, may well proceed with the following steps:

Influence Studies: This method has often centred on influences between Chinese and Western playwrights, reception and comparison of works, directing, acting system or theatre theories, Chinese and Western. Examples can be found in studies on Stanislavski's Method system on modern Chinese theatre or on the applicability of Stanislavski's Method in traditional Peking opera, the impact of Chinese style of acting on Bertolt Brecht's dramaturgy or even the latter's reverse influence on contemporary Chinese theatre, etc. Studies characterized by this method are quite numerous. They could cover as wide a range of contents as Eugene O'Neill and Taoism (*Chung-wai Literary Monthly*, Vol. 7, No. 7), Strindberg and his oriental outlook (*Chung-wai Literary Monthly*, Vol. 13, No. 6), Brecht's Epic Theatre and traditional Chinese theatre (*Ming Pao Monthly*, Feb. 1981), Ts'ao Yü and Chekhovian and O'Neillian influences (*Ming Pao Monthly*, Sept. 1969), etc., to name just but a few.

Parallel and Affinity Studies: Methods of study in this category mainly focus on the affinity between dramatic works which have no *rapports de fait* whatsoever, except stylistic, structural or ideological resemblances. These examples can consist in parallel study of plays, Chinese and European, such as *Romeo and Juliet* and *Chiao hung chi* 嬌紅記 (*Essays in*

Comparative Literature Studies. Tianjin: Nankai University Press, 1984), *Macbeth* and *Fa tzu tu* 伐子都 (*Tu shu*, 1986.5), *Hsi hsiang chi* 西廂記 and *Romeo and Juliet* (*Kwang Hua University Bi-monthly*, Vol. 4, Nos. 1 & 3, Oct./Nov. 1935), *Hamlet* and *Hu-tieh meng* 蝴蝶夢 (*Chung-wai Literary Monthly*, Vol. 4, No. 4), etc. All in all, these methods could cover the so-called "rapports exterieurs" as well as "rapports interieurs" between Chinese and Western dramatic works.

Genology Studies: Examples of this nature in general borrow Western generic concepts such as tragedy, comedy or melodrama to study Chinese dramatic works with a view to shedding some light on the structural, ideological and typological constructs of Chinese drama. Perhaps one of the earliest pioneer works is Ch'ien Chung-shu's 錢鍾書 article, "Tragedy in Old Chinese Drama" published in *T'ien hsia* 天下 magazine in 1935. More recent examples have run the gamut from Ku T'ian-hung's 古添洪 "*Tou O* as Tragedy" (*Chung-wai Literary Monthly*, Vol. 4, No. 8), Cheung Ping-cheung's 張秉祥 "*Tou O Yüan* as Tragedy" (*Chung-hsi pi-chiao wen-hsüeh lun chi*. Taipei: Shih Pao Book Series 203), Chang Han-liang's 張漢良 "Kuan Han Ching's *Tou O Yüan*: A Melodrama" (*Chung-wai Literary Monthly*, Vol. 4, No. 8), to Y. T. Luk's 陸潤棠 "Tragedy as Genre and Its Applicability in Chinese Drama" (*Literature Quarterly*, Vol. 24, Dec. 1982) and Chiao Teh-wen's 喬德文 "On the Differences between the Concept of Chinese Tragedy and the Concept of Western Tragedy" (*Hsi-chu i-shu*, Vol. I, 1982).

Though the three kinds of approach pertaining to Chinese-Western comparative drama can be subsumed in the general parameters of Chinese-Western comparative literature study, however, we need to pay attention to the fact that drama study has two sides of a coin, the other side being drama as theatre, which, as its mediumistic nature entails, has to be different from literature study after all, be it general or comparative. Besides, theatre study or analysis involves performance and performance has its most essential human dimension, which comes from actors acting their roles, i.e., their particular actorly artistry, systems of performance, and the playwright-director-audience triangle, all of which form a very complex and multi-level matrix of relationship. These are matters germane to the theatre as a means of expression, and require thus special methods and practices suitable to the theatre to body forth its expression. Hence, they should, in accord with its medium, transcend methods and practices pertaining to general and comparative literature study. It follows then that a viable and distinct methodology for the investigation and study of Chinese-Western comparative drama is in order, in addition to what has already been made available by Chinese-Western comparative literature study in general.

At this point in time, some initial steps have been taken. One has seen works addressing themselves to comparing the concept of theatre in China and the West, Grotowski's Poor Theatre and Chinese theatre, aesthetic ideals in the system of Brecht, Stanislavski and the Chinese theatre, etc. One cannot expect an instant methodology, least of all a poetics. Certainly, theoretical and methodological fruition needs time to come to being. In the future, comparative study on Chinese-Western drama and theatre will have to be armed with more genre and medium conscious methodology and practice, which will have been the convergent efforts of both theatre practitioners and scholars interested in the Chinese-Western comparative perspective. Presumably, these efforts will and should concern themselves with comparing the concept of theatre in China and the West, systems of performance as well as directing, uses of theatre language and space, audience response, etc. These efforts or endeavours should enhance the viability of Chinese-Western comparative drama as academic discipline, the research methods of which embrace yet transcend the scope of mere comparativism and nominal internationalism, with a view to eventually establishing a Chinese-Western comparative drama poetics.

In view of this aim, the present collection of essays is a modest step taken in that direction. It is, nevertheless, significant and important to note that this is the first collection of essays in English, devoted to Chinese-Western comparative drama. All of the articles were read at the Fourth Hong Kong International Comparative Literature Conference held in 17–21 August 1987 and sponsored by the Comparative Literature Research Unit of the English Department of The Chinese University of Hong Kong. The collection shows a wide range of topics of Chinese-Western comparative drama interest, and represents to a large extent the general concern and quality of the conference. Moreover, it reflects efforts by drama scholars and theatre practitioners in this rather new territory of research. By no means does this collection claim to be authoritative or presume to lay down guidelines or directives. However, it does hope to demonstrate some possibilities in the area of Chinese-Western comparative drama and serve important informative and inspirational purposes.

The present collection contains fourteen articles, which by their thematic and methodological nature can be arranged in five categories for discussion and review. The articles by Drs. Fong, Sato and Tam are concerned with the influence and reception of European drama in modern Chinese and Japanese drama. Dr. Fong's article, "Western Influence and the Rise of Modern Chinese Drama," offers an appropriate area of investigation for Chinese-Western comparative drama scholars, analyzing and comparing three modern Chinese plays, *The Greatest Event in Life* by Hu Shih, *Yama Chao* by Hung Shen and *Wang Chao-chün* by Kuo Mo-jo, with their respective Western prototypes, *A Doll's House* by Ibsen, *Emperor Jones* by O'Neill and *Salomé* by Oscar Wilde. Though with only three case studies, the article is a legitimate attempt at establishing *rapports de fait* between these three sets of plays, shedding light on certain issues about adaptation and indigenization. Perhaps, one may feel a little uneasy with the configurations to the rise of modern Chinese drama to be provided by three individual plays.

Compared with Fong's panoramic view of the rise of modern Chinese drama, Dr. Tam's "Drama of Dilemma: Waiting as Form and Motif in *The Bus-stop* and *Waiting for Godot*" is more specific in its thematic parallel approach, dwelling on the existential theme of waiting and the passage of time as main aspects of comparison; though distinguishing the Chinese play's social and political implications from the Western play's philosophical and religious concerns, Tam seems to have dwelt a bit too often on thematic parallelism and explication, and has to justify the first half of his title, "Waiting as Form" more, in addition to mentioning only in passing both plays share a circular structure. If there is another caveat one has to make, perhaps, it is his enthusiasm in analogizing the time parallels in both plays, which at times strikes one as a bit passionate for sameness.

Dr. Toshihiko Sato's article, "Ibsen's *The Lady from the Sea*, T'ien Han's *Return to the South*, and Satō Kōroku's *The Disabled Horse*: A Comparative Study," is what its title tries to suggest. Through textual analysis, Dr. Sato points out that the two Asian plays were written under the influence of Ibsen's romantic play, and that among them, there are enough parallels in dialogue, characterization and dramatic techniques to warrant a case of influence and reception. Reasonable as it sounds, Sato's article is informative, pointing out what has already been known generally, and could use more in-depth cultural and aesthetic analysis. The interesting aspect of Sato's article, however, lies in its intra-Asian comparative literature perspective, and raises a curious question: How do the Chinese and Japanese writers, in this case, T'ien Han and Satō Kōroku, differ or resemble each other in their cultural and literary adoption of Ibsen's ideas and dramaturgy, conditioned as they were by their own cultural, traditional, aesthetic and social milieu? This would seem a very crucial and enriching aspect to the reinforcement of a somewhat generalized comparison.

The second group of articles by Professors C. H. Wang, Han-liang Chang and Mr. Sai-shing Yung share a structural concern in their respective analyses. Professor Wang's article, "The Double Plot of *T'ao-hua shan*" is an analysis of the interrelationship between fiction and historicity embedded in a double plot, which dramatizes respectively the representation of a romantic love affair on the one hand, and the fall of the Ming empire on the other. This dual representation is interwined by the double plot structure in such a way, according to Professor Wang, that "it employs the emotions entailed by separation and union to depict feelings about the rise and fall." Though without expressly claiming to define the tragic theme or spirit of the play, his analysis of the double plot framework converges on what he describes as "theatrically moving and literarily powerful," which is just the tragic essence of this particular play.

More structuralist in argumentation, Professor Han-liang Chang's article, "Mimetic Desire/Dramatic Structure: Racine's *Phaedra* and Ma Chih-yüan's *Han-kung ch'iu*," begins with an elucidation of Rene Girard's triangular model of desire, mediator and vaniteur, and A. J. Griemas' actantial matrix of desire, communication and power; he follows in the second part with the application of these two models interchangeably to two dramatic texts widely separated in time and space as Racine's *Phaedra* and Ma Chih-yüan's *Han-kung ch'iu*. Professor Chang's objective is to point out relationships between desire and writing, verbal relations between characters in the dramatic discourse, or relationships between the playwright and his precursor. In the course of applying Girard and Griemas, he also makes reference to Freud's Eros and Thanatos, concerning the character analysis of Hippolytus and Khan Hu-yen of the two plays in question.

Mr. Sai-shing Yung's article, "*Tsa-chü* as a Lyrical Form," is a lucid account of the aesthetics of Yüan *tsa-chü* as being constituted by two structural elements, the narrative act and the lyrical act which govern the movement of events and the movement of mind respectively. Mr. Yung points out the significance of the actor-oriented system of Chinese theatre is attributed to centring the main character in the lyrical act, and thereby explains one of the most salient features of traditional Chinese theatre. Though Mr. Yung is traditional in his elucidation as a whole, he at times cross-refers to Russian formalism as well as semiotics to help clarify his argument.

The third group of articles by Miss Shu-chu Wei, Dr. Sheng-chuan Lai and Mr. William Hui-zhu Sun are more theatre-oriented in their analyses. Miss Wei's article, "English Renaissance Acting: With Reference to Peking Opera," is an application of Peking opera techniques to some of the Elizabethan plays, especially Shakespeare's, with the intention of "re-presenting" the Elizabethan acting style, an attempt inspired by Professor Leonard Pronko's application of Kabuki to the Elizabethan plays for the same purpose. Miss Wei points out the open stage, simplicity of properties, fluidity of location, imaginative participation of the audience as constituent points of parallels, taking examples from *Romeo and Juliet*, *A Midsummer Night's Dream*, *The Tempest*, *Dr. Faustus*, *Hamlet* and *King Lear*. Miss Wei's speculation is interesting and is not far-fetched as it may seem at first. In fact, what she is proposing is not an imposition of foreign model but an exposition of the salient features shared in general by all non-illusionistic theatres.

Dr. Sheng-chuan Lai's article, "The Structuring of Spontaneity: An Assessment and Documentaion of Improvisational Creative Methods in the Modern Taiwan Theatre," begins with a general background to the use of improvisation in the arts; then it moves on to detail the rise of improvisation in the decade from 1978 to 1987 in modern Taiwanese theatre, with a specific and personal illustration of the writer's own works. With an eye on the theatre, Dr. Lai states how he works with the method through a continual process of interaction between director and actors. According to him, the objective of this improvisational method is twofold: to experiment new forms of expression and to rebel against traditional forms and methods in Chinese theatre. Nevertheless, he acknowledges that such a rebellion eventually takes on certain characteristics of the traditional forms and method, and hence, he ends his articles not without some ambivalence, registering the feelings of how a die-hard tradition-conscious psyche grapples with the fact of assimilating Western methods and influence.

Mr. William Hui-zhu Sun's article, "Blurring Line between Stage and Life: 'Poor Theatre' in China," borrows more Grotowski's terminology than his concept of theatre to discuss the rural theatre in Ting Hsien of northern China between 1932 and 1936, led by Hsiung Fo-hsi 熊佛西 , one of the pioneers of modern Chinese theatre. Mr. Sun's article touches on a topic of theatrical interest, which surprisingly has seldom been heeded by scholars. Mr. Sun is to be credited with having called our attention to it.

However, Mr. Sun seems a bit so carried away with his Grotowskian parallel that he raises a few methodological loose ends. Speaking of the "poorness" of the pre-modern Chinese experimental theatre, led by Hsiung Fo-hsi, Mr. Sun suceeds in demonstrating the poorness of this theatre in its socio-economic sense, which is not exactly Grotowski's "back to the essentials" poorness, with its emphasis on actor-training and actor-audience relationships. Hsiung's theatre, though involving peasants and amateurs, may lend itself to be "poor" in view of its actor-audience proximity, being ritualistic and paratheatrical in nature; but it shows hardly any concern for rigorous training of actors.

The fourth group of articles is represented by two Shakespeare-related studies. Professor Mei-shu Hwang's article, "The Deaths of Cordelia and Tou O: Morality or Theatricality," does not purport to make a case of affinity study between *King Lear* and *Tou O yüan*. Instead, he attempts to use elements of their plots, i.e., the deaths of Cordelia and Tou O, more specifically, Tou O's three wishes and their eventual fulfilment, to show the playwright's choice between logical probability and theatrical effectiveness. Thus, it may not be necessary to cavil at the logic of their development as Hwang's argument seems to suggest, if the desired theatricality is to be realized. Hence, moral feelings about these two plays should be secondary to what Professor Hwang calls theatricality.

At first glance, Miss Louise S. W. Ho's article, "Shakespeare and Possibilities of Comparison: Notes on Ideas of Order," is strictly a Shakespearean study. However, it displays a possible analogy between the Elizabethan cosmic system and the Chinese counterpart as formalized in the Han dynasty: The five elements, the *Yin* and *Yang*, the trigrams or hexagrams of the *Book of Changes*. At one point, she offers to rewrite Shakespeare by using the imagery and ideas of Chinese cosmology, an idea resembling Miss Wei's re-presenting the Elizabethan acting with reference to Peking opera in an earlier article of this collection.

The fifth group of articles coverges on the theme of China and the Chinese in the perception of Europe and America. Professor A. Owen Aldridge's article, "The First Chinese Drama in English Translation," is informative about the diverse stage adaptations of the Yüan play, *Chao-shih ku-erh* (The Orphan of the House Chao), in the eighteenth-century Europe and specifically provides a clear exposé on the first Yüan play, *Laou-seng-urh*, ever to be translated in English by the pioneer British sinologist, John Francis Davis. In introducing this English translation of a Yüan play,

Professor Aldridge touches upon a very important issue, that is, what is the purpose of the translator? To "portray the taste and genius of another nation"? If one takes Davis' view, one cannot but query the peculiarity and exoticism with which the Europeans greeted this Chinese play, and that one may submit that their reactions provide clues more suited to the study of chinoiserie than of Chinese drama.

In connection with the eighteenth-century perception of China and Chinese drama in Europe, Professor Adrian Hsia's article, "*The Orphan of the House Chao* in French, English, German and Hong Kong Literature," makes a good sequel to the above article. While Professor Aldridge is concerned with the first Chinese drama in English translation, Professor Hsia is more concerned with the evolution and reception of the Yüan play, *The Orphan of the House Chao*, from its many versions in the hands of Joseph Henri Premare, J. B. Du Halde and Voltaire to the 1964 Hong Kong production by Mr. Li Chüeh-pen 黎覺奔 . According to Professor Hsia's analysis, the range of these adaptations is often determined by the different perception of China of the authors who adapted the play, a perception which is again determined by the individual temperament or preference as well as the collective consciousness of the society of the adaptors. The Europeanization or appropriation of the Chinese orphan/revenge motif provides a classic example of influence and reception in comparative literature studies, revealing more about cultural, social and aesthetic values of eighteenth-century Europe than China and Chinese drama, Professor Hsia's argument suggests. His inclusion of the 1964 Hong Kong production by Mr. Li Chüeh-pen which stresses the importance of *yi* (righteousness) and justice endows his analysis with a very timely relevance to Hong Kong readers, in view of 1997.

Like the preceding articles of Aldridge and Hsia, Professor Moy's "Bret Harte and Mark Twain's *Ah Sin*: Locating China in the Geography of the American West" is concerned with foreign perception or representation of China and the Chinese. However, instead of arguing against its subjectivism and distortion on an ethnic vantage point, he proceeds to deconstruct its my tification and hypocrisy in a Derrida fashion. In Bret Harte and Mark Twain's collaborated play, *Ah Sin*, opened in the Daly's Fifth Avenue Theatre of New York on 31 July 1877, he examines the dialectic struggle between the "popular" and the "literary" representation of the Chinese in nineteenth-century America. Not only does he demonstrate how the Chinese had fallen victim to the political, racial and imaginary stereotyping, but more importantly, through his deconstructive analysis, how the American effort or desire to represent the Chinese had ended ironically in creating a "presence of absence," a mirage or what Edward Said would call "Orientalism."

In sum, the fourteen articles in this collection synchronically represent a fair variety of approaches, covering influence and affinity studies, genological and structural studies, theatre and Shakespeare studies, translation and adaptation studies; diachronically, they span from the classical to the modern periods of Chinese and Western dramatic literature. It is hoped that these articles not only provide a rich and varied complex of dramatic experiences but also open up new vistas of possibilities thematically and methodologically for the future study of Chinese-Western comparative drama as a discipline. If this collection could ever be recognized as having moved a step or two closer to the eventual emergence of a Chinese-Western comparative drama poetics, in spite of its variety and plurality, it would have at least staked a small claim to its share of contribution in the field.

1. Western Influence and the Rise of Modern Chinese Drama

Gilbert C. F. Fong

The rise of modern Chinese drama has to be seen in the wider context of the Literary Revolution. The proponents of new drama, such as Li Ta-chao 李大釗 , Ch'en Tu-hsiu 陳獨秀 , Hu Shih 胡適 , Ch'ien Hsüan-t'ung 錢玄同 , were the same intellectuals who advocated the creation of a new literature of realism and social criticism. They refuted the old idea of "literature to convey the *Tao* 道 " (of Confucianism), but they also propagated their own *Tao* of reformism and revolution, and looked upon drama as a didactic means in the "new wave of thought." In 1904, Ch'en Tu-hsiu already equated the reform of society with the reform of drama.[1] And it was no accident that the first performance of the new "spoken drama" (*hua-chü* 話劇), staged by a group of overseas Chinese students in Tokyo in 1907, was an adaptation of Harriet Beecher Stowe's novel *Uncle Tom's Cabin*, a story about the oppression of the black slaves in America. The Evolution Society (*Chin-hua t'uan* 進化團), a famous drama troupe around the time of the 1911 revolution, propagated revolutionary ideology and actively supported the new Republic. The promotion of drama as the means of social and political reform culminated in the manifesto of the Popular Drama Society (Min-chung hsi-chü-she 民眾戲劇社) in 1921:

> Bernard Shaw once said: "The theatre is a place for propagating ideas." This is not necessarily so, but at least we can say this much; the time is past when people took theatre-going as (mere) recreation. The theatre occupies an important place in modern society. It is an X-ray searching out the root of society's maladies. It is also a just and impartial mirror, and the standards of everybody in the nation are stripped stark naked when reflected in this great mirror, that allows no slightest thing to remain invisible.... This kind of theatre is precisely what does not exist in China at present, but it is what we, feeble though we are, want to strive to create.[2]

The Popular Drama Society was part of the movement to dissociate

hua-chü from the commercialized "civilized plays" (*wen-ming-hsi* 文明戲)
which regarded drama as a recreational pastime. At the same time, the stylized acting in classical drama was also under attack. Cheng Chen-tuo 鄭振
鐸 argued for a new and "reasonable" drama. By associating newness with
reasonableness, he implicitly attacked the old drama for its implausible representation of life, the detachment from reality which minimized its useful-
ness to social criticism. And Ch'ien Hsüan-t'ung advocated that "If China
were to have 'real' drama, it must naturally be Westernized drama, not the
drama of the school of painted faces. If we do not totally reject the actors
who do not act like human beings, and the dialogues which do not sound
like dialogues, how can we promote 'real' drama?"[3] The thrust of the arguments was the repudiation of non-reality in favour of representationalism
and the realistic dramatization of life.

As the key concepts of reality and social concerns were found to be lacking in classical drama, the logical choice for the foreign-educated writers
was to look for guidance and inspiration from the West. T'ien Han 田漢
once pointed out that the spoken dialogues and realistic movements, scene
division, realistic make-up, costumes, setting, and lighting, and the depiction of the struggles in contemporary life were direct imports from the West
together with capitalistic culture.[4] The question arose of how to view translations. Contemporary opinions concluded that literal translations, without
changes and alterations to suit the Chinese cultural and social background,
greatly reduced accessibility, and therefore were unacceptable as performance texts, valuable only as models for playwriting.[5] Other critics called
for original creations and the adaptation of Western plays to suit the conditions of the Chinese theatre. Wang Chung-hsien 汪仲賢 argued for drastic
"tailoring" in adapting Western drama. "As long as the original idea is pre-
served, superfluous scenes should be deleted, and amplifications should be
made to clear up obscurities. In the most extreme cases, even a whole act
can be added or omitted without hesitation."[6]

Whether translation, original creation or adaptation, Western drama was
revered as the paragon of producing new drama. Here the dramatist's role
as both initiator and interpreter was an important one, as he had to encode
his Western-inspired products to suit his audience. And as the early dramatists were also the intellectuals closely identified with the New Culture
Movement, they were overtly concerned with the ideological message in
their plays. The important factor in the understanding of Western influence
thus lies not in the professed acceptance or imitations of Western realism,

naturalism, romanticism, expressionism, or any other "isms" used as catch-phrases in the May Fourth period, but in the process of adaptation, i.e., how Western plays were understood and Sinicized for the purpose of enlightenment and reform.

In this paper, we have chosen three early plays for analysis. Hu Shih's *The Greatest Event in Life* (*Chung-shen ta-shih*) 終身大事 inherits the basic dramatic situation in Ibsen's *A Doll's House*; Hung Shen's 洪深 *Yama Chao* (*Chao yen-wang* 趙閻王) adopts the story in Eugene O'Neill's *The Emperor Jones*; and Kuo Mo-jo's 郭沫若 *Wang Chao-chün* 王昭君 is interesting in that it attempts to re-evaluate a popular classical Chinese story and incorporates the finale of Oscar Wilde's *Salomé* for its ending. Our emphasis is not on the similarities of the plot but on the changes, the omissions and amplifications, and the difference in their meaning-generating functions.

The Greatest Event in Life and A Doll's House

The first Chinese translation of Henrik Ibsen's *A Doll's House* appeared in a special "Ibsen number" of *Hsin ch'ing-nien* (New Youth 新青年) in June 1918. Entitled *Nuola* 娜拉 (Nora), the translation was collaborated on by Hu Shih and Luo Chia-lun 羅家倫 . Since then, an Ibsenite cult emerged in China, and the Nora syndrome and its variations became the favorite subject matter in modern Chinese literature. The issue of women's rights, or feminism, was adopted not so much because it was a genuine concern but because women, after centuries of being dominated by a patriarchal society, were the most apt symbol as the victim of feudalistic morality. And the voluntary submission of women to male domination, as dictated by the teachings of Confucianism, also underscored the urgent need for their awakening. As Nora was upheld as the model of courageous rebellion, didacticism went hand in hand with iconoclasm.

To Hu Shih, Ibsenism was a social rather than literary phenomenon. It was the exposure of the degeneracy and corruption in the family system and society and the awakening of the people to the adverse reality which inevitably led to revolution and reform. In a 1918 article entitled "Ibsenism" (Yi-pu-sheng chu-yi 易卜生主義), Hu Shih vehemently attacks the old society with examples drawn primarily from Ibsen's social plays such as *A Doll's House* and *An Enemy of the People*. The family system, he argues, is infested by the diseases of egotism, hypocrisy, subservience, and coward-ice; the legal system has been dehumanized; religion has been converted into a money-making enterprise; and morality, which frowns upon individ-uality, is no more than obsolete conventions.[7] Noticeably absent from the article is any discussion of Ibsen's dramaturgy, and the father of modern European drama is considered not as an artist, but as a social thinker arguing his point with visual images on the stage.

The assimilation of literature with ideology and the super-imposition of the Western worldview onto the Chinese scene were typical of the May Fourth mentality. It was not that Hu Shih was ignorant of Ibsen's dramatic art: the social and political conditions, as interpreted by the intellectuals themselves, forced upon them a utilitarian view of literature. And drama, because of its accessibility as a public medium, could more easily propagate didactic messages than fiction, poetry or other literary genres. In 1919, Hu Shih published the one-act play *The Greatest Event in Life*, which incorpo-rates all the ideas discussed in his article on Ibsenism. The plot is vintage Nora: the heroine decides to run away from home because her parents re-fuse to sanction her marriage with her beloved. Elopement is a common-place and universal subject-matter. In *The Greatest Event in Life*, the elopement motif is given a new twist: the heroine is motivated less by ro-mantic sentiment than by her desire to assert her individuality. Her note to her parents reads: "This [marriage] is the greatest event in your daughter's life. Your daughter ought to make a decision for herself."[8] Her action is a rebellion against her parents' wishes and her duties as a daughter, a procla-mation of her rights to make up her own mind. The absence of love essentially changes the complexion of the play into a social problem drama. Nora in *A Doll's House* also rejects the notion of love for the "duties of myself":[9]

> I believe that before all else I am a reasonable human being, just as you [Helmer] are—or, at all events, that I must try and become one ... but I can no longer content myself with what most people say, or what is found in books. I must think over things for myself and get to understand them.[10]

To Nora, being a person is given higher priority than her duties as wife and mother. Both Nora and T'ien Ya-mei 田亞梅 challenge the stereotyping of women and their social obligations, which for women's own social needs, have proven to be violations of their selfhood.

Despite T'ien Ya-mei's Ibsenite proclamation, which remains seminal in the play's meaning, "The Greatest Event in Life" falls short of the radicalism in *A Doll's House*. In the last scene, Nora confronts her husband Helmer with the declaration of her independence, a slap on the face of conventional morality which has been the covert persecutor of her selfhood and to which he expediently subscribes. Instead of this frontal attack on society, T'ien Ya-mei chooses to sneak away and leave a brief explanatory note. Here, Hu Shih adopts a less radical position than in his article on Ibsenism. He steers clear of the total condemnation of traditional morality by attacking the system but sparing its representatives. T'ien Ya-mei's mother is a traditional woman, loving, caring, concerned about her daughter's welfare, and eager to cater to her husband's every whim. She is portrayed comically, a caricature of the ignorant woman who clings to superstition to direct the course of her life. Her encounter with the blind fortune-teller borders upon the farcical and sets the comical tone of the play. The father, Mr. T'ien, is the most interesting character in the play. His reversal of attitude provides suspense to the otherwise simplistic plot. He chastises his wife's superstitious beliefs and forbids her to consult fortune-telling, but his liberalism also belies his patriarchal authoritarianism and stubborn adherence to the "clan shrine law," insisting that he "will not for the sake of your [T'ien Ya-mei's] marriage suffer the ridicule and scorn of our clan elders."[11] Mr. and Mrs. T'ien are not the orges of tyrannical parents, only the unwitting antagonists, the obstacles blocking the heroine's goal. In Ibsen's play, Helmer is a duplicitous villain. He is apparently a successful provider and an ardent husband, but his love for Nora is infuriating in its condescension: "But no man would sacrifice his honour for the one he loves."[12] Egotism and self-preservation lead to his demeaning treatment of Nora as a mere plaything, a doll-wife. Clearly his is the case of what is wrong in a male-dominated society whose double standards have been Nora's covert persecutor. Hu Shih's play demonstrates to a great extent the tolerance towards the absurd and the abnormal typical of satirical comedy, and has the effect of insulting the targets from a direct attack and lessening the dramatic impact of its predecessor.

Towards the end, *The Greatest Event in Life* regains its posture of a problem play. T'ien Ya-mei's departure, however, is not without hesitation: she looks back and pauses. Despite her earlier demonstration of childish petulance, her assertion of independence, signified by the disowning of her family, is apparently effective. Mrs. T'ien is stunned, and Mr. T'ien "looks back with a wide-eyed, helpless look of hesitation and uncertainty."[13] The new morality has claimed T'ien Ya-mei and has taken her under its wings; even though her maturity and reasoning remain a question mark, the ending nevertheless is a happy one. In a similar manner, one can argue back and forth whether Nora has made a wise decision and if she has the certainty of being right. She does not storm out of the door in celebration of emancipated womanhood. She walks out in self-disgust, with the realization that her secret pride and joy (forging her father's signature for a loan to save her husband) has turned into her nemesis, and that in the eyes of her husband, she has become a criminal and his ruin. Along with the social conventions she has been espousing, her world is shattered into pieces. Disillusionment and discovery are the essential qualities which bestow on Nora the status of a tragic heroine. (Ibsen referred to his play as a "modern tragedy.") Importantly, her gradual understanding of her plight parallels her growing awareness of her selfhood. With T'ien Ya-mei, our judgement of her inner strength is hampered by the sketchy and "flat" characterization. Rather than a self-discovery, her conviction is forced upon her by the disappointment in her parents' intransigence, and especially by her fiancé's encouragement to "make your own decisions."[14] Unlike Nora's departure, hers is induced by external forces and points to the search for a social meaning for her action. *A Doll's House* can be read on two levels, as the conflict between society and the individual, and as the development of selfhood within the individual. In disregarding the inner growth of his heroine, Hu Shih has chosen the route of social criticism.

The Greatest Event in Life is the dramatization of Hu Shih's understanding of *A Doll's House* as a social problem play. The rather detailed and realistic description of the setting, which was new to Chinese drama, signifies the treatment of the play as a clash of ideas:

> The walls are hung with scrolls of Chinese paintings and calligraphy, along with two Dutch-style landscape paintings. The East-meets-West arrangement on the walls strongly indicates an atmosphere of a family in transition from tradition to the modern age.[15]

The setting is metonymic in that the properties set the stage for the conflict between "tradition" and "the modern age," the old and new ideologies. Mrs. T'ien's laughable dependence on superstition (what Hu Shih considers old "religion") and Mr. T'ien's insistence on Confucianism and the old clan system combine forces to repudiate the newly found freedom represented by the Westernized Mr. Ch'en. The heroine is caught in the middle of this tug of war. In the May Fourth context, the battle is that of superstition and "science" (Mr. Ch'en's automobile is a symbol of scientific advancement), authoritarianism and "democracy." The interpersonal factors are dismissed from playing any role in the conflict, as Mr. Ch'en, being rich and a "very dependable person"[16] is an acceptable, even desirable son-in-law. The play is thus not about characters, but the conflict of ideologies personified by the characters. That T'ien Ya-mei happens to be a woman is incidental, as womanhood is the backdrop for the assertion and affirmation of individualism. In the process, the Nora story is reduced to a problem play of social polemics.

Yama Chao and *The Emperor Jones*

Hung Shen's *Yama Chao* (1922) follows closely the story of Eugene O'Neill's *The Emperor Jones*, adopting its scene divisions, motifs, and technical devices.[17] However, the adaptation process is more than a mere transference of the plot to a Chinese setting and the change into Chinese names. To Hung Shen, drama is correlated with its age and reflects its contemporary environment. He insists that:

> The dramatist has a great responsibility on his shoulders. He first starts with his own experiences and observations on life. After a process of selection, he dramatizes them into meaningful and interesting stories on the stage in the manner of everyday living (the subjects usually concern clothing, food, and shelter). The audience, excited and delighted by their deep impressions of the plays, will then be able to contemplate the meanings, so that their intelligence and sense of beauty are enhanced. Drama thus directly improves their mind and indirectly reforms humanity.[18]

His concerns are fundamentally audience-oriented: drama should serve the dual functions of "instruction and delight," and in order to be more effective in these two functions, it should be readily comprehensible and acceptable ("in the manner of everyday living"). This utilitarian view of drama provides the proper perspective for our analysis of his adaptation of *The Emperor Jones*. The pragmatics of message transmitting is tied in with audience acceptance, and realism becomes the guideline in the encoding processes of rewriting and performance.

The main action of both plays evolves around the pursuit of the hero in a dark forest. But the significance lies beyond the superficial narrative. Brutus Jones's journey is a personal quest for identity in a recognition of his self-betrayal (thus his name Brutus). On his way to become emperor, Jones has rejected his black culture and heritage, having taken on the white man's violence, greed and trickery, and ironically—as the white man's reckless way of values are corruptible, and he has sold his soul for material posses-sion—his rise in social status represents a moral decline.[19] His visions are encounters with the past "sins" of his personal consciousness (the Little Formless Fears, the killing of the dice-throwing Jeff, and the murder of the white prison guard) and of his collective consciousness (the slave auction, the slave boat, and the witch doctor and crocodile). The flight into the forest is metaphorically not a flight from the natives but the discovery of funda-mental self which is ineluctable and from which his arrogant majestic ways and self-image have for so long alienated him. The movement into the for-est symbolizes self-understanding: as piece by piece his "emperor's" cloth-ing is ripped from his back, he strips away the veneers making up his mask, until at the end he must in nakedness confront the historical destiny of his own race and ultimately of his self.[20]

The vision scenes are arranged to trace the distant past of the history of the hero. The sequence arranged in temporal displacement is an attempt to reproduce the haphazard recall of memory in his inward journey, his psy-chological jungle, so to speak. With *Yama Chao*, the temporal sequence of the visions follows an orderly time inversion pattern, designed to probe into the causes and progress of Chao Ta's corruption, and the scheme clearly outlines the progression from personal experiences to the events of national significance and their correlation. A reconstruction of the scenes in their chronological order shows an obvious causal relationship among them. Scene 8 refers to the Boxer Rebellion in 1900 and the domination of the for-eign powers over China. The effect of foreign oppression of the Chinese people is shown in Scene 7 (set in the same year), as a foreign missionary and his lackey (Wang the Tiger) rob Chao Ta of his land and livelihood and are also responsible for the deaths of his wife and his mother. Chao Ta is also persecuted in the hands of a corrupt government (in Scene 6, 1905), being wrongfully convicted of murder by a magistrate who tortures the witnesses into false accusation. At this point, Chao Ta the common peasant, who aspires only to lead a simple life, is at the end of his tether. As he suf-fers from homelessness and a broken family, he is forced into exile and enlists himself in the warlord's army. Scene 5 (1915) describes how he and his unscrupulous comrades commit the crimes of rape, slaughtering the innocent, and laying waste to their homes. The mould of Chao Tao becoming the feared and ruthless Yama Chao is cast, and he throws himself into one misdeed after another. He commits perjury for personal revenge (Scene 4, 1916) and buries alive his wounded fellow-soldier to steal his money (Scene 3, 1922). The corruption of Chao Ta is thus complete. However, he is by nature a "good" person who is not totally indifferent to his own wrongdoings. As Lao Li says of him at the end,

> You! Your heart was too bad for you to be a good man, and too good for you to be a bad one. But good or bad, you weren't at home being either. I watched you running helter-skelter. Wherever you went, you found trouble. In your whole life, you never had a single good day.[21]

Chao Ta has no control over his own life; his passivity places him squarely at the mercy of society. His visions puts forth the rather naturalistic determinism that environment shapes the fate of the individual, or as Hong Shen explains: "No one is born to be good or bad. Both good and bad people are only the products of their environment."[22]

Both plays evolve around the relationship between individual and the collective for their effectiveness. In *The Emperor Jones*, the focal point is the self, defined by its inherent kinship in the larger community. Once the definition is completed and the search for identity becomes successful, the heroic Jones is carried away by the natives, the members of his own race, metaphorically in celebration "in the 'eight o' style."[23] *Yama Chao* highlights the collective and its pitfalls, which are underscored by the sufferings inflicted by it upon the individual. At the end of the play, Lao Li steals Chao Ta's money and prays to the soul of his dead comrade to protect him. The dawn breaks as the marches into the forest, another Yama Chao in the making. The implication of a vicious cycle is clear, that as long as injustice and corruption are allowed to persist in society, they will continue to force the honest and the innocent onto the path to ruin, perpetrating more injustice and corruption. It would not be inappropriate to regard *Yama Chao* as a study of the hero's environment, as the play turns out to be an outcry against the debilitating woes leading to the decline of modern China as a nation. Therein lies the main difference between *The Emperor Jones* and *Yama Chao*: one launches into an intensive examination of the personal psyche, and the other proceeds to depict the external, pointing to an unequivocal condemnation of social and political evils.

The difference in focus translates itself into the divergent stage settings and styles of presentation. Both plays start and end with scenes presented on the conscious level in the present, and the intervening scenes set in the forest are played out in the hero's deranged imagination which takes him further back into the past. In *The Emperor Jones*, reality is distorted when filtered through Jones' consciousness, and the expressionistic techniques effectively present the vision scenes as a psychic phenomenon. The lighting ranges from the blazing afternoon sunlight in Scene 1 when Jones is confident and proud, to the darkness of fear, and to the moonlight "merged into a veil of bluish mist" in Scene 7, signifying hauntedness and death. The interplay of sound and silence of the shrill cries and the dumb show, and the growing sound of the tom-tom punctuated by the revolver shots, in combination convey the intensification of Jones' fear and the assimilation and uncertainty of reality and hallucinatory vision. *Yama Chao*, on the other hand, concentrates on the physical and the concrete to get its point across. The setting is more direct and indexical, demonstrating the cause and effect. Some of the technical devices such as the moonlight and the drumbeat are retained, but they are conceived as referents to reality, or their symbolic values are reduced to atmospherics.

The Emperor Jones' dependence on the expressionistic setting as a meaning-generating mechanism is evident in Scene 1:

> The audience chamber in the palace of the Emperor—a spacious, high-ceilinged room with bare, white-washed walls. The floor is of white tiles. In the rear, to the left of centre, a wide archway giving out on a portico with white pillars....[24]

The colour is conspicuously and predominantly white. As the black hero emerges, the colour symbolism takes on a racial as well as a moral significance, pointing to the denial of his own blackness. The whiteness of the audience chamber, which at first appears factual, turns out to be substitutive, revealing Jones' longing for purity and his lack of it.[25]

> The room is bare of furniture with the exception of one huge chair made of uncut wood which stands at centre, its back to rear. This is very apparently the Emperor's throne. It is painted a dazzling, eye-smiting scarlet.[26]

The huge thorn highlighted at centre stage underlines Jones' delusion of grandeur—the uncut wood, of which the throne is made, has been uprooted from the "black" forest where it should belong. There is in the air "an oppressive burden of exhausting heat,"[27] making "the palace like a 'bleeding' tomb."[28] Jones is spiritually dead in his own palace, and his flight into the forest is a quest for life; the quest concludes at a gigantic "sacred tree," alongside which is a boulder-like altar where he is to be sacrificed in an expiation of his sins. The irony is that in living he clings to the dead (the tree-stump throne) and in death he regains life (the living tree). The setting thus provides the dynamics of the symbolic signification of the main action, which moves from non-recognition to knowledge, and from living to death and to rebirth.

The Emperor Jones relies on symbolism for its effectiveness. In a play which depicts as its subject-matter an interior landscape, the supernaturalistic symbols are fitting devices in a refutation of external reality. *Yama Chao*, with a keen eye on social problems, cannot afford such excursions from the real world.

> The scene is the bedroom of the Battalion Commander. Against the rear wall on the extreme left is a metal, military folding cot, and on it a white wolfskin rug with a Western style pillow and a pink silk comforter on top. Against the left wall is a low dresser with an attached mirror above and storage for clothes below. Piled in a disorderly heap on top are a pistol, an army sword, a military hat and unbuckled belt which have been casually tossed there, plus a face- powder compact perfumed soap, a mirrored case, and a perfume bottle....[29]

Hung Shen spares no pains to furnish the stage with realistic properties, and the detail leaves no doubt as to their denotation of society and its squalor. The attempt to incorporate life with art is clearly evident even in the vision scenes:

> The scene is the place where the road ends. Ahead is a forest of large trees which screen the sky and block off the ground. The forest is thick with interconnected vines forming a vague black mass.... Outside of the forest are several straight old trees and piles of squat, rough rocks, all evil-looking. The night has become deeper. A tiny bit of starlight shines on the frozen ground. The cold is bone-chilling....[30]

The darkness, the bone-chilling cold, and the evil-looking rocks make up the background of an adverse surrounding in which the woeful past is evoked. The setting is extroversive, signifying a massive social determinant dictating the fate of the hero, something over which he has little or no control. Documentation of social conditions is the least of interests in *The Emperor Jones*, where the setting is introversive. It is viewed as metaphorical or metonymic, and depends on the correlative between the hero and his surroundings for its effects.[31] Whereas the times of the vision scenes in *The Emperor Jones* are unspecific, conveying the "contemplative stasis"[32] of a mental phenomenon, their counterparts in *Yama Chao* are given actual dates and sometimes the exact locale (e.g. Ch'ang-hsin-tien 長辛店 , Nanking 南京), pointing to historical events. The time dimension is closely contrived, and chronology becomes the major factor in the structure of causality. This is also an authentication process, an attempt to heighten the topicality and to shorten the aesthetic distance between stage and society, and thus the thematic relevance.

In *The Emperor Jones*, stage presentation is characterized by stylized movements. This is particularly evident in the vision scenes. The Little Formless Fears are "black, shapeless, only their glittering little eyes can be seen.... They move noiselessly but with deliberate, painful effort, striving to raise themselves on end, failing and sinking prone again."[33] The dice-throwing Jeff, the prisoners, the slaves, and the witch doctor all conduct themselves in a "rigid, slow, and mechanical" manner with rhythmic "unreal and marionettish" movements. The juxtaposition and interaction of Jones and these expressionistic "haunts" obfuscate the line between appearance and reality and indicates Jones's spiritual flaw, his inability to distinguish between the two. Such dichotomy is not a concern in *Yama Chao*, where appearance and reality are fused in the revelation of Chao Ta's guilt and fear of retribution. The hallucinatory figures are presented as ghostly apparitions, which to the Chinese audience are concrete and actual entities. As referents to reality, their appearances remain more on the level of conscious experience. Scene 8 is a good example of this conversion of the symbol to the index. Here Chao Ta goes into a trance and performs a ritualistic dance to the hounding drumbeat. In the background is a group of men "dressed in tatters; they look like beggars"[34]—symptomatic of the squalid poverty due to the country's decline. There are banners proclaiming "Support the Ch'ing and Destroy the Foreigners" and "Kill the Big Hairy Barbarians,"[35] which point to the shame and disaster of the Boxer Rebellion. The Boxers' rites signify Chao Ta's physical and mental collapse, a ritualistic showing of the hatred against foreign oppression with which the hero associates his own persecution, thus identifying the cause of his personal misfortune with the worsening destiny of the nation.

The key concepts in *Yama Chao* are realism and social criticism. In 1928, Hung Shen claimed that the play was "taken straight from life, based on my own experience and observation, and charged with genuine feelings.... The theater should serve mankind, should voice the sorrow of man." The story, he continued, was inspired by a conversation he overheard on the train, describing how the soldiers buried their wounded enemies alive to rob their money during the war among the warlords. "I thought of all the crimes committed by the Northern warlords and their soldiers. This aroused my sympathy towards the victimized masses, and even towards the soldiers who perpetrated the crimes."[36] His compassion for the downtrodden found an ally in O'Neill's *The Emperor Jones*, which describes the exploitation of the black prisoners by the white guard, and the auction of black slaves uprooted from their African homeland. The insistence on the validity of the social theme,[37] however, necessitates a realistic presentation on a more empirical level.

Insofar as *Yama Chao* adopts the story of *The Emperor Jones*, both plays depict the spiritual and physical downfall of the hero, and the structures follow a similar pattern of past recollections pointing towards their judgement. (Yama, *yen-wang* in Chinese, is the king of Hades who hands down judgements on the dead. Ironically, Chao Ta is the judged rather than the judging.) In the O'Neill play, the judgement is a personal one, with its terms of reference the individual consciousness as an inseparable part of the totality of the collective conscious (the unfolding of the true identity behind the majestic mask). The hero's relationship with society at large is at best tenuous; society, even when it matters, remains on the peripheral. *Yama Chao* treats as its starting point the examination of the relationship between the individual and the collective in light of society's persecution of the individual, forcing the latter into immorality despite his good conscience. In its refusal to imitate external reality, *The Emperor Jones* turns towards the soul to "capture its movement in the prearticulate purity" in an effort to abstract from reality. *Yama Chao* is a less metaphysical treatment of the story, attempting to modify the expressionistic disjointed syntax for a more coherent and true-to-life presentation. The urge of the irrational and the visionary is suppressed to depict reality in a detailed manner, portraying human miseries in no uncertain terms within the context of social inequities.

Wang Chao-chün, *Autumn in Han Palace*, and *Salomé*

There is no other country in the world like China which has been controlling women, harrying women, and discriminating against women to such a degree. Because of the moral code of the three obediences: obey your father at home, obey your husband in matrimony, and obey your son after your husband's death, women's lives have been wasted away. If we are to save China, we have to totally liberate women, and if we are to liberate women, should we not advo- cate the morality of "the three disobediences" in opposition to "the three obediences"?[38]

These are the fiery words on the status of women expressed by Kuo Mo-jo in his postscript to *Three Rebellious Women (San-ke p'an-ni-de nü-hsing* 三個叛逆的女性), a trilogy of short plays consisting of *Cho Wen-chün* 卓文君 (1923), *Wang Chao-chün* 王昭君 (1923), and *Nieh Ying* 聶嫈 (1925). In the context of the fervent iconoclasm of May Fourth reformism, *Wang Chao-chün* is a deliberate attempt to "reverse the verdict" (*fan-an* 翻案) on an historical figure. Intertextuality therefore looms large as the dominant factor from which the impact and the shocking value of the play are derived.

As a historical figure, in the popular imagination, Wang Chao-chün has been lavished with praise and sympathy for her plight. The beautiful palace lady, who sacrificed her own happiness to marry a barbarian king, has been the favourite subject of many stories down the ages. The famous Yüan drama *Autumn in Han Palace (Han-kung ch'iu)* written by Ma Chi-yüan 馬致遠 is representative of the traditional perception of the heroic and vir- tuous Wang Chao-chün and is largely responsible for the making of her legend. The play is a romantic story of the trials and triumphs of love, cap- italizing on the sorrows of separation and death for its emotional impact. Wang Chao-chün is a paragon of filial piety and a dutiful wife in the royal household. Right to the end, she carries herself with the dignity that exem- plifies noble Confucian womanhood. She never blames others for her or- deal and in a typical Chinese fashion, she find solace by resigning her sufferings to fate: "An ill fate befalls all those born fair; the fault is not the world's but theirs."[39]

Kuo Mo-jo commented that in his *Wang Chao-chün* he has remade the tragedy of fate into a tragedy of character through the emphasis on the heroine's iron-clad will.[40] Unlike the demure and submissive beauty in the Yüan drama, the modern Wang Chao-chün is charged with defiance and self-righteousness bordering on excess. She is unyielding in her refusal to be victimized by sexual slavery as Emperor Yüan's plaything, and chal- lenges the rights of the supreme power of the monarch, which usually dete- riorates into despotism at the expense of human dignity.

You [the Emperor] have the power to let people live or die. If today you don't like me, you can send me into exile, or if you like me tomorrow, you can use me to satisfy your lustful appetite, and order those women you find wanting into exile. Do you know the private sufferings of the women tortured by your sexual abuses? Who are you that you can rule over thousands and be so unscrupulous?[41]

Wang Chao-chün never minces her words. Uncompromising even when pushed into a corner, she retaliates by running away to the desert and offering herself to the barbarian king, depriving Emperor Yüan of his sexual gratification. Her self-imposed exile, a reversal of the tearful farewell in the Yüan drama, is not motivated by love or by patriotism; it is a triumphant exit, an expression of her free will which sends shock waves through feudalistic morality. At this time she willingly abandons everything, and the wish for self-destruction is her vindication.

> Now I have nothing. I feel neither happiness nor pain. Oh, all I have left is my body. I wish to have it scorched on red-hot sand, or let it be torn apart in the jaws of the ruthless wolves. Only if I could have my heart gnashed and gnawed to pieces by the white teeth of the wolves, or my eyes pecked away by the wild ravens, and tossed away in the cold on an island in the northern sea, perhaps then I could feel some pain, or even some pleasure.[42]

The repressed rage is total repudiation of society's corrupted values, an impassioned urge which mixes revenge with defiance and rebellion. Kuo Mo-jo finds unacceptable the Confucian contentedness of the heroine in the Yüan drama; in his judgement, Wang Chao-chün represents the "rebellious" woman intent on shattering the myths of patriarchal morality, in other words, a modern-day Nora in a historical setting.

> For thousands of years, women have been harried spiritually and now it is time for them to be awakened. When they are awakened, it is natural that they should demand their rights as human beings and the absolute equality between men and women.[43]

Whereas the Yüan drama celebrates effacement of the self for the common good, the modern play extols the individualism of the newly awakened woman. Wang Chao-chün's fight against the authoritarian Emperor Yüan, insists Kuo Mo-jo, represents a daring challenge of the revered moral code of obeying one's husband.[44]

Autumn in Han Palace is dominated by the presence of Emperor Yüan. (He is given the singing role.) His emotions, ranging from joy at the discovery of Wang Chao-chün's beauty to rage and fury for his own helplessness, and finally to heart-rending sorrow for his love's loss, constitute the play's structural framework. As Emperor, he is incompetent, but as lover, his devotion and helplessness evoke our sympathy. In *Wang Chao-chün*, Emperor Yüan becomes the perpetrator of evils, a manipulator of emotions and a hypocrite who disguises himself as a humane ruler. Emperor Yüan in *Autumn in Han Palace* executes the treasonous Mao Yen-shou 毛延壽 to avenge the death of his beloved and to show that justice is properly served. In the modern play, he offers Mao Yen-shou's head to Wang Chao-chün to procure her sexual capitulation. The final scene reveals the true face of the depraved Emperor:

> Emperor Yüan: Alas! Khan Huhanyeh of the Huns, your are really the favorite son of Heaven!... (*He puts Mao Yen-shou's head on the railing of the bridge and unrolls the picture of Wang Chao-chün in admiration. Then he turns to Mao Yen-shou's head.*) Yen-shou, my old friend, you are the more fortunate after all! You painted the pictures of beautiful women and your name will be immortalized. You are dead, but your face has been slapped by a beautiful woman. Oh, you are much more fortunate than I. (*He puts down the picture and holds up the head.*) Oh, Yen-shou, my old friend! She slapped you, was it on the left cheek, or the right one? Her sweet fragrance still lingers on your face. Let me share it a little! (*Repeatedly he kisses both cheeks.*) Oh! Your eyes, they are staring at me. You cursed that I would die and go with you within this year. But I have lost my will to live. Yen-shou, why don't you stay with me at Yeh-ting palace for one more year. (*He puts down the head and rolls up the picture.*) I want to hang the picture of this beauty on the wall and place your head on my desk. I swear I'll never leave this place, Yen-shou. Follow me to Yeh-ting palace. (*He puts the picture under his arm, holds the head in his hands and kisses the cheeks repeatedly as he walks towards Yeh-ting palace.*)[45]

The metamorphosis of a sentimental lover to a sexual pervert is a reflection of the zealous iconoclasm typical of the early Kuo Mo-jo. In his hands, Emperor Yüan becomes the personification of feudalistic morality and is the more wicked for his deceptiveness. The death wish, the homosexual overtone, and the perversion bordering upon fetishism are to be taken literally, as the unnatural behaviour (certainly unbecoming for an emperor) is symptomatic of the perverted values of the ruling class morality.

The ending of *Wang Chao-chün* bears marked resemblance to that in Oscar Wilde's *Salomé*. Veil by veil, Salomé is stripped of her outward facade until she emerges as a primordial terror. Pale and naked, she feasts on the head of the dead Jokanaan.

> Ah! I have kissed thy mouth, Jokanaan. I have kissed thy mouth. There was a bitter taste on thy lips. Was it the taste of blood?... But perchance it is the taste of love ...

They say that love hath a bitter taste ... but what of that? What of that? I have kissed thy mouth, Jokanaan.[46]

Throughout the play, Salomé lusts after Jokanaan, the blind prophet who persistently denounces lust in a repression of his own desires. Deathlike, chaste like the moon, and "very cold, cold as ivory." he is a natural choice for Salomé, for despite her outward abandon, she is unwilling to part with her virginity, and his sterility poses no threat to her chastity. After Jokanaan's repeated rejections, she knows that the only way to control him is to kill him. As she kisses the head of Jokanaan, all hatred has vanished— she can do whatever she wishes at the height of her passion.

What shall I do now, Jokanaan? Neither the floods nor the great waters can quench my passion. I was a princess, and thou didst take my virginity from me. I was chaste, and thou didst fill my veins with fire ... Love only should one consider ...[47]

The ending forces the audience into a shocking realization of the evil in human nature, but it is also an exaltation and deification of the heroine and her sinful lust. The decadents, as suggested in *Salomé*, saw human nature as evil and regarded it not only as a reality but also celebrated it as the primordial impulse unrestricted and inbridled by conventions. Moral judgement of the good and evil, therefore, loses its relevance. The qualities of evil and naturalness converged in Salomé are divided in Kuo Mo-jo's play between Emperor Yüan and Wang Chao-chün. The process, however, is modified by the insistence on moralistic judgement. Didacticism creeps in with the identification of "evil" as morally repugnant and naturalness and individualism as valuable attributes of human dignity, and Wang Chao-chün becomes a moral battleground resulting in the victory of the good and the shocking unmasking of the hidden evils in society.

As an intertext to *Wang Chao-chün*, *Salomé*'s impact is minimal. The overwhelming sense of urgency, of impatience, and the excessive intensity in *Wang Chao-chün* are more akin to German expressionism.[48] The adaptation of the finale in *Salomé* remains a literary curiosity, intriguing in the sense that Kuo Mo-jo has chosen to convert decadent passion into a bizarre and freakish spectacle. Here intertextuality refers back to the Yüan drama for its impact, relying on the "distortion" of not only the heroic ideal of Wang Chao-chün but more importantly, of the romantic image of Emperor Yüan and the relationship between the two characters. Love is conspicuous by its absence, having been displaced by lustful perversion; what has been sanctioned as love by Confucian morality suddenly becomes inhuman sexual abuse in light of the new morality inspired by Western ideas. In adapting materials from various sources, *Wang Chao-chün* transforms a traditional heart-rending love story into a problem play, condemning in a struggle of the sexes the covert male chauvinism in traditional morality and its social implications. In spite of Kuo Mo-jo's romanticism and self-expressive view of literature, the eulogy of individualism and self-fulfillment is at the same time an anatomy of the rotten state of society. The conclusion is uneqivocal, that the oppressive society strangles self-expression and debases human dignity.

Conclusion

There are two important phases in the development of early modern Chinese drama. The first is "destruction," the total rejection of the traditional themes and the highly formulaic style of representation. The new generation of dramatists felt that the traditional dramatic devices, which survived mainly at the technical level, could no longer give adequate expression to the new sensibility, the new concepts of selfhood, liberation, and human relations. In order to establish their credibility in a takeover bid of the old drama, they had to create their own drama with new conventions, which would be new and "living," instead of being old and "dead." This is the second phase of "construction." Here the formal aspect was part of the New Culture Movement determined to reform society by means of "science" and "democracy." The social concern and empiricism demanded topicality and relevance, which in turn necessitated a realistic depiction of social conditions. Realism, with its many variant definitions and re-interpretations by the Chinese intellectuals for their own purposes, became the vogue of the age.

To many May Fourth writer, realism was "simply a lively, vigorous and plain style" and was intended to be combined "with a humanitarian and idealistic approach to the problem of modern life in society."[49] For example, Hu Shih equates realism with a brave new worldview, the courage to tell life as it really is, with all its depravities and squalor.[50] Thus Ibsen's *A Doll's House*, and not the later visionary plays became the logical model for the struggle against a corrupt patriarchal morality in a realistic setting. The importance of Hu Shih's *The Greatest Event in Life* lies not in its literariness but in its assimilation of drama with social phenomena. In combining literature and ideology, the Nora syndrome became the dominant theme not only in drama but also in all forms of literary writing.

Hung Shen once admitted that as a dramatist he aspired to be an Ibsen rather than a Shakespeare,[51] apparently referring to his preference for the ideological Ibsenism as it was understood. In his adaptation of *The Emperor Jones*, he therefore suppresses the expressionist impulse to examine the inner consciousness in favour of external references in an attack on the distressing consequences of the prevailing social conditions. The early Kuo Mo-jo was attracted by the ideas of aestheticism, and along with his Creation Society colleagues, advocated "art for art's sake" and the unrestrained expression of emotion in literature. But in his *Wang Chao-chün*, poetic exuberance and the new-found barbarism are associated with defiance of old conventions, and individualism gives way to an active desire for social revolution.[52] The adaptation of the finale of *Salomé* represents a total break with tradition, shattering the myth of Confucian morality in favour of a new social order. The celebration of "evil" (in *Wang Chao-chün*) is given a didactic interpretation, regarded as the rebellion against a society which sanctions degeneracy and debauchery, or as the unswerving dedication to liberate the self from a society of deceptive moralism and self-abnegating ascetism.[53]

The preference for dramatic illusionism[54] was to an extent necessitated by practical concerns of audience acceptance. "Absolute freedom is not available: a dramatist must win the consent of his audience to any particular means that he wishes to employ ... for even if the audience is sympathetic, too great a consciousness of the novelty or strangeness of the means may as effectively hamper the full communication of a play as would even hostility."[55] In 1920, the famous dramatist Wang Chung-hsien staged Bernard Shaw's *Mrs. Warren's Profession* in Shanghai, but the hostility of the audience (some even walked out during the performance) and the dismal box office forced the play to be cancelled after only three performances. The reason, besides some technical flaws in the production, was attributed mainly to the thoughtless imposition of foreign devices and modes of expression.[56] Conversely, Hung Shen's production of Oscar Wilde's *Lady Windermere's Fan* was a big theatrical success, because the play transposed to a Chinese setting (Shanghai) with Chinese characters and mannerisms was rewritten, not literally translated, and the story was transposed to audience acceptance was a major concern, and sinicization at least helped to shape the dramatic form and was a controlling factor in the dramatists' urge for a total "adoption of Western ways." This is why Hu Shih dispensed with the long discussions in *A Doll's House* in his *The Greatest Event in Life*, and Hung Shen chose to focus on the concrete, relying on a realistic presentation of his adaptation of O'Neill's expressionistic play.

The main reason behind the preference for realism, however, remained the view of drama as a tool for the audience's edification. The modern Chinese writer was obsessed with the concern of "China as a nation afflicted with a spiritual disease and therefore unable to strengthen itself or change its set ways of inhumanity."[57] This "obsession" led to the depiction of society as the writers saw it, as the persecuting environment which had to be reformed for its own survival. In this regard, modern Chinese plays were invariably more or less problem plays. The Chinese dramatists adopted from Western modernism the intellectual conventions of plight, alienation, and nihilism bound up with the consciousness of disorder, despair, and anarchy, but their reformist zeal led them to repudiate the hostility to civilization and the disenchantment with culture of the Western modernists. Individualism was not an end in itself; it represented the fervent hope for a better world in the struggle between the individual and society. The insistence on a realistic treatment of subject-matter was justified, that if man were to be shown as a product of his environment, against which he must struggle to assert his selfhood, then the environment had to be shown, and shown forcefully on stage. Despite and because of Western influence, early modern drama set the stage for its successors in its persistent refusal to be self-reflexive both in theme and in technique. Instead of "all the world a stage," the stage became the whole world.[58] And the attempt to substitute drama for experience in the outside world turned out to be a renewal of old didacticism.

NOTES

1. Ting Luo-nan 丁羅男 , *Chung-kuo hua-chü hsüeh-hsi wai-kuo hsi-chü te li-shih ching-yen* 中國話劇學習外國戲劇的歷史經驗 (Shanghai: Chung-kuo hsi-chü ch'u- pan-she, 1983), p. 7.

2. William Doby, "The Appearance of Western-style Drama," in his *A History of Chinese Drama* (London: Paul Elak, 1976), p. 205.

3. Ting, op. cit., p. 9.

4. See T'ien Han 田漢 , "Chung-kuo hua-chü yi-shu fa-chan te lu-hsien he chan-wang" 中國話劇藝術發展的路綫和展望 *Hsi-chü lun-ts'ung* 戲劇論叢 , 2 (1957).

5. Hung Shen 洪深 , *Chung-kuo hsien-tai tso-chia t'an ch'uang-tso ching-yen* 中國現代作家談創作經驗 (Chinan: Shantung jen-min ch'u-pan-she, 1980), p. 29.

6. Ting, op. cit., p. 31.

7. Hu Shih 胡適 , "Yi-pu-sheng chu-yi" 易卜生主義 , in *Chung-kuo hsin-wen-hsüeh ta-hsi, Chien-she li-lun chi*, 中國新文學大系 · 建設理論集 (Shanghai: Liang-yu t'u-shu kung-szu, 1935), pp. 179–92.

8. Hu Shih 胡適 , *The Greatest Event in Life*, trans. by Edward M. Gunn, in Edward M. Gunn (ed.), *Twentieth-Century Chinese Drama* (Bloomington: Indiana University Press, 1983), p. 9.

9. Henrik Ibsen, *A Doll's House*, in his *Four Major Plays* (New York: Airmont Publishing Co., 1966), p. 67.

10. Ibid., p. 69.

11. Hu, *The Greatest Event in Life*, p. 69.

12. Ibsen, op. cit., p. 71.

13. Hu, *The Greatest Event in Life*, p. 9.

14. Ibid., p. 8.

15. Ibid., p. 1.

16. Ibid., p. 3.

17. David Ch'en, "Two Chinese Adaptations of Eugene O'Neill's *The Emperor Jones*," *Modern Drama* (Feb. 1976), p. 435.

18. Hung, op. cit., pp. 65–66.

19. Egil Tornqvist, *A Dream of Soul, Studies in O'Neill's Supernaturalistic Technique* (New Haven and London: Yale University Press, 1969), p. 238.

20. Doris V. Falk, *Eugene O'Neil and the Tragic Vision* (New Brunswick, New Jersey: Rutgers University Press, 1985), p. 67.

21. Hung Shen, *Yama Chao*, trans. by Carolyn T. Brown, in Edward M. Gunn (ed.), *Twentieth-Century Chinese Drama*, p. 39.

22. Hung, *Chung-kuo hsien-tai tso chia t'an ch'uang-tso ching-yen*, p. 282.

23. Eugene O'Neill, *The Emperor Jones*, in his *Anna Christie. The Emperor Jones. The Hairy Apes* (New York: Vintage books, 1972).

24. Ibid., p. 5.

25. Tornqvist, op. cit., p. 55.

26. O'Neill, op. cit., p. 5.

27. Ibid., p. 6.

28. Ibid., p. 7.

29. Hung, *Yama Chao*, p. 11.

30. Ibid., p. 24.

31. Warren Austin and Rene Wellek, *The Theory of Literature* (3rd ed.; New York: Harcourt, Brace & World, 1956), p. 221.

32. Ibid., p. 215.

33. O'Neill, op. cit., p. 28.

34. Hung, *Yama Chao*, p. 36.

35. Ibid., p. 36.

36. Hung, *Chung-kuo hsien-tai tso-chia t'an ch'uang-tso ching-yen*, p. 70.

37. Ibid., p. 273.

38. Kuo Mo-jo 郭沫若, "Hsieh tsai san-ke p'an-ni-te nü-hsing hou-mien" 寫在三個叛逆的女性後面, in *Kuo Mo-jo chü-tso ch'üan-chi* 郭沫若劇作全集 (Peking: Chung-hua hsi-chü ch'u-pan-she, 1982), p. 192.

39. Ma Chih-yüan 馬致遠, *Autumn in Han Palace*, in *Six Yuan Plays* (Middlesex: Penguin Books, 1972), p. 213.

40. *Kuo Mo-jo chü-tso ch'uan-chi*, p. 195.

41. Kuo Mo-jo, *Wang Chao-chün* 王昭君, in his *Kuo Mo-jo chü-tso ch'üan-chi*, p. 146. Quotations from the text are my translations.

42. Ibid., p. 145.

43. Kuo, *Kuo Mo-jo chü-tso ch'üan-chi*, p. 189.

44. Ibid., p. 196.

45. Ibid., p. 148.

46. Oscar Wilde, *Salomé* in his *Plays* (Middlesex: Penguin Books, 1983), pp. 347–48.

47. Ibid., p. 347.

48. Martin Esslin, "Modernist Drama: Wedeking to Brecht," in Malcolm Bradbury and James McFarlane (eds.), *Modernism* (Middlesex: Penguin Books, 1976), p. 537.

49. Bonnie S. McDougall, *The Introduction of Western Literary Theories into Modern China 1919–1925* (Tokyo: The Centre for East Asian Cultural Studies, 1970), p. 149.

50. Hu, "Yi-pu-sheng," p. 179.

51. Ting, op. cit., p. 163.

52. McDougall, op. cit., pp. 200–201.

53. Ke Ts'ung-min 葛聰敏, "'Wu-ssu' hua-chü ch'uang-tso yu wai-kuo wen-hsüeh" 「五四」話劇創作與外國文學, *Wen-hsüeh ping-lun* 文學評論, 1 (1987), p. 99.

54. Luk Yun-tong 陸潤棠, "Chung-kuo hsien-tai hsi-chü so shou chi hsi-fang ying-hsiang" 中國現代戲劇所受之西方影響, in *Tian-ying yu wen-hsüeh* 電影與文學 (Taipei: Chung-hua wen-hua ta-hsüeh ch'u-pan-pu, 1984), p. 161.

55. Raymond Williams, *Drama from Ibsen to Brecht* (Middlesex: Penguin Books, 1968), p. 8.

56. Ting, op. cit., p. 29.

57. C. T. Hsia, "Obsession with China: The Moral Burden of Modern Chinese Literature," in his *A History of Modern Chinese Fiction* (New Haven and London: Yale University Press, 1971), p. 533.

58. John Fletcher and James McFarlane, "Modernist Drama: Origins and Patterns," in *Modernism*, p. 511.

2. Drama of Dilemma: Waiting as Form and Motif in *The Bus-stop* and *Waiting for Godot*

Kwok-kan Tam

The search for a new theatre beyond that represented by the trinity of social-ist realism, Ibsenism and Stanislavsky's system, which has dominated the contemporary Chinese stage for almost thirty years, has become the major concern of the new generation of playwrights in China.[1] The experimen-tation since 1979 with other forms of expression than the conventional Western realistic theatre has brought about the large-scale introduction of Brechtian and absurdist drama to the Chinese audiences.

Although Brechtian drama was first introduced to the Chinese audiences in the late 1950s for the reason, firstly, that it is a Marxist theatre and, secondly, that it has its source in traditional Chinese theatre, it has never been so consciously considered by both the Chinese playwrights and audi-ences as an alternative to the Ibsenian theatre in China. When Bertolt Brecht's *Galileo* was staged in Peking by the Chinese Youth Art Theatre in 1979, it aroused a stir and was hailed as a breakthrough from the stagnant Chinese stage. The performance was originally construed as a debate on the pursuit of truth and blind doctrinism and valued for its political implication, but the real effect of the play lies in its offering a new perspective on the nature of the theatre.

From 1979–1981 there were a considerable number of Chinese plays written under the influence of Brechtian drama, the most successful of which is undoubtedly Sha Yeh-hsin's 沙葉新 *The Imposter* (*Chia ju wo shih chen ti* 假如我是眞的 , or *If I Were Real*), published in the summer of 1979. The introduction and subsequent imitation of the Brechtian style was not so much the result of a programmed effort in replacing Ibsen by Brecht as a desire to look forward to something new in the theatre. Thus Arthur Miller's *Death of a Salesman* was also staged in Peking in 1984, while Shakespeare was sinicized on the Shanghai stage several times since 1980.

The general trend in today's Chinese theatre is to break away from doctrines and formulae in playwriting and performance. This break-away has more artistic significance than political implication for the playwrights.

Accompanying this breakthrough was the introduction of the Theatre of the Absurd to China. As early as 1978, the Chinese journal *World Litera-ture* (*Shih-chieh wen-hsüeh* 世界文學) published a translation of Harold Pinter's *The Birthday Party* along with Chu Hung's 朱虹 "A Critical Introduction to the Theatre of the Absurd" (Huang-tan-p'ai hsi-chü shu-p'ing 謊誕派戲劇述評). Chinese playwrights and readers were thus given an opportunity to know the more recent developments of Western theatre and drama. Two years later, a collection of drama, in Chinese translation, from the contemporary Western avant-garde theatre came out in Shanghai, included in which were such typical plays as *Waiting for Godot, Amedee or How to Get Rid of It, The Zoo Story,* and *The Dumb Waiter.* Although the process of introducing Chinese readers to the most avant-garde works of the Western theatre has been rather slow, it allows Chinese readers and playwrights time to readjust their way of appreciation which is necessary for a culture in which the prevalent interpretive code remains to be that of nineteenth-century Western realism. In recent years, essays introducing Western absurdist dramatists can be found in Chinese journals from time to time.[2]

The first Chinese attempt at an absurdist play was made by Kao Hsing-chien 高行健 , a Shanghai playwright who has a great interest in French literature, in 1983 when his play, *The Bus-stop (Ch'e chan* 車站), appeared in the literary magazine *October (Shih yueh* 十月). In many respects, Kao Hsing-chien's *The Bus-stop* can be considered a Chinese version of Beckett's *Waiting for Godot.* In his book *Techniques of Modern Fiction (Hsien-tai hsiao-shuo chi-ch'iao ch'u t'an* 現代小說技巧初探), Kao openly shows his admiration of Beckett, especially Beckett's contribution to the contemporary theatre.[3] It is, however, the absurd social condition in con-temporary China that forms the basis of Kao's play, which was an immedi-ate stir to both the Chinese audiences and critics for its shocking effect and apparent violation of the traditional style of stage presentation. When the Peking People's Art Theatre performed it in a small theatre-in-the-round studio to a limited audience, it was obvious that the play was considered mainly as an experiment to be conducted with control to test the theatre-goers' response. The controversy this play aroused, however, was chiefly on its ideological inclination and challenge to the social doctrine of literature and art rather than on its artistic achievements and innovations, which are unique among contemporary Chinese plays. The critic Ho Wen 何聞 blames Kao Hsing-chien for being pessimistic about Socialism as well as for his "blind worship" of Beckett.[4] But the more senior drama critic Ch'ü Liu-i 曲六乙 defended the play for its originality and optimistic views about social reality.[5] The controversy over the social implication of Kao's play has made it one of the most controversial Chinese plays of the 1980s.

Like *Waiting for Godot*, *The Bus-stop* can be interpreted as a piece of pessimistic writing as well as an optimistic treatment of the belief that there is always hope in waiting. Godot may be allegorized as "little God" or taken as a combined form of the names of the two tramps, Gogo and Didi, thus representing their false hope and imagination in salvation. It is true that in Beckett's play there are a number of philosophical and religious references, which all tend to point at the basic absurdity of the human situation. Yet it is not simply a morality play; nor is it merely an Existentialist play in the vein of Sartre or Camus. It is an absurdist play with its mode of expression characteristic of the abandonment of the rational approach. In this respect, the social and political references in *The Bus-stop* are not as important as the act of waiting, for what matters is not so much in for what and where the passengers are waiting as in the fact that they are waiting. If in *Waiting for Godot* what counts is not Godot but the subject of waiting and the hope, frustration and anxiety thus caused, then in *The Bus-stop* the bus or the bus company is only of secondary importance. Actually, the uniqueness of both plays lie in their treatment of the subject of waiting, that is, how the devices in structure, characterization and language are used to present the theme of waiting. A major and easily noticed technique employed in *Waiting for Godot* is the device of contrast and dilemma, which is also successfully used in the Chinese play, *The Bus-stop,* by Kao Hsing-chien. The technique of contrast and theme of dilemma fully used and developed in the two plays include the freedom of choice but with no alternative, expectation for change and unchangeability, the waiting and the drifting, and the absurdly rapid flight of time and the sense of indivision of time. These technical as well as thematic devices have all become the basis for presenting the absurdist motifs of waiting, boredom, time passing, anxiety, and anguish in the two plays.

The playwright Kao Hsing-chien calls *The Bus-stop* "a lyrical comedy of life with no division of acts and scenes." Although there is no physical division of scenes in the play, there are actually six repetitive episodes with the coming of the bus or the sound of the bus as division, in which nothing happens. It makes more sense to say that it is the situation of waiting and hope deferred in *Waiting for Godot* and *The Bus-stop* that give both plays a circular structure with the ending repeating the beginning. At the end of both Act I and Act II, the two tramps Estragon and Vladimir in Beckett's play say that they will go, but in fact they stay there and continue to wait. In the Chinese play, all the seven passengers also remain at the bus-stop though they say that they will go. Besides the contradiction between what the passengers say and what they do, which is a comic and absurdist device, there is also the suggestion that the passengers have no choice except for staying on.

Nothing is more frustrating to the characters in both plays than the fact that they are presented without any alternative except continuing to wait. Estragon and Vladimir say that they are tied to the situation and the only alternative they have is to attempt suicide. Thus Estragon and Vladimir have to think of some way to end their lives as an alternative to the Existentialist frustration of waiting:

Vladimir: … What do we do now?
Estragon: Wait.
Vladimir: Yes, but while waiting.
Estragon: What about hanging ourselves?
          ....
Estragon: Let's hang ourselves immediately!
Vladimir: From a bough? (*They go towards the tree.*) I wouldn't trust it.
Estragon: We can always try.
Vladimir: Go ahead.
Estragon: After you.
Vladimir: No, no, you first.
Estragon: Why me?
Vladimir: You're lighter than I am.
Estragon: Just so!
Vladimir: I don't understand.
Estragon: Use your intelligence, can't you?
          Vladimir uses his intelligence.
Vladimir: (*finally*). I remain in the dark.
Estragon: This is how it is. (*He reflects.*) The bough … the bough …(*Angrily*). Use your head, can't you?

Vladimir: You're my only hope.

Estragon: (*with effort*). Gogo light—bough not break—Gogo dead. Didi heavy—bough break—Didi alone. Whereas—

Vladimir: I hadn't thought of that.

Estragon: If it hangs you it'll hang anything.

Vladimir: But am I heavier than you?

Estragon: So you tell me. I don't know. There's an even chance. Or nearly.

Vladimir: Well? What do we do?

Estragon: Don't let's do anything. It's safer.

Vladimir: Let's wait and see what he says.

Estragon: Who?

Vladimir: Godot.

Estragon: Good idea.[6]

The only hope the two tramps have in life is to wait for Godot and see what he will say about their situation. Hence, at the beginning of the play the two tramps are full of the hope that they will be saved and do not expect to do anything themselves. When they talk about suicide, they take it as a funny thing. On the one hand, they want Godot to come and change their situation. On the other hand, they fear that if they try to make the change themselves, the worse may happen to them. Estragon therefore says that it is safer not to do anything. But in Act II, after so much distress and anxiety, they begin to consider suicide seriously and decide to hang themselves again. This time they also fail as they have not even got a rope strong enough to hang either one of them. But how about the next day? Vladimir says, "We'll hang ourselves tomorrow. (*Pause.*) Unless Godot comes."[7] This remark serves as a conclusion to their situation: either they keep on waiting for Godot or they keep on trying to hang themselves. But what has happened previously in the play suggests that neither will come true. What is more despairing is the fact that they cannot even kill themselves and in this way they have lost the only alternative to waiting.

Actually all the while the two tramps are waiting for Godot, they have tried to do something constructive or meaningful, which they expect will change their situation while they are waiting. Only that whatever they do will amount to nothing:

Vladimir: Nothing you can do about it.

Estragon: No use struggling.

Vladimir: One is what one is.

Estragon: No use wriggling.

> Vladimir: The essential doesn't change.
> Estragon: Nothing to be done.[8]

The most distressing thing for the two tramps is fully expressed here that whatever they do will not change the essence of their situation. Since they cannot change their situation by their own effort, they expect and have to rely on something from the external to save them.

As in *Waiting for Godot*, the passengers in *The Bus-stop* are tormented between the proper wish of achieving something through waiting and the Existentialist frustration of doing nothing. The play begins with an allegorical stage direction:

> In the middle of the stage is a bus-stop sign. The words on the sign have become illegible due to long exposure to the natural erosion of weather. Next to the bus-stop sign are two rows of iron railings for people to line up. The railings are arranged in such a way that they form the shape of a cross of different lengths, which is symbolic of a cross-road, an intersection, or a stop in the lives of various people.[9]

Like the barren willow tree, which is a sign of the place of appointment, in *Waiting for Godot*, the bus-stop sign serves as a link between the passengers and the bus, as well as a device linking up all the passengers. But the implication of both plays does not lie in the tree or in the bus-stop sign. Nor does it lie in Godot or in the bus. The message is in the characters themselves and in their act of waiting.

Right at the beginning of *The Bus-stop*, the Old Man complains about the absurdity of life:

> Do you smoke? (*The Silent Man shakes his head.*) It is a good thing not to smoke. Actually it is impossible to get good cigarettes anyway, not to mention that smoking is a money-causing way to get bronchitis. When people hear that the "Great Front Gate" is available, they will all flock to buy it and the line will be so long that it winds round the street corner several times. One person is allowed to buy only two packs. When your turn comes, the sales person may leave the counter without even glancing at you. If you ask why, there will not be any answer. Is this what is called "Serve the People?" It is only lip-service. The "Great Front Gate" has already silently slipped away through the back door! This is like waiting for a bus. Are you not waiting for the bus in an orderly way? But someone may just have to run a little bit further ahead and wave to the driver, then the front door will open for him. He must be a "man of connections," gee, always this trick. When you reach the front door, it will close with a bang. If this is called "Serve the Passengers," won't you open your eyes wide? Everybody knows this, but none can change it.[10]

The Old Man's complaint sets the play against the backdrop of a society which is so chaotic and unreasonable that whatever happens in it has gone far beyond rational human thinking. The cigarette brand "Great Front Gate" provides an ironic image for such an absurd social phenomenon as "Back-doorism." Similar to the "Great Front Gate" in its effect of irony and degree of absurdity is the slogan "Serve the People," which has turned to its opposite and is totally beyond the Old Man's comprehension. The failure of the Socialist ideal, which is so moral and religious in nature and has had an impact in China no less strong than that of Christianity in the West, can be seen in the light of the human condition in an absurd world described by Ionesco: "Absurd is that which is devoid of purpose.... Cut off from his religious, metaphysical, and transcendental roots, man is lost; all his actions become senseless, absurd, and useless."[11] The Old Man's feeling of being lost in a strange world is actually a result of this crisis of belief and his alienation from a world which is within his comprehension, as Camus puts it:

> A world that can be explained by reasoning, however faulty, is a familiar world. But in a universe that is suddenly deprived of illusions and of light, man feels a stranger. His is an irremediable exile, because he is deprived of memories of a lost homeland as much as he lacks the hope of a promised land to come. This divorce between man and his life, the actor and his setting, truly constitutes the feeling of Absurdity.[12]

At the metaphorical level, both *Waiting for Godot* and *The Bus-stop* can be considered modern morality plays, referring subtly to social and religious absurdity. G. S. Fraser considers the message of *Waiting for Godot* as something nearer a message of religious consolation.[13] References to the Christian faith are obvious in the play, but the play does not simply pose a question of the validity of religion, for it has generalized the situation of waiting to cover all aspects of the human condition of hope and hope deferred in waiting. Similarly, *The Bus-stop* is not merely about the chaotic and absurd social condition in China in the 1980s. It brings forth to the audience the question of waiting and its senselessness, for as in *Waiting for Godot* the image of waiting is given a generalized and philosophical significance. Hence, in *The Bus-stop* the actor, who plays the double role as Director Ma and later as a detached observer, says as a metacomment on the theme of waiting:

> Sometimes we really need to wait. Haven't you had the experience of queuing in a line to buy fish? Oh, suppose you don't cook! How about waiting in a line for a bus?

Queuing is waiting. Even if you have queued for half a day, what is for sale is not hairtail, but washing boards—fine washing boards which do not damage clothes, and you've already got a washing machine, then you have wasted half a day queuing for nothing. There is no way you don't get angry. Hence, what matters is not waiting, but that you must make sure what you've been waiting for is what you want. Otherwise you're just making a fool of yourself if you waste half or even the whole of your life waiting for nothing.[14]

The Existentialist dimension of the theme of waiting in *The Bus-stop* is explicitly stated in the comment made by the actor, who plays the carpenter, in response to the above comment: "… I don't mind waiting. When someone is waiting, it means that he has a hope. It will be really bad if one doesn't even have a hope…. To borrow the words of the bespectacled young man [Glasses], this is called hopelessness."[15] This is reminiscent of the remark made by Vladimir: "Hope deferred maketh the something sick."[16]

To the passengers in the play, the purpose of waiting is related to the meaning of life, which is metaphorically presented as a process of waiting. They ask such questions as those follow:

Mother: What Chaos.
Glasses: Ah, life …
Girl: Do you call this living?
Glasses: Sure it is. Despite everything we are still alive.
Girl: We might as well be dead.
Glasses: Why don't you end it all, then?
Girl: Because it seems like such a waste to come to this world and then get nothing out of life.
Glasses: There should be some meaning to life.
Girl: To live on like this, not really alive and not dead either—it's so boring![17]

It is exactly the same kind of boredom as that experienced by the two tramps in *Waiting for Godot* or Rosancrantz and Guildenstern in *Rosancrantz and Guildenstern Are Dead*. In *The Bus-stop*, Glasses says, "We can't wait any longer; it's useless to keep on waiting. This is meaningless torture."[18] While the two tramps in *Waiting for Godot* look upon suicide as an alternative to waiting and try but fail to commit suicide, the passengers in *The Bus-stop* think that it is a waste not to get anything out of life. However, the characters in both plays recognize the fact that it is boring to live on, waiting for something that will change their situation or fate to happen.

Like what Rosancrantz and Guildenstern do in the play *Rosancrantz and Guildenstern Are Dead*, the passengers in *The Bus-stop* also think that life is as absurd as flicking a coin and there is no logical and sensible way to predict the result. Yet, they believe that since life or fate is absurd, it should be dealt with in an absurd way when they finally resort to the flicking of a coin to determine whether they should continue to wait or to go:

> Glasses: You can think of life as a coin. (*Takes a coin out of his pocket.*) Do you believe in this? (*He flicks the coin in the air and then catches it.*) Head or tail? *Pig, book, desk, dog,* that's decided! *Are you teachers? No, Are you pig?* No, I'm none of those. *I am I.* I am who I am. You don't believe in yourself, but you do believe in this? (*Self-mockingly he flicks the coin again and catches it.*)
>
> Girl: What do you think we should do?I don't even have the strength to make a decision.
>
> Glasses: Let's gamble with Fate: heads we wait, tails we go. It all depends on the coin—(*He flicks the coin into the air. It falls to the ground and Glasses covers it over with the palm of his hand.*) Do we stay or do we go? Stay or go? Let's see what Fate has decreed.[19]

The resolution to flicking a coin in order to determine whether or not to stay stands for not only the passengers' loss of confidence in approaching problems in life in a rational way, but also their submission to Fate and the absurdity of life. In this sense, the Existentialist theme of waiting is explored in *The Bus-stop* as well as in *Waiting for Godot*, though treated in different situations.

Martin Esslin defines the Theatre of the Absurd as an expression of the "sense of the senselessness of the human condition and the inadequacy of the rational approach by the open abandonment of rational devices and discursive thought…. The Theatre of the Absurd has renounced arguing *about* the absurdity of the human condition; it merely *presents* it in being—that is, in terms of concrete stage images."[20] In this respect, *The Bus-stop* is still in line with the main tradition of the Theatre of the Absurd, although in the play there are arguments here and there about the absurdity of life and the passengers try many times to seek a rational explanation for such absurdity, as the purpose of using "rational devices and discursive thought" in the play is to show the inadequacy of them and the impossibility of reaching a conclusion by the rational approach. That is why the Old Man says, "What logic is this; (*coughs*) making passengers stand around waiting till their hair turns grey…. (*Suddenly becoming decrepit.*) Absurd … too absurd…."[21]

The act of waiting in *The Bus-stop* is only a metaphor of life in China. There is nothing absurdist or Existentialist in the act of waiting itself, but once the act of waiting is turned into a metaphor of life and the question of the meaning of life is asked but not answered, then the act of waiting is no longer simply a matter of waiting for the bus, for it has become life itself, in which there is hope which is never realized but always promised. It is absurd to make a waste of one's life waiting for something that has posed itself as a promise of change to the passengers, but at the same time there is always the promise, which is symbolically represented by the sound of the bus approaching from all directions at the end of the play. It is the same situation of dealing with the effects of hope in waiting and hope deferred upon the characters as in *Waiting for Godot* that is explored in *The Bus-stop*.

Related to the theme of waiting is the flight of time, which is used both as a theme and as a dramatic device to intensify the anxiety of waiting in the two plays. Time is one of the most significant elements in the two plays as it links the act of waiting with the value of life and how the time during the waiting should be spent. The characters' lament of the absurd flight of time not only shows their metaphysical anguish, but also provides one of the major comparative aspects of *Waiting for Godot* and *The Bus-stop*. The rapid passage of time is contrasted with the age-old lamentation of the short span of human life. The dilemma of how significance can be achieved in a seemingly insignificant life becomes one of the central questions in both plays, in which the flight of time serves not only as a technique of contrast, but also to provide a thematic dilemma. As Martin Esslin says,

> The subject of the play [*Waiting for Godot*] is not Godot but waiting, the act of waiting as an essential and characteristic aspect of the human condition. Throughout our lives we always wait for something, and Godot simply represents the objective of our waiting—an event, a thing, a person, death. Moreover, it is in the act of waiting that we experience the flow of *time* in its purest, most evident form. If we are active, we tend to forget the passage of time, we *pass* the time, but if we are merely passively waiting, we are confronted with the action of time itself.[22]

While the two tramps in *Waiting for Godot* are not sure how long they have been waiting for Godot and how much longer they still have to wait for him to come, the passengers in *The Bus-stop* are becoming more and more confused about the passage of time and less and less sure how long they have been waiting. Yet, to the characters in both plays, the most contradictory thing is that, on the one hand, they want the time to pass rapidly so that they do not have to invent ways to kill time, but on the other, they lament over the fact that time passes so rapidly that they grow old and also that they have wasted their time in waiting. Estragon says that the visit of Pozzo helps pass the time,[23] but Vladimir thinks that the passage of time makes them grow old.[24] The passengers in *The Bus-stop* are tormented by the absurdly rapid flight of time, which is even more unbearable when it is given the "illusion of value":[25]

> Glasses: (*Looks at his watch. Shocked.*) I don't believe it.
> (*The Girl goes over to look at his watch. They count the numbers indicated on the face of the watch in time with music.*)
> Glasses: (*continuously pressing the indicator button on his digital watch*) Five, six, seven, eight, nine, ten, eleven, twelve, thirteen months ...
> Girl: ... one month, two months, three months, four months ...
> Glasses: ... Five months, six months, seven months, eight months ...
> Girl: ... one year and eight months altogether.
> Glasses: Another year has just gone by.
> Girl: That makes it two years and eight months.
> Glasses: Two years and eight months, ... no, it's three years and eight months. No, I'm wrong—five years and six months.... Seven, eight, nine, ten months.
> (*They all look at each other in amazement.*)
> Lout: This is crazy.
> Glasses: I am sane!
> Lout: Wasn't talkin' about you. I said this watch's had a nervous breakdown!
> Glasses: Mechanical devices don't have nerves. A watch is a device for measuring time, which is not affected by the psychological state of man.[26]

Although Glasses affirms that time is not affected by the psychological state of man, the audience will wonder whether it is time that passes so rapidly or it is the anxiety of waiting that gives the passengers the feeling. Both are possible. The absurdly rapid passage of time in *The Bus-stop* is comparable to the sudden growing of leaves on the previously barren tree in *Waiting for Godot*. In this respect, *The Bus-stop* is even more explicit in its absurdist treatment of time than *Waiting for Godot*, in which the two tramps only feel the confusing indivisiveness of time and circular repetition of events but do not take the fast growth of leaves on the tree as a sign of time passing, which is objective and indifferent to their anguish. In *Waiting for Godot*, time passes but is at first not consciously noticed and seriously taken by the two tramps. The waiting thus seems an endlessly long process, in which what counts is boredom. Yet, in *The Bus-stop* the rapid passage of time is contrasted with the passengers' sudden awakening that they have already grown old, thus producing a strong sense of anxiety and futility of action.

Actually the anxiety, boredom, and the absurd flight of time in both plays are presented in a framework, which is based on a dramatic structure of circular repetition. Commenting on the structure of *Waiting for Godot*, Michael Robinson says:

> Nothing ends in this infinity which is composed of an infinite number of periods of finite time for ever repeating themselves. This is demonstrated by the principle of renewal in the conventions of drama, and in the structure and dialogue of *Godot* itself. The second act repeats the first: both open with the tramps coming together again after the night, end with their motionless withdrawal, and are punctuated, in the middle, by Pozzo and Lucky on their journey.[27]

The Bus-stop is structured on the same principle. There are five episodes in the play, each is a repetition of the previous one, with the bus coming and going but not stopping for the passengers, as Martin Esslin points out: "What passes in these plays are not *events* with a definite beginning and a definite end, but types of *situations* that will forever repeat themselves."[28] In each of these episodes, the passengers' patience is stretched to its limit until finally all of them feel frustrated and angry. Like the two tramps in *Waiting for Godot*, the passengers in *The Bus-stop* do not move, though they have said several times that they will go. This pattern of circular repetition provides the dramatic foundation for the belief that life is cyclical and essentially unchanging, as Vladimir remarks, "The essential doesn't change."[29] The essential here refers, of course, to the essence of the characters' predicament rather than to the objective passage of time and the growth of the tree in *Waiting for Godot*, which signifies that "something is still taking its course in time."[30] The effect of time passing is noted by Vladimir:

> All I know is that the hours are long, under these conditions, and constrain us to beguile them with proceedings which—how shall I say—which may at first sight seem reasonable, until they become a habit. You may say it is to prevent our reason from foundering. No doubt. But has it not long been straying in the night without end of the abyssal depths?[31]

The most awful thing for the more philosophical Vladimir is that time passes without bringing about any change in their life or predicament but making life a habit, which is "a great deadener."[32] At the intellectual level, there is of course change in the two tramps, for they finally understand that there is no way to rationalize the world they live in. This kind of change can never be found in the wandering pair, Pozzo and Lucky, as they only change in appearance. However, to Pozzo and Lucky, who wander and change in their appearance, time passing is equally awful as Pozzo remarks,

> Have you not done tormenting me with your accursed time! It's abominable! When! When! One day, is that not enough for you, one day like any other day, one day he went dumb, one day I went blind, one day we'll go deaf, one day we were born, one day we shall die, the same day, the same second, is that not enough for you? (*Calmer.*) They give birth astride of a grave, the light gleams an instant, then it's night once more.[33]

In contrast to the two tramps, who note that it is safer not to do anything at the beginning of the play,[34] Pozzo and Lucky are changing, though superficially, from bad to worse, and to the latter pair, time passing only signifies the worsening of their situation.

The change in the outside world as well as in other people technically provides a contrast to the stagnant situation of the two tramps in *Waiting for Godot* and the passengers in *The Bus-stop*. This contrast reminds them of two things: time passing and change in the outside world; and time passing but no change in themselves. It is the Hegelian concept that time is measured by the change in the objective world that confuses the characters in both plays as they do not see any change in themselves. Thus Estragon says in *Waiting for Godot*, "Very likely. They all change. Only we can't."[35] And Glasses notes in *The Bus-stop*, "You don't know what pain is—that's why you're so indifferent. We've been cast aside by life, forgotten. The world is fleeting by in front of you and you don't even notice it. Do you understand? You don't."[36] Martin Esslin's comment on *Waiting for Godot* is also applicable to *The Bus-stop*: "Waiting is to experience the action of time, which is constant change. And yet, as nothing real ever happens, that change is in itself an illusion. The ceaseless activity of time is self-defeating, purposeless, and therefore null and void."[37] But the longer they keep on waiting, the less they feel about the change of time and the more they are confused about the passage of time. In *Waiting for Godot*, the two tramps have lost the sense of time and date:

> Estragon: (*very insidious*). But what Saturday? And is it Saturday? Is it not rather
>   Sunday? (*Pause.*) Or Monday? (*Pause.*) Or Friday?

Vladimir: (*looking wildly about him, as though the date was inscribed in the landscape*). It's not possible!
Estragon: Or Thursday?[38]

In *The Bus-stop*, however, the characters are too much confused by the long time they have been waiting for the bus that they do not know exactly when they began waiting there. When they talk about whether the bus-stop has been cancelled, they argue about the date as the two tramps do in *Waiting for Godot*:

Mother: What? This bus-stop has been canceled? But last Saturday I was still ...
Girl: Which last Saturday?
Mother: That Saturday before the last, or that before ... before ... before ...
Glasses: The Saturday of which month and which year are you talking about? (*Looking very closely at his watch.*)[39]

In this respect, both plays can be viewed as a study of the effects of waiting on human psychology and the causes of frustrations, anxiety, confusion, and anguish. The sense of nothingness and forever-repetition is so strong in both plays and that this sense of timelessness is reinforced by the loss of the consciousness of time and date in the characters. To the characters in both plays, what can be sure of are the events in the present. The endlessness of waiting "reduces everything in time to the same level of significance— insignificance."[40]

While the characters' expectation for change is contrasted with the unchangeability of their situation, the waiting is juxtaposed with the drifting. In *Waiting for Godot*, the intrusion of the drifting pair Pozzo and Lucky, unfortunately, does not bring about any change to the two tramps, but serves technically as a contrast to them. This contrast is skillfully used by Beckett as a device to intensify the effect of monotony in waiting. While Estragon and Vladimir wait, Pozzo and Lucky wander and seek for change, but Pozzo and Lucky are no better than Estragon and Vladimir. For Estragon and Vladimir, nothing changes; for Pozzo and Lucky, their change is from bad to worse. But this change is already an envy to Estragon and Vladimir, who are like audiences of a drama performed by Pozzo and Lucky but expect to participate in the performance:

Vladimir: How they've changed!
Estragon: Who?
Vladimir: Those two.
Estragon: That's the idea, let's make a little conversation.

Vladimir: Haven't they?
Estragon: What?
Vladimir: Changed.
Estragon: Very likely. They all change. Only we can't.[41]

In Act II when Pozzo and Lucky return, Estragon and Vladimir also hope for change. They begin to ask for something "tangible"[42] and think that what they did in the past was just to kill time in the expectation that Godot would come soon. Now the change in Pozzo and Lucky is so tempting that they do not want to waste their time any more:

Vladimir: Let us not waste our time in idle discourse! (*Pause. Vehemently.*) Let us do something, while we have the chance! It is not everyday that we are needed. Not indeed that we personally are needed. Others would meet the case equally well, if not better. To all mankind they were addressed, those cries for help still ringing in our ears! But at this place, at this moment of time, all mankind is us, whether we like it or not. Let us make the most of it, before it is too late! Let us represent worthily for once the foul brood to which a cruel fate consigned us! What do you say? (*Estragon says nothing.*) It is true that when with folded arms we weigh the pros and cons we are no less a credit to our species. The tiger bounds to the help of his congeners without the least reflection, or else he slinks away into the depths of the thickets. But that is not the question. And we are blessed in this, that we happen to know the answer. Yes, in this immense confusion one thing alone is clear. We are waiting for Godot to come—[43]

It is obvious that the two tramps are confused and are full of contradictory thoughts in their mind. The most fearful thing in their waiting, however, is the sense of boredom and lack of direction, as Vladimir laments:

We wait. We are bored. (*He throws up his hand.*) No, don't protest, we are bored to death, there's no denying it. Good. A diversion comes along and what do we do? We let it go to waste. Come, let's get to work! (*He advances towards the heap, stops in his stride.*) In an instant all will vanish and we'll be alone once more, in the midst of nothingness.[44]

Almost at the end of the play after the two tramps have tried every possible means to change their situation and done something to remind themselves of their existence and value, Vladimir comes to an understanding of their situation and the ineffectuality of individual struggle:

All I know is that the hours are long, under these conditions, and constrain us to beguile them with proceedings which—how shall I say—which may at first sight seem reasonable, until they become a habit. You may say it is to prevent our reason from foundering. No doubt. But has it not long been straying in the night without end of the abyssal depths? That's what I sometimes wonder.[45]

This understanding of their situation is not necessarily a good thing to Vladimir as he says, "What is terrible is to *have* thought."[46] What can the two tramps do if they even cannot end their boredom by killing themselves? The act of waiting is an absurd combination of doing something and doing nothing. For the more contemplative Vladimir, this is even more distressing as he cannot find any rational explanation in the combination. At any rate, they have to do something in order to pass the time. It does not matter whether what they do is meaningful or meaningless, for it will finally amount to nothing. Vladimir's final comments on the horror of having thought and the contrast between the change in Pozzo and Lucky and their unchangeability and their idling away the time technically serve to intensify the dramatic irony that whatever change in the objective external world may not necessarily cause any change in them and that Godot may only be a false hope for change.

The technique of ironic contrast by using a foil is also employed in the Chinese play *The Bus-stop*, in which the Silent Man, who wanders and has the same function of contrast as that of Pozzo and Lucky, at first stands with the group waiting for the bus but later departs and continues his own journey without the notice of any of the passengers. Portrayed as a mysterious figure of wanderlust and quest, the Silent Man is a character-type based on the lonely traveller in Lu Hsün's one-scene play, *The Passer-by*, written in 1925, whose reappearance in a play in 1983 symbolizes the motif that the quest is an endless process, which can be allegorically equated with "the journey and struggle of the Chinese people for a more hopeful albeit uncertain future."[47] Although the Silent Man's departure can be interpreted as a constructive and positive action as some critics do, the endlessness of his quest also gives the audience a strong sense of uncertainty. Thematically the Silent Man is an ambiguous figure whose quest, like the drifting of Pozzo and Lucky, may not necessarily be a better alternative than waiting and not doing anything, as Glasses remarks:

> What if the bus comes after we leave? (*Faces the audience and continues as if thinking out aloud.*) And if it comes but fails to stop again? Looking at the problem rationally, I know I should start walking; it's just that I'm not one hundred percent sure. What's stopping me is the nagging suspicion that it'll come. I must make a plan! *Desk, dog, pig, book*, should I stay or go? It's the enigma of our existence.

Perhaps Fate has decreed that we must wait here forever, till we grow old and die. But why do people accept the capricious rulings of Fate? Then again, what exactly is Fate? (*Addressing the Girl*.) Do you believe in Fate?[48]

This speech by Glasses is so far the most illuminating of the dilemma in which the characters are involved and very Existentialist in perspective, which renders invalid all interpretations of the passengers' waiting as negative and of the Silent Man's quest as positive, particularly when it is taken into consideration that the Silent Man has already travelled a long way and for many years, but this time he also tries to wait before he makes up his mind "to go in great strides without looking back, with the accompaniment of light music to express his pain but stubbornness in the quest."[49] Actually, most of the drama at the bus-stop occurs after the Silent Man has departed and, therefore, the contrast between the Silent Man and the other passengers is not so much a dilemma between the positive and the negative ways to go to the city as one between quest and waiting, either one of which may not be less painful and frustrating than the other. In the dramatic context of *The Bus-stop*, the Silent Man is presented mainly as a foil to the group of passengers and thus has as much technical as its thematic significance.[50] In contrast to the mysterious Silent Man, the babbling Director Ma is also a foil who serves the technical purpose of intensifying the failure of the rational approach to their problems, social and metaphysical. In this sense, his effort to explain rationally the absurdity of Socialism provides an ironic contrast to the long speech of complaint made by the Old Man at the beginning of the play.

As is true in *Waiting for Godot*, what matters in *The Bus-stop* is not the referential but the dramatic form.[51] The play can be allegorized at many levels, thus yielding various, even contradictory, interpretations. As a drama, what is more important is not its reference to the social reality in China, but its use of dramatic devices that deviate from the main current of modern Chinese drama. If *Waiting for Godot* can be considered as a play with an Existentialist situation presented in an absurdist dramatic form, then *The Bus-stop* is a Chinese experiment with an allegorical social situation, which on the surface seems to be presented in a realistic mode of the commonly-seen scene of a group of passengers waiting for the bus, but is actually presented in a symbolic way, signifying the whole drama of the socialist promise of a utopian society, and in a dramatic form which questions the validity of rational thinking and defies the tradition of realism.

Like *Waiting for Godot*, *The Bus-stop* is undramatic but theatrical.

The Bus-stop is purposely written to question the validity of rational thinking and the tradition of dramatic realism by beginning with a realistic scene and rational dialogue and moving gradually toward a greater degree of absurdity in its mode of presentation. In terms of form, the play has a mixture of both realistic and absurdist elements, which are juxtaposed against each other, but its ending emphasizes the absurdity of the realistic and rational approach to life. Hence, in the play absurdism presents itself only gradually as a replacement of realism. Perhaps, this is the reason why some Western readers consider the play mainly as a realistic one, while the Chinese critics who are used to the realistic tradition regard it as an absurdist play.

The sense of absurdity is also expressed in the peculiar form of dialogue employed in the two plays. Martin Esslin points out that most plays of the Theatre of the Absurd present the authors' "intuition of the human condition by a method that is essentially polyphonic; they confront their audience with an organized structure of statements and images that interpenetrate each other and that must be apprehended in their totality, rather like the different themes in a symphony, which gain meaning by their simultaneous interaction."[52] This can be seen in the language of the two plays. The sense of absurdity and insignificance of life can be found in the tramps' invention of various kinds of games with words and engaging themselves in artificial conversation:

> Vladimir: Ceremonious ape!
> Estragon: Punctilious pig!
> Vladimir: Finish your phrase, I tell you!
> Estragon: Finish your own
>   *Silence. They draw closer, halt.*
> Vladimir: Moron!
> Estragon: That's the idea, let's abuse each other.
>   *They turn, move apart, turn again and face each other.*
> Vladimir: Moron!
> Estragon: Vermin!
> Vladimir: Abortion!
> Estragon: Morpion!
> Vladimir: Sewer-rat!
> Estragon: Curate!
> Vladimir: Cretin!

Estragon: (*with finality*). Crritic!
Vladimir: Oh!
     He wilts, vanguished, and turns away.
Estragon: Now let's make it up.
Vladimir: Gogo!
Estragon: Didi!
Vladimir: Your hand!
Estragon: Take it!
Vladimir: Come to my arms!
Estragon: Your arms?
Vladimir: My breast!
Estragon: Off we go!
     They embrace. They separate. Silence.
Vladimir: How time flies when one has fun![53]

The purpose of this artificial conversation is twofold. First, it gives them fun. Second, it gives them the impression that they exist: "They speak, therefore they are." Director Ma and the Old Man in *The Bus-stop* also make similar comments on what they do in life:

Dir. Ma: (*Turns to the Old Man balefully.*) I'm telling you it's not worth it, old man. Why not grow old in the peace and calm of your home. All this playing of the lute, chess, calligraphy and painting is for whiling away the hours at home. Why do you have to go into the city to find yourself a partner anyway? Is it worth throwing your last years away here on the road?

Old Man: What would you know about it? All you can think of is your infernal wheeling and dealing. The whole point of chess is the feeling of exhilaration you get from it; it's all a matter of the spirit of the thing. The spirit of the thing, that's what life's all about.[54]

For the Old Man, the meaning of his life is equivalent to the significance of a game of chess in that both are as meaningful as they are trivial. Yet, no matter how insignificant the game of chess is, it gives the Old Man a point of reference in life as well as a sense of his own existence. The Old Man's going to the city for a game of chess is thus no less important than the Girl's going to the city to meet her boyfriend, for the game of chess has been inflated to signify the purpose of his life. On the other hand, it is no more important than Vladimir's and Estragon's game with words for they have the same purpose of giving significance to an insignificant life. Though the characters in *The Bus-stop* accuse each other of going to the city for nothing great and significant, they all think in their own ways that their purposes of going to the city are great and significant enough for them to spend years and years waiting on the road. In this way the two tramps' imitating a manikin, squirming like an aesthete, playing at Lucky and Pozzo, permuting their hats, doing exercises, examining their boots, or trying to kill themselves can be considered equivalents of the different life pursuits of the characters in *The Bus-stop*. Besides showing that there is no absolute standard to measure the significance of things, the play is also an allegory of the meaninglessness of life, in which all the seven characters as a whole serve to symbolize different stages of man's life rendered meaningless, irrespective of their difference in sex. It is in this allegorical nature of the seven characters that the greatest metaphysical anguish of life lies.

Absurdism is further reinforced by the incongruity and contradiction between dialogue and action in *The Bus-stop*. Toward the end of the play, the characters all talk together at the same time in a disjointed way. The scene is reminiscent of that in a mental hospital with all the lunatics speaking together, each talking about his/her own things. Yet, what they say and the style in which they speak are related to the theme of the play. In his "Playwright's Suggestions for the Performance of *The Bus-stop*," Kao points out that "the speech of the characters is at times clear and direct, while at other times it is vague and purposely inept, or uttered merely for the sake of speaking, just as the act of endlessly waiting for the bus gradually makes the characters forget the reasons and meaning for doing so."[55] This technique of babbling, multiple soliloquy and mismatched conversation is for the first time used in a contemporary Chinese play. In his book, *Techniques of Modern Fiction*, Kao Hsing-chien points out that a common technique in modern literature is the use of a fool or a mentally sick person to tell a profound truth. It is probably the inspiration of Lu Hsün's *Diary of a Madman* (*K'uang-jen-jih-chi* 狂人日記), in which the author conveys his message of social criticism through the seemingly insane words of a madman, that Kao Hsing-chien has learned to use this technique in his play.

The device of multiple soliloquy, polyphonic dialogue and mismatched conversation resembling that of lunatics reinforces the sense of absurdism and loneliness in the play *The Bus-stop*, for although the passengers gather together at a bus-stop and can be seen as a group sharing a common goal of expecting the bus, they are in fact separate. Each of them is a loner in the world, entertaining his/her own hope and pursuing his/her own goal in life, the nature of which is so insignificant. What counts in the play is the fact that they all participate in the waiting. This is equally true in *Waiting for Godot*, in which the two tramps are different in all aspects, and it is their common goal of waiting that brings them together as figures reflecting the predicament of modern man. In short, nothing is particularly significant or bears any great meaning in both plays except that all the major characters are waiting for something to change their situation, but nothing happens. In view of its technical innovations and philosophical treatment of the theme of waiting in relation to the crisis of belief and loss of roots, *The Bus-stop* signifies the most important milestone in the endeavour of contemporary Chinese playwrights to break away from the tradition of Ibsenian drama and to introduce the Chinese audiences to the Theatre of the Absurd.

NOTES

1. For more details of the recent changes in the contemporary Chinese theatre, please refer to my article, "From Social Problem Play to Socialist Problem Play: Ibsen and Contemporary Chinese Dramaturgy," *The Journal of the Institute of Chinese Studies of The Chinese University of Hong Kong*, Vol. 17 (1986), pp. 387–402.

2. An example of the Chinese reception of absurd drama can be found in the following article: Kuo Chi-teh 郭繼德 , "Ah-erh-pi yü huang-tan p'ai hsi-chü" 阿爾比與謊誕派戲劇 (Albee and Absurd Drama), *Wai-kuo wen-hsüeh yen-chiu* 外國文學研究 (Studies in Foriegn Literature), No. 3 (1986), pp. 32–38.

3. Kao Hsing-chien, *Hsien-tai hsiao-shuo chi-ch'iao ch'u t'an* (Canton: Hua-ch'eng ch'u-pan-she, 1981), p. 50.

4. Ho Wen, "Hua chü *Ch'e chan* kuan hou" 話劇《車站》觀後 (A Note to the Play *The Bus-stop*), *Wen-i pao* 文藝報 , 1984.3, pp. 21–25.

5. Ch'ü Liu-i, "P'ing hua-chü *Ch'e chan* chi ch'i p'i-p'ing" 評話劇《車站》及其批評 (On the Play *The Bus-stop* and the Controversy It Aroused), *Wen-i pao*, 1984.7, pp. 29–33.

6. Samuel Beckett, *Waiting for Godot* (London: Faber and Faber, 1975), pp. 17–18.

7. Ibid., p. 94.

8. Ibid., p. 21.

9. Kao Hsing-chien, "Ch'e chan," *Shih yüeh*, 1983.3, p. 119.

10. Ibid., p. 120.

11. Martin Esslin, *The Theatre of the Absurd* (Revised and enlarged edition; London: Penguin, 1977), p. 23.

12. Quoted by Esslin, ibid., p. 18.

13. G. S. Fraser, *The Modern Writer and His World* (Westport, Connecticut: Greenwood Press, 1975), p. 62.

14. "Ch'e chan," p. 137.

15. Ibid.

16. *Waiting for Godot*, p. 10.

17. Ch'e chan," p. 133.

18. Ibid., p. 129.

19. Ibid., pp. 129–30.

20. Esslin, op. cit., p. 24.

21. "Ch'e chan," p. 131.

22. Esslin, op. cit., p. 49.

23. *Waiting for Godot*, p. 49.

24. Ibid., p. 91.

25. Michael Robinson, *The Long Sonata of the Dead: A Study of Samuel Beckett* (London: Rupert Hart-Davis, 1969), p. 246.

26. "Ch'e chan," p. 131.

27. Robinson, op. cit., p. 247.

28. Esslin, op. cit., p. 75.

29. *Waiting for Godot*, p. 21.

30. Robinson, op. cit., p. 247.

31. *Waiting for Godot*, p. 80.

32. Ibid., p. 91.

33. Ibid., p. 89.

34. Ibid., p. 18.

35. Ibid., p. 48.

36. "Ch'e chan," p. 136.

37. Esslin, op. cit., p. 51.

38. *Waiting for Godot*, p. 15.

39. "Ch'e chan," pp. 136–37.

40. Robinson, op. cit., p. 249.

41. *Waiting for Godot*, p. 48.

42. Ibid., p. 79.

43. Ibid., pp. 79–80.

44. Ibid., p. 81.

45. Ibid., p. 80.

46. Ibid., p. 64.

47. Geremie Barmé, "A Touch of the Absurd—Introducing Gao Xingjian, and His Play *The Bus-stop*," *Renditions*, Nos. 19 & 20 (Spring & Autumn 1983), p. 374.

48. "Ch'e chan," p. 129.

49. Ibid., p. 125.

50. The simplistic interpretation of the Silent Man as a positive hero is perhaps a

reflection of the mentality of mechanically dividing the characters in the play according to the traditional standard of the good (*chung* 忠) and the evil (*chien* 奸), and also the morality of blaming a person who waits for gains without pains as what the stupid farmer in a famous traditional Chinese story does by waiting behind a tree for a hare to break its neck by running into the tree. It is precisely with this mentality that some critics interpret the Silent Man as the embodiment of a positive message in the play and subsequently regard Kao's work as a didactic play with a "moral undertone."

51. Raymond Williams, *Drama from Ibsen to Brecht* (London: Penguin, 1978), p. 345.
52. Esslin, op. cit., p. 51.
53. *Waiting for Godot*, p. 76.
54. "Ch'e chan," pp. 131–32.
55. Ibid., p. 138.

3. Ibsen's *The Lady from the Sea*, T'ien Han's *Return to the South*, and Satō Kōroku's *The Disabled Horse*: A Comparative Study

Toshihiko Sato

With the coming of Ibsen's drama in the West, which contributed significantly to the development of the genre, many young playwrights in Europe and America were influenced by his ideas and dramaturgy and adapted them into their own productions. How was the reaction in China and Japan? In those countries, Ibsen was introduced as a social reformer during the last decade of the nineteenth century in Japan and in the early twentieth century in China respectively. Nevertheless, as time advanced, they became more inclined to viewing Ibsen as a romanticist. Thus, during the 1900s in Japan and the 1920s in China, they produced two plays which are said to have been written under the influence of Ibsen's *The Lady from the Sea* (1888): T'ien Han's (1898–1968) *Return to the South* (1929) and Satō Kōroku's (1874–1949) *The Disabled Horse* (1909).

In this paper, I propose to study these two Asian plays in relation to *The Lady from the Sea* and to detect the influence of the Norwegian drama on the Chinese and Japanese plays. I will examine some parallels and similarities in the main characters of the three plays—the first group: Ellida, Chung and Tamaki; the second group: Dr. Wangel, Cheng-ming and Andō; and, the third group: Friman, Sing the wanderer and Mutsuo—as well as some dramatic techniques used.

I

I begin with a question: "Why did Ellida, Chung and Tamaki long to leave their homes?" We can think of two possible reasons.

Mrs. Ellida Wangel, the wife of Dr. Wangel, is attracted to a stranger named Friman who has a supernatural power over her. Feeling imprisoned

while living in a small village near a fjord with Dr. Wangel, she longs to follow the stranger and return to the sea. Dr. Wangel, perceiving Ellida's unhap-
piness, tells her of their prospect to move to a new place near the open sea.

Chung, in *Return to the South*, is a local farmer's daughter who lost her
father half a year earlier and lives with her mother in the countryside. Now
she has come of age, and her mother is anxious to see her get married for
the security of the family, so that, when Li Cheng-ming, a young farmer,
comes to visit them, she tells him that she would allow him to marry Chung.
Yet, Chung is reluctant to accept his proposal, because she is tormented by
her memories of the wanderer Sing with whom she had a romantic encounter under a peach tree the previous year. Longing for reunion, Chung now
awaits his return.

Let us examine the dialogue between Chung and Cheng-ming and their
talk about the wanderer:

Girl: Yes, brother Cheng-ming! At least I cannot forget him. Look under the peach
    tree beside the well. Doesn't he always like to sit there? Doesn't he always like
    to hold my hands and sit with me against the tree, and tell me the stories of his
    past? Look again at the poem he wrote to me on the tree. Funny that the tree is
    still alive, and the flower is still blossoming, and the words on the tree are still
    so fresh. Oh, how can I forget him?

Young Man: Well, sister Chung …

(The girl doesn't say anything.)

Young Man: Then, when can you forget him?

Girl: Brother Cheng-ming, I'll tell you when: When the tree is dried up, the fruit is
    dead, and the flower will never blossom again, and the words on the tree go
    away …

Young Man: That, that will be for your whole life …

Girl: Yes, I will never forget him, never in my life, believe me, brother Cheng-ming.

Young Man: *(kneel down and beg her)* Sister Chung, if you love him this much, can
    you love me this much as well? Didn't we all grow up together? Did I ever
    leave you? Didn't I say that I will always wait for you?

Girl: Brother Cheng-ming. Just because you grew up with me, just because you said
    you will always wait for me and never leave me; you and he are very different.
    I neither know where he came from nor do I know where he is going. In my
    heart, he is my god. Regardless where or when he is standing or sitting, his eyes
    can see so far away. Although I don't know much, deep inside me that far away
    place is where my dream lies. He is just simply the god I was looking for. Even
    when he is away from me, I still feel his presence. Someday he will come back
    and take me with him to wherever he is going. May be far, far away …

Young Man: Oh, no, sister Chung, he must be a ghost rather than a god; he must be a wizard, and you are bewitched.[1]

The above dialogue reveals the romantic emotion and atmosphere when the wanderer visited Chung, the romance which Chung still remembers so dearly and vividly. On the other hand, the later part of the dialogue in which Chung says, "Just because you grew up with me ... He is just simply the god I was looking for," shows pathetic feeling on the part of Cheng-ming who wants to be united with Chung, but is rejected as Chung is completely hypnotized by the magnetic power of the wanderer and looking forward to the day of his revisit.

The above dialogue immediately echoes the following between Ellida and Dr. Wangel:

Wangel: This man must have had a strange power over you, Ellida.

Ellida: Oh, yes. He was terrifying man.

Wangel: But you mustn't think about this anymore. Never! Promise me, please, Ellida my dearest! Now we're going to try a different cure for you. A more bracing air than up here in the fjords. The fresh salt tang of sea air. What do you say?

Ellida: Ah! You mustn't speak of these things! You mustn't think about it! There is no salvation for me there. I know only too well that ... I shall never be rid of this thing, not even out there.

Wangel: What thing? Ellida my dear, what exactly do you mean?

Ellida: All horror of it, I mean. This mysterious power he has over my mind ...

Wangel: But you have rid yourself of this. Long ago. When you broke with him. All that was over long ago.

Ellida: (*jumps up*) No, that's not just it. It isn't!

Wangel: Not all over!

Ellida: No Wangel, it isn't all over! And I'm afraid it never will be. Never in this world!

Wangel: (*in a choked voice*) Are you trying to say that deep down you have never been able to forget this strange man?

Ellida: I had forgotten him. But then it was as though he seemed to come back.[2]

As we can see from the dialogues in *Return to the South* and *The Lady from the Sea*, the common element in the characters of Ellida and Chung is that both are yearning for being united with their lovers. When Chung desires to be united with the wanderer whose home is "white mountains and black jungles," we expect T'ien Han's intention to recapture a symbol of the sea, in the form of the land in the character of Chung; nevertheless, we fail to recognize it, because, we find that the reason why Chung wants to leave home is that "Chung is longing for a break from her roots, signifying boredom and the lack of aspiration,"[3] and that "she does not want to be tied to any one place."[4] In the case of Chung, unlike Ellida, there is no demon-like power that pushes her to her destructive action of her present environment, but she is simply enchanted by the wanderer, in addition to the fact that she is bored with her countryside life. In Act I of *The Lady from the Sea*, there is a scene where Ellida returns to the shore from swimming and appears before Wangel and Arnholm and complains that the water there is sick and warm: "Fresh! Good Lord, this water's never fresh. So stale and tepid. Ugh! The water's sick here in the fjord."[5] To Ellida, it had to be the ocean water since the sea is the source of her being. Realizing this, Wangel tells her that they could move to the seaside, but Ellida is so caught up in the dream of the wanderer, she refuses Wangel's proposition. Chung refuses Cheng-ming's proposal not because the land is the source of her being, but because she is simply bored with her life in the countryside. If she accepts it, she would have to spend the rest of her life in the same place; thus, Chung wants to leave. Being frustrated, she resents the situation, she is overcome with an appetite for sensation, and looks forward to a life in the primitive world, yet she is still not the child of nature like Ellida.

In China during 1920s playwrights became interested in Ibsen's romantic works, and thus during this era, T'ien Han interpreted *The Lady from the Sea* as a romantic piece unlike his earlier view of it as a play dealing with the idea of "human responsibility."[6] It seems that he tried to create a romantic Ellida-like character in this play but failed to put the breath of Ellida into the character of Chung.

The play *The Disabled Horse* shows Tamaki, the wife of Andō, a retired army officer, who remembers well a red sail ship she had seen in a mirage in her childhood. She is greatly attracted to Mutsuo, a seaman, who tells her about the freedom of sea life. She is so attracted to him that she decides to leave home and desert her husband. Andō's batman, upon learning it, in a rage, attempts to shoot Tamaki and Mutsuo, but instead kills the disabled horse that had been wounded in the Russo-Japanese War which Andō had loved most dearly.

Tamaki, like Ellida, lives in an inappropriate environment so that her individuality is always encroached upon. Let us examine the dialogue between Tamaki and her sister Yasue when the latter discovers the former out of sorts:

Yasue: Were you here? Why, what makes you feel so depressed? I don't see you this way too often.

Tamaki: Don't you see me like this too often?

Yasue: You always look gay and happy!

Tamaki: I feel depressed all the time; so I try to make myself look happy. Otherwise, I will suffocate …

Yasue: Why so?

Tamaki: Listen! You could hear the sounds of the sea waves, couldn't you? Each time the waves lap the beach, I feel as if my body rises to the surface of the water and I become so restless![7]

The last line of Tamaki, "Each time the waves lap the beach, I feel as if my body rises to the surface of the water …," reveals that she feels confined like Ellida and "the neurotic symptoms as a result of the tension between her defensive inner life and the free, loving outer life"[8] and "the forces," in Tamaki's character "that hold her captive and the form her struggle for self-liberation takes are similar"[9] to Ellida.

The above Japanese dialogue reminds us of what Dr. Wangel says to Ellida in Act II:

Yes. The fact is, you can't bear these surroundings. The mountains oppress and weigh down your spirit. There's not enough light for you here. Not enough space. Not enough strength and sweep to the wind.[10]

As seen above, Ellida, like Tamaki, has a strong yearning for the ocean. She considers that she herself belongs to the sea and that the sea is the source of her being, so that she, like Tamaki, could not resist herself—she is possessed by a demon called the sea which pushes her to destroy her present self and drives her to go forward to the ocean. This is what differs from Chung.

When we consider the common element in Tamaki, Ellida and Chung that I discussed above for comparison, we may say that, although all the three wanted to leave home, Chung cannot be mermaid of the land since no demon of the land is living in her, while Ellida and Tamaki are both mermaids of the sea.

II

At a different level, another reason in common as to why Ellida, Chung and Tamaki desired to leave home is freedom which they all wanted to gain.

Ellida and Tamaki are encouraged to break with their circumstances by the wanderer who desired to take them away from the false world. Ellida made a secret promise long before she married Dr. Wangel and Tamaki was first fascinated by the sea when she was only ten years old. They have not been living in the real world, but a world of falsehood and hypocrisy; and so, they are obsessed by the sea where their fate is to join their old lovers, Friman and Mutsuo. In the Chinese play, Chung longs to leave for a new world after she becomes bored with her life in the country; thus, she awaits her lover Sing's visit to fetch her and take her to a new world. In each case, their longing is a symbol of man's strong inner drive and desire to enter and create a new life of his own, leaving the secular world and society where conventional duty and the established old morality are entangled. Hence, it is safe to say that all three looked forward to freedom.

However, two of them succeed to gain freedom while one fails. Chung meets the wanderer Sing who comes to fetch her, but her mother already had promised Cheng-ming one hour ago to give her to him, so Sing is disappointed and leaves Chung for good, as did Friman in *The Lady from the Sea*; thus, Chung's dream to free herself did not materialize. In the case of Tamaki, Andō's batman attempts to shoot Tamaki and Mutsuo when he discovered them eloping, but he shot a disabled horse instead, so Tamaki eventually succeeds to go with Mutsuo to the sea. How about Ellida's case? When Friman asked Ellida to go to the sea with him, Wangel gradually understands what she wanted—freedom.

> Wangel: (*To Ellida*) I'm beginning to understand you ... little by little. You think in images ... Your mind works in visual terms. Your yearning for the sea ... your attachment to this man, this stranger ... these things were nothing more than an expression of your growing desire for freedom. That's all.[11]

When Ellida was given the freedom to choose Friman or Wangel, she decided not to go with Friman. Friman left. In this case, her decision to stay with Wangel means that her aspiration and yearning for freedom has been fulfilled. Accordingly, her dream to free herself materialized and she was able to start a life of true marriage with Wangel as she gained the freedom she sought on land.

All the three characters are regarded to have been sick and seeking a "cure" from the disease: the "cure" for them was freedom. Nevertheless, it was only Ellida who was "cured" because she was given the freedom to choose between Wangel or Friman, while Tamaki and Chung were not given it, so they began to pursue it by deserting their partners.

III

Now let us look at another group of characters: Andō, Dr. Wangel and Cheng-ming who all failed to keep their partners satisfied. The common element in all three is that they are all insecure psychologically and that they tried their best to make their partners happy but failed, not because of their inability but because of their partners' nature. All three are good men and well-to-do people in their profession and dependable ethically and financially—Cheng-ming has some property he inherited from his father, and Dr. Wangel is a physician while Andō is a retired major who now lives comfortably on his retirement allowance pay check. Therefore they are considered to be therefore a symbol of security and trust.

IV

When it comes to the matter of the characters of the wanderers, we find even closer parallels. Sing, having lived with Chung and her mother for a year in the countryside, became homesick and left, just as Friman, having visited and met Ellida at the lighthouse, left for the sea which is his home. Then, Friman returns to Ellida, as Sing does as a hidden character of shadow through the world of Chung's imagination. Sing this time returned to the North having had travelled through the South, just as Friman came in an English ship and met Ellida over the fence in order to fetch her as Sing did Chung. In the case of the Japanese play too, Mutsuo, the wanderer, tells Tamaki about freedom of sea life with the intention of taking her with him to the sea.

Nevertheless, at the end, the expectations of the two wanderers are destroyed. Ellida, realizing her human responsibility when she was given the freedom of choice by Dr. Wangel, decides to stay with Dr. Wangel, so that Friman goes away with a wounded heart in search of the free world. In the case of *Return to the South*, when Sing comes to visit the house, he is told that he should have come one hour earlier and that Chung's mother had already given her daughter to Cheng-ming, so that, like Friman, he leaves the scene in search of the free world. But, in the case of the Japanese play, the situation in the end is slightly different, because Andō's batman, upon learning Mutsuo's intention of taking Tamaki with him to the sea, in a rage, attempts to shoot them; and yet, there is no question about that, as far as Mutsuo is concerned, he is the wanderer and the same character essentially like Friman as a manmaid of the sea and Sing as a manmaid of the land. Ibsen once remarked, "There is something extraordinarily captivating in the sea. When one stands and stares into the water, it is as if one sees that life which stirs about on land, only in another form. There is connection and similarity in everything."[12] Therefore, Friman, Sing and Mutsuo are all regarded as symbols of nature.

V

Besides the characters of Ibsen, some parallels of dramatic techniques are found in the Chinese and Japanese plays such as the use of symbolism, retrospective method, etc.

The use of symbol in the works of Ibsen written during 1880s is a special feature of his, and, "with the publication of *The Lady from the Sea* in 1888, Ibsen's position as a symbolist had become clear to everyone."[13] The most representative use of symbol may be that of "the sea" which appears throughout the Norwegian play to represent (1) Ellida's ambivalent feeling; (2) Ellida's yearning for the wanderer; and (3) Ellida's yearning for freedom as I have already discussed earlier. Another example is that, when it comes to the ending part, as Ellida decides to stay with Wangel, Friman vaults over the fence and says to Ellida before he leaves her, "From now on you're nothing more than—a shipwreck I barely remember."[14] Here the word "shipwreck" symbolizes to mean (1) forgotten lady; (2) episode in life; (3) heart broken lady, etc. Likewise, in the later part of the Chinese play, we find that Chung keeps a worn-out shoe of Sing as if it is a treasure of the house. This is something Sing left when he left the house, and in the end, Sing will take it with him when he leaves the house with a broken heart. It symbolizes: (1) Chung herself as one being forgotten and left alone by Sing, or Chung without the wanderer; (2) the wanderer's trodden tracks of past journey—he wandered all over in China, so that the shoe became worn out; (3) a part of the wanderer's body; (4) memories of the wanderer; (5) re-opening of the scars of the wanderer's wounded heart; and (6) a partner who nurses the wanderer's wounded heart. In the Japanese play, a "red ship" appears. This is what Tamaki had seen in a mirage in her childhood, which symbolizes Tamaki's yearning for the sea, or in a broader sense "sea" itself, because like Ellida, the sea is the source of Tamaki's being. In the Chinese and Japanese plays, the land and the sea are used as symbols of nature and also to mean "freedom." It is Ibsen's device to have a word signified more than two things.

Another technique of Ibsen which the Chinese and Japanese playwrights seem to have learned is that, as Henning Kehler, a Danish Ibsen scholar, pointed out, "When a figure is attracted by others, Ibsen made the latter symbolic."[15] Ellida is attracted by Friman and the sea. Likewise, Tamaki is attracted by Mutsuo and the sea, as Chung is attracted by the wanderer and the primitive land. T'ien Han and Satō Kōroku seem to have used Ibsen's curious habit in their own productions.

The retrospective method is not Ibsen's invention since Sophocles had already used it in the fifth century B.C. Nonetheless, Ibsen made extensive use of it in his plays. In *The Lady from the Sea*, Ibsen created a premarital past relationship between Ellida and Arnholm before her marriage to Wangel which disclosed through the dialogues between Ellida and Arnholm. In the case of the Chinese play, the past relationship between Chung and the wanderer Sing is revealed through the dialogue between Chung and Cheng-ming when he asks her why she is reluctant to marry him. Further revelation about the past relationship between the two is made through the world of Chung's imagination in which Chung and the wanderer speak. In the Japanese play, the dialogues between Andō and Tamaki, who live on a seashore, reveals that Tamaki was a nurse in a Japanese army hospital during the Russo-Japanese War which was where she met Major Andō when he was hospitalized after being wounded in a battle. T'ien Han and Satō, using the method, could have saved space; both of the Asian plays are one-act plays.

Another parallel in dramaturgy is "separation" as the backbone of these plays. Francis Fergusson says, "all of the characters we meet in Dr. Wangel's household feel that they are missing out; that they are somewhat separated from life and the love they need and cannot find."[16] In this drama of Ibsen's, all of the characters leave after all—Friman isn't the only one to leave in the end, but also Lyngstrad the sculptor who goes abroad seeking freedom recalling a sweet memory of Bolette. Bolette also leaves for a new life in a big city in Norway. This is also the case in the Japanese and

Chinese plays. Andō remains home but Mutsuo and Tamaki leave for sea, while Chung leaves her mother to pursue the wanderer and seek freedom when Sing leaves the house. In this respect, every character in each of the three plays is different from each other.

Furthermore, the Chinese and Japanese writers seem to have utilized a method called *scène à faire*. "This involves the treatment of protagonist and antagonist in the scene in which the final decision is reached."[17] As we have already observed, there is a scene in which Ellida confronts Dr. Wangel for the freedom to choose (Wangel or Friman) in *The Lady from the Sea* and there are scenes in *The Disabled Horse* in which Tamaki confronts Andō for her freedom and another occasion she confronts Ando for her freedom of choice (Mutsuo or Andō), and on another occasion instance, Andō confronts Tamaki over the horse, and in *Return to the South*, Chung confronts Cheng-ming to choose him or the wanderer.

VI

As seen above, it is clear that there are a number of parallels in characterization and dramatic techniques used in the Norwegian, Chinese and Japanese plays.

When and how did the Chinese and Japanese playwrights become interested in Ibsen, then? T'ien Han studied in Japan in the early twentieth century where he became interested in Western drama and, with an expectation of the appearance of new drama in China, he organized the Spring Willow Society which consisted of Chinese students in Japan and which closely associated with Japanese Shimpa (a new school in Japan opposing to the Kabuki which overemphasizes the picturesque form of drama. In 1907 this group produced one act of Alexandre Dumas fil's *La dame aux camelias* and an adapted version of Harriet Beecher Stowe's *Uncle Tom's Cabin* in Shimpa form in Tokyo. In this production, lighting, dialogue, acting as well as the scenery used were different from the Chinese traditional ways, and, this experience became an impetus for reforming the Chinese traditional drama. It is interesting to note that this production by the Spring Willow Society coincided with the Japanese Free Theater's (Jiyu Gekijo) production of *John Gabriel Borkman* directed by Osanai Kaoru (1881–1928), a Japanese drama critic and playwright, with an intention of reforming the Japanese traditional drama. T'ien Han, having returned to China, founded with his wife the South China Society in 1923 which became one of the earliest companies in China devoted to the study, writing and production of modern drama.

T'ien Han read a good number of Ibsen's plays while he was studying in Japan and became so interested in Ibsen as to call himself "Budding Ibsen of China."[18] After 1920, he became more attracted by the romantic side of Ibsen rather than his social side. In fact, his views of *The Lady from the Sea* while he was in Japan and after he returned to China were different. In a letter to Kuo Mo-jo in 1920, he expressed his earlier view, interpreting the drama as one dealing with the idea of human responsibility when making a choice between duty and freedom. But, by 1929, when he wrote *Return to the South*, his view had been changed as to see it as a romantic piece of work; so T'ien Han tried to realize and recapture in his play the romantic theme, the romantic mood and characters of the Norwegian drama. About Ibsen's influence on *Return to the South*, Kwok-kan Tam affirms it as follows: "Ibsen's influence on T'ien Han is subtle and at the same time obvious—subtle in the treatment of longing as a theme and obvious in the similarity in mood, diction and characterization."[19]

The Japanese playwright Satō began reading Ibsen early in the twentieth century. *Engei Gahō* (Jan. 1908) reveals that in November 1907, a reporter of the magazine paid Satō a visit for an interview article titled "Plays Which I Have Written," in which Satō mentioned regretfully, "The time for Ibsen's play production on stage has not yet arrived in Japan; the audience does not understand Ibsen well yet, for example, they are only interested in the plot and the change of the incident in his works, but not in the nature of the characters."[20] Satō had already read Ibsen's major works in Japanese and other languages by November 1907; and, we can understand, viewing this comment he made on Ibsen that Satō had a considerably good knowledge of Ibsen and his works by the end of 1907. During the years of 1908–1909, Satō read all Ibsen's works in English about which Fujiki Hiroyuki remarks, "Satō Kōroku read almost all of Ibsen's dramas by and through 1909. Being so impressed, he immediately began translating Ibsen's works such as *Little Eyolf*, etc., into Japanese."[21]

About Ibsen's influence on his work, Satō himself says, "*The Disabled Horse* is my first work after having read and been moved by Ibsen's plays."[22] Fujiki further comments, "In *The Disabled Horse*, we can see clearly the footmarks of Ibsen."[23] Furthermore, Akiba Tarō points out, "It was in 1909 that a new Japanese drama was written in the Ibsenian style by a playwright named Satō Kōroku. The title of the drama was *The Disabled Horse* and was published in a magazine *Chūō-Kōron* (April 1909)."[24] On another occasion Akiba said, "Satō Kōroku and Nakamura Kichizō were the earliest among those young Japanese playwrights who digested Ibsen's modern thought and dramaturgy so well."[25]

In this way, considering the external testimonies together with the internal evidences shown above through comparative textual analysis, I can positively conclude that T'ien Han and Satō Kōroku wrote *Return to the South* and *The Disabled Horse* respectively under the influence of Ibsen's work *The Lady from the Sea*.

NOTES

 1. T'ien Han, *Chu-tso hsüan* (Peking: Jen-min wen-hsüeh ch'u-pan-she, 1955), pp. 137–38.
 2. James McFarlane (trans.), *Oxford Ibsen*, Vol. VII (New York: Oxford University Press, 1966), pp. 64–65.
 3. Kwok-kan Tam, "Ibsen and Modern Chinese Dramatists: Influence and Parallels," in *Modern Chinese Literature* (San Francisco: San Francisco State University, Spring 1986), p. 54.
 4. Ibid.
 5. Rolf Fjelde (trans.), *Henrik Ibsen: The Complete Major Prose Plays* (New York: Farrar, Straus, Giroux, 1978), p. 604.
 6. *T'ien Han san-wen chi* (Shanghai: Chin-tai shu-tien, 1936), p. 68.
 7. Satō Kōroku, "Haiba," *Chūō-Kōron* (Tokyo: Chūō-Kōron sha, April 1909), pp. 14–15.
 8. James Hurt, *Catalina's Dream* (Urbana: University of Illinois Press, 1972), p. 143.
 9. Ibid., p. 140.
10. Rolf Fjelde, op. cit., p. 623.
11. McFarlane, op. cit., p. 122.
12. Halvdan Koht, *H. Ibsen: Eit Diktarliv, II* (Oslo: Aschehoug, 1954), p. 186.
13. Maurice Valency, *The Flower and the Castle* (New York: Macmillan, 1963), p. 380.
14. Rolf Fjelde, op. cit., p. 686.
15. Henning Kehler, "Studier i det ibsenske Drama," *Edda, V* (Oslo: Universitetsforlaget, 1916), p. 97.
16. Francis Fergusson, "*The Lady from the Sea*," in *Contemporary Approaches to Ibsen* (Oslo: Universitetsforlaget, 1966), p. 51.

17. Toshihiko Sato, "Ibsen Parallels in Modern Japanese Drama," in *Yearbook of General and Comparative Literature* (Bloomington: Indiana University Press, 1962), p. 62.

18. *T'ien Han san-wen chi*, p. 54.

19. Kwok-kan Tam, op. cit.

20. *Engei Gahō* (Tokyo: Engei Gahō sha, Jan. 1908), pp. 94–95.

21. Fujiki Hiroyuki, "Ipusen," in *Obei Sakka to Nihon Kindai Bungaku*, edited by Fukuda Mitsuharu et al. (Tokyo: Kyōiku Shuppan Sentā, 1976), p. 238.

22. Satō Kōroku, "Haiba," *Kabuki* (Tokyo: Kabuki Hakkōsho, May 1912), p. 68.

23. Fujiki, op. cit.

24. Akiba Tarō, *Nihon Shingeki Shi*, Vol. I (Tokyo: Risōsha, 1955), p. 566

25. Akiba Tarō, *Meiji Kindai Geki Shū* (Tokyo: Chikuma-Shobō, 1967), p. 387.

4. The Double Plot of *T'ao-hua shan*

C. H. Wang

K'ung Shang-jen 孔尚任 (1648–1718) revitalizes a good technique of classical poetics by approaching the vernacular in *T'ao-hua shan* 桃花扇. The interaction of two major motifs in a single composition, ever since Ch'u Yüan's 屈原 *Li sao* 離騷, creates a process that allows them to illuminate each other in an incremental manner. Politics and love are entwined, imagistically, throughout the plot of that poignant song. The thematic intents of one contribute to identifying what the other purports to mean. No student of classical poetry would understand *Li sao* correctly without constantly checking the two motifs in reciprocity, or, for the better, reading the one against the other as backdrop, and vice versa. In the Prelude to his play, K'ung Shang-jen has the old Master of Ceremonies, who appears to impersonate the dramatist himself, define the method of *T'ao-hua shan* as follows:

> It employs the emotions entailed by separation and union to depict feelings about rise and fall.[1]
>
> 借離合之情，寫興亡之感。

The emotions and feelings, two significant entities generated by related experiences, interact closely in the play to produce an effect that is both theatrically moving and literarily powerful. It is a fully developed masterpiece of Chinese drama.[2]

Indeed, the two motifs of separation and union, which entail emotions in the lovers, are presented in parallel and, by themselves, organized into a plot; so are the motifs of the rise and fall of political powers, viewed in successive scenes, sufficient to become another plot. The parallel structure is not contained within a single plot only. It extends to the whole play of *T'ao-hua shan*. The structure of the play is set forth according to a rhetorical device of antithesis which seems ontological in substance. The two plots progress together, complementing and interpreting each other, in the discovery of the drama. They fulfill themselves in the end, and, combined, offer a resolution toward the denouement, where there is poetic justice risen from illusion, a consolation of philosophy based on religious faith, and there is the persistent doubt whether history and fiction can be distinguished and if the world is not just a stage.

K'ung Shang-jen believes that drama, which he specifies as *ch'uan-ch'i* 傳奇, is an effective vehicle to arrive at many important goals. It is, to begin with, a serious institution derived from respective functions of some classical subjects. In style, it absorbs the features of all types of poetry, parallel prose, and tales; in the description of characters and scenes it resembles graphic art. K'ung Shang-jen also asserts that, as far as thematic stress is concerned, *ch'uan-ch'i* attempts to imitate what is found in *Shih Ching* 詩經, and *Ch'un Ch'iu* 春秋, and other histories from antiquity.[3] The type of drama he handles, he believes, is as weighty as history, as expansive as fiction, and as exquisite and resounding as poetry. It certainly would not be adequate if a play deals only with romantic love, or political intrigues, or military adventures. A play aspires to comprehend several topics and weave them organically into a whole. By the same token, a play is good only when it is variably embellished with all the stylistic devices typical of many poetic genres while the action takes place in a double plot. In the case of *Tao-hua shan*, it is clear that the love theme that directs the first plot is fascinating by itself, but it is not weighty enough to sustain drama as a serious institution, K'ung implies. It takes the second plot, a national catastrophe brought about by numerous factors, to complete the play as drama. The relationship between these two plots is not one of balancing but of opposition. Sometimes they tend to confront each other in order to yield the correct meanings which the action conveys. In Scene 14, for example, Hou Fang-yü 侯方域, the hero of the play, drafts a letter on behalf of General Shih K'o-fa 史可法, President of the Board of War, in response to Ma Shih-ying 馬士英, Governor of Feng-yang, in which he outlines the crimes of Prince Fu (福王), whom the villainous Ma and his clique have conspired to support as emperor. They express strong objections to Ma's proposal. The incident reveals a confrontation between the righteous and the wicked among the intellectuals soon after the fall of Peking in 1644. It progresses in this plot without blemish. The incident, too, intensifies the misery which permeates Scene 25, where Li Hsiang-chün 李香君, the heroine, is given a "peach-blossom palace fan" (桃花宮扇) by the same Prince, now Emperor Hung-kuang 弘光 , as a token of patronage. The irony is obvious because it is just in Scenes 22 and 23 where we see how a fan (the authentic token of love bearing Hou Fang-yü's poem), which Hsiang-chün had brandished "like a sword" in defence of her chastity and stained with her own blood, was painted to become a "peach-blossom fan" (桃花扇) and sent to Hou far in North China.[4] An event in the second plot cuts across the first and generates meanings to what it touches there.

In order to maintain the structure in such active equilibrium K'ung Shang-jen searches through classical metaphysics for principles to follow. The "fan-li" 凡例 he sets out preceding the play shows his earnest intention to create a work not only for folk theatre but also for the literati's studio. Of all points he puts stress on, K'ung assumes a *historicity* of the plots as a primary concern. He seeks perfection in all aspects of the play, such as the use of verse in juxtaposition with prose, the preciseness of stage directions, and the arrangement of an exact number of scenes in balance. The play proper is composed of forty scenes, divided equally into two parts, the *shang* 上 (Part One), and the *hsia* 下 (Part Two).[5] In addition, Part One is preceded by a so-called "Enquiry" (Prelude) and followed by an "Inter-calary Scene," whereas Part Two is preceded by an "Additional Scene" and followed by a "Sequel" (Epilogue).

If the antithetical arrangement of the scenes is literarily crafty, strongly savouring of the style common in some classical writings such as parallel prose, regulated verse, and especially the "eight-legged essay," the distribution of the *dramatis personae* is ingenious. K'ung first assigns his thirty characters to four departments, namely *left*, *right*, *odd* and *even*; then he adds one more, called the *general department* (總部). The left department is led by Hou Fang-yü the hero and the right by Li Hsiang-chün the heroine; all the characters in these two departments are represented in diverse positive modes (色). The odd department is led by Shih K'o-fa and the even by Tso Liang-yü 左良玉; they are then represented in various negative moods (氣). The fifth department is occupied by just the Taoist Priest Chang Wei 張薇 and the old Master of Ceremonies. Now, the characters in the diverse modes are positive because they enact the plot of separation and union in romantic love and, as a consequence, conclude their life in a reverent way delivered by the Taoist Priest. The characters in the various moods are negative, because they participate mainly in the political strug-gles that cause the fall of one dynasty and give rise to another, while almost all of them, without blessing from the supernatural, meet violent death one by one, to be lamented by the old Master of Ceremonies who, in turn, is the playwright. K'ung Shang-jen points out that the arrangement is done according to the way *yin* and *yang* operate.

T'ao-hua shan is the best example of a vernacular piece of work intentionally elevated by an erudite man of letters to convey messages for the audience in both low and high cultures. As it is not easy, however, to predict if the first plot of romantic love appeals more to the literati or the common people, so it is hard to tell whether the second plot, the transition of dynasties, finds more enthusiasm in one class than another. Drama is such a unique art that it often mingles itself with other cultures easily. The power of drama rises from its mimetic nature, or the delightful confusion of the real and unreal, the pathetic and comic, the grandiloquent and feeble, and the horrible and beautiful. All of these elements are present in *T'ao-hua shan*. One of the most significant innovations for which K'ung is always commended, specifically, is his meticulous handling of historical figures. All the thirty characters, either major or minor, and most of the events celebrated in the play, can be traced and verified in history, while many literary references are made to extant works authored by the characters, such as Hou Fang-yü and Juan Ta-ch'eng 阮大鋮. The dramatist, being a lineal descendant of Confucius in the sixty-fourth generation, may find it necessary to be faithful to history when he takes up a vernacular attempt in such a critical age.[6] Through the old Master of Ceremonies, he comments on Part One of his own play: "As if it were written with Ssu-ma Ch'ien's 司馬遷 historical approach, involving Tung-fang Shuo 東方朔 on the stage."[7] The dramatist assumed an historian's attitude in recounting events which occurred roughly half a century before, and he accentuated the work with implicit criticism typical of Tung-fang Shuo's rhetoric.[8]

The unique quality of *T'ao-hua shan*, therefore, has much to do with the dramatist's manipulation of the relationship between the historical and the fictitious. While most Chinese writers endeavour to charge their fictitious works with a quasi-historicity, K'ung Shang-jen treats history as fiction.[9] The play opens, with the Prelude, or "Enquiry," in the year 1684 (most likely the very year in which K'ung initiated the writing project), and immediately proceeds to 1643, through a flashback, as the two plots are identified in a total of twelve scenes. The conflict between the Revival Club (復社) and Ma Shih-ying's clique resulted in the separation of the hero and the heroine at the end of Scene 12, in early winter of 1643. Events occurred historically in 1644 are, then, covered in the next twelve scenes, with the most momentous incident, the death of Emperor Ch'ung-chen 崇禎 in late spring, reported in the beginning of this section. Those occurred in the following year, 1645, are celebrated in the last seventeen scenes, in which the Manchu conquest of South China is manifested after the suicide of General Shih K'o-fa in midsummer that year while the eventual reunion of the hero and heroine in early autumn, though brief, leads toward the interpretation that life without a Chinese monarch is vanity. The Epilogue, or "Sequel," picks up an episode dated in 1648, in which the surviving Ming loyalists, now disguised as a woodcutter and a fisherman, and the old Master of Ceremonies join in a crescendo in trio lamenting the loss of glory that once shone over the city of Nanking.

The play deals mainly with history dated from 1643 through 1645. Most of the events which had taken place during that period of time were, in fact, well remembered not only by intellectuals but also by common folk at the end of the seventeenth century: the excessively pathetic death of Ch'ung-chen, the treacherous conspiracy of Ma Shih-ying, the corruption of Juan Ta-ch'eng the poet, the integrity of the Revival Club members, the martyr-dom of the generals, especially Shih K'o-fa, and the dubious royalty of Hung-kuang. There is no doubt that people in all walks of life, toward the end of the seventeenth century, were familiar with these stories, and many people remember them even down till today. For the literati in particular, the "four distinguished young lords" (四公子), the superior personality of popular artists like Liu Ching-t'ing 柳敬亭 and Su K'un-sheng 蘇崑生 in contrast with that of a scholar like Ch'ien Ch'ien-i 錢謙益 , the legendary life of Liu Ju-shih 柳如是 , and those of other dissenters, such as Huang Tsung-hsi 黃宗羲 , Ku Yen-wu 顧炎武 and Wang Fu-chih 王夫之 , are standard exemplars in their consideration of what knowledge and person-ality signify during a time of crisis. All the events and personages are historical, and though they are shown in different strata they rarely seem to be twisted. In other words, there was, by the time when K'ung Shang-jen assumed to write the play, definite consensus among literate and illiterate alike as to how one should pass judgment on them.

There was little chance for K'ung Shang-jen to depart from the standard interpretation of this history. He, however, was not writing strictly as an historian, despite his claim that in doing the play he was as earnest as his ancestor was in writing *Ch'un Ch'iu*. Ironically, the only subject on which he might be able to offer a truly original opinion, one that could be different from what the court would accept, was the meaning of the 1645 Manchu Conquest, and that was one which he had to avoid tackling directly. Ku Ts'ai 顧采, his collaborator on an earlier work, *Hsiao Hu-lei* 小忽雷, which also deals with an historical theme from the T'ang period, commented most rationally on *Tao-hua shan*: "Though peopled with historical personages and proceeding according to real events, as though there were no refrains from any taboo, I still would not necessarily take it as a history written in dramatic verse."[10] K'ung Shang-jen created a piece of artistic, fictitious work after history by adhering closely to the standard evaluation of historical figures. For the fiction of it, he singles out the heroine Li Hsiang-chün to preside over the first plot. The conventions of the theatre demand a female role to be complemented by a male, and he has Hou Fang-yü, who at the same time also cuts actively into the second plot in order to maintain an historical veracity for the drama. Hou Fang-yü, consequently, occupies more scenes than his lover does, and, under such circumstances, interacts intensely with other historical figures in the identification of his role in history and fiction. The characterization of Hou is done through such a process toward composition, by relating him with several groups of people in different times and places. His role in the play can be understood best through an analysis of his contacts with three groups of historical figures.

Hou Fang-yü's relationship with Liu Ching-t'ing and Su K'un-sheng is that of an elite scholar with popular artists, i.e., classical learning *vis-à-vis* vernacular entertainment. The meeting of Hou and Liu occurs rightly in Scene 1, when the former, in the company of two famous scholars, Ch'en Chen-hui 陳貞慧 and Wu Ying-chi 吳應箕, visits the latter in Nanking. The scholars request Liu to tell them a story. "I'm afraid things like popular tales and folk stories cannot meet your approval," Liu Ching-t'ing says. "What can I do? I'll tell you something from the book you read, the *Analects*!" The dramatist writes with great enthusiasm about Liu Ching-t'ing's performance, elevating his language and contents to a height equal to that of classical literature. Consequently, Hou Fang-yü comments: "I see that Ching-t'ing is a man of extremely high personality; his mind is broad and carefree. He belongs to our group—storytelling must just be a habit." Indeed, Liu Ching-t'ing knows very well that he uses the skill for didactic purposes and that he is not a simple entertainer. When Hou Fang-yü needs a man to deliver a letter to General Tso Liang-yü, in order to prevent a national calamity, Liu volunteers to go (Scene 10). With that as a start, Liu participates in witnessing the downfall of the Ming dynasty on the side of the loyal intellectuals. And two years later, when he again volunteers to deliver another letter, which contains a denunciation of Nanking politics, from General Tso to Ma Shih-ying, now the Grand Secretary, he is compared to Ching K'o 荆軻 (Scene 31). By bringing him together with Hou Fang-yü, Ch'en Chen-hui and Wu Ying-chi in a Nanking jail, the dramatist indicates that he is indeed spiritually an equal of the Revival Club members (Scene 33). Finally, when he enters the stage as a fisherman, Liu Ching-t'ing is recognized as the wisest man of his age.[11]

Su K'un-sheng, who accompanies Liu Ching-t'ing in the denouement, is dressed as a woodcutter. Similarly, he is now a wise man of his age. At first, as Li Hsiang-chün's music tutor, he also appeared to be a lowly professional only. He distinguished himself as a messenger, too, when he agreed to send the peach-blossom fan on Hsiang-chün's behalf to Hou Fang-yü. The first plot of the play reaches a climax with the fan as a recurrent image (Scene 23). His faithful friendship is amplified in the scene as he strives to keep the fan from soaking in the water when he was pushed into the Yellow River. K'ung Shang-jen intends to portray an ideal folk hero of the highest loyalty through this incident (Scene 27). One of the most theatrically exciting episodes in the play, however, is the one in which Su K'un-sheng tries to provoke Tso Liang-yü to arrest him, so that he may supplicate the general to go for Hou Fang-yü's rescue (Scene 31). When it is done, with Liu Ching-t'ing gone on an errand, the singer replaces the storyteller as the artist in company with General Tso. Eventually, it is Su K'un-sheng who is left alone to mourn Tso's death:

> The hero has died of anger, people all gone,
> Leaving here but a hollow casket.
> I'm just a friend summoning his soul by the river,
> Having nowhere to buy a cup of wine.

> 氣死英雄人盡走，撇下了空船柩。
> 俺是個招魂江邊友，沒處買一杯酒。

(Scene 34)

The next time Su K'un-sheng appears, he is protecting Li Hsiang-chün to hide in Mount Ch'i-hsia 棲霞山 (Scene 36), a scene paralleling exactly the one in which Liu Ching-t'ing guides Hou Fang-yü in the same direction (Scene 38). The two groups approach each other very closely in the mountain, but, interfered with by Taoist precepts, fail to make contact (Scene 39). Su K'un-sheng disappears in the woods. His identity as a recluse confirms in the classical manner an image of superlative wisdom, one that transcends social classes to reach a status of absolute morality.

With the elevation of Liu Ching-t'ing, a storyteller, and Su K'un-sheng, a singer, K'ung Shang-jen intends to justify his attempt at drama. Vernacular art, when deliberately attended to, can become a power greater than classical literature perhaps, and this is especially true during a time of political emergency. The rise of drama itself under the Mongol rule foreshadows the celebration of Liu and Su as men of integrity now at the start of the Manchu dynasty. When the Confucian scholars lose their strength, in one way or another, the royal family becomes a laughingstock, and as the social ethic breaks down the folk hero is the one who insists on the freedom to be both delightful and melancholy. When the classics prove weak in the face of Tartar horsemen, the theatre, K'ung Shang-jen insinuates, prevails as the meeting hall of the conquered, who are deprived but not completely overcome.

The corruption of Confucian scholars is shown ruthlessly in the characters Ma Shih-ying and Juan Ta-ch'eng.[12] The former, who has distinguished himself through superior literary talent, exposes his personality in a monologue addressed directly to the audience:

It is fortunate that this country is in trouble,
A time for us to get what we want and be successful.
幸遇國家多故，正我輩得意之秋。

(Scene 15)

The latter, in addition to his scholarship, is known to be the best playwright of the time. When Su K'un-sheng, alone, extemporizes a good song for his own contentment, he sighs: "Such a wonderful song—nobody but Juan Ta-ch'eng would be able to appreciate it" (Scene 31). Nevertheless, K'ung Shang-jen depicts this excellent scholar and talented poet unreservedly as avaricious, shameless, wicked, and ridiculous. Juan's soliloquy after the incident in which he was expelled from the Confucian temple by the Revival Club members is most revealing of a condemned soul. He introduces himself first as a famous poet and successful candidate in the civil service examinations, and describes how later on he has been despised by the intellectuals for his disgraceful behaviour in association with the eunuchs, and how he now lives in Nanking awaiting the opportunity to regain a good reputation. "If by chance I should come across a righteous gentleman who would pity and accept me, I would not miss it to become a repentant soul," he says. "If the way of heaven should turn to my advantage, the cold ashes would be kindled fiery again—I, Whisker Juan, would then ignore virtuous principles and do something terrible to make the world upside down" (Scene 4).

Juan Ta-ch'eng's harassment is the immediate cause of Hou Fang-yü's separation from Hsiang-chün (Scene 12). Here there is an overt conflict between the beautiful and the ugly, love and hatred. It is clear, too, that his harassment on the lovers is an act of revenge for the insult he has received not only from Hou and his friends but especially from Hsiang-chün. The fact that the most excruciating contempt for him is expressed by Hsiang-chün, a woman, indicates the low reputation Juan enjoys. Positively, it also conforms to a long-standing convention in the Chinese theatre, or vernacular literature in general, that the woman possesses great spiritual power and that she is never hesitant to express it. Juan Ta-ch'eng's plan for revenge is fulfilled, so he thinks, by the abrupt order Ma Shih-ying makes to drag her down the stairs, when Hou is away, and marry her to someone else. The farcical episode, in which her foster mother is married in her stead, proves the confusion Ma Shih-ying and Juan Ta-ch'eng have fallen into, unable even to bully correctly (Scene 22). The audience is exempted from any pity or fear, eventually, when this pair of villains are attacked by the mob in the wake of Nanking's fall (Scene 36). When they are executed by the thunder god and mountain spirits, respectively, in the visionary procession enacted by the Taoist Priest, the audience, despite the Priest's pathetic comments, celebrate it as the return of justice (Scene 40).[13]

Hou Fang-yü's relationship with Generals Tso Liang-yü and Shih K'o-fa completes his role as an active intellectual in the second plot of *T'ao-hua shan*. For the peace of Nanking, Hou Fang-yü assumed his father's name and wrote Tso Liang-yü, the old General Hou's protégé, to stop moving his troops eastward. This gave Juan Ta-ch'eng a pretext to slander him before Shih K'o-fa and, consequently, to force him out of Nanking (Scenes 9–12). While Tso Liang-yü's loyalty to the Ming throne is manifested in his ritualistic mourning for Ch'ung-chen, as witnessed by Liu Ching-t'ing, who serves on behalf of Hou to befriend him, Shih K'o-fa has accepted Hou Fang-yü as an advisor in his camp and instructed him to draft a denunciation of Prince Fu. Hou Fang-yü's participation in the bewildering development of the diminishing Ming royalty proves nearly tragic along with the bloody struggles of the two military leaders. Amidst the chaotic disputes of his inferiors, General Shih predicts the collapse of his army, while Hou is given the chance in North China to observe how the soldiers riot and defect to the Manchu camp. The detailed dramatization of the corrupt military morale and discipline, from Scenes 18 to 20, and then resumed in Scene 26, to end in the grotesque death of Kao Chieh 高傑, is certainly one of the most disturbing appraisals a literary man has written about the foolhardiness of the military.[14]

Nevertheless, the death of General Tso Liang-yü is registered with passion and courage (Scene 34). His desperate lamentation of the emperor earlier was witnessed by Liu Ching-t'ing and now his own death is eulogized by Su K'un-sheng. The scene is particularly dolorous because it is presented with an action that blends the straightforward loyalty, which the General holds toward the crown prince, with the heartbreaking disappointment he has over his own rebellious son. K'ung Shang-jen invents this interpretation to fulfill a dramatic tension built upon the conflicts between loyalty and filial piety or something equivalent, one which is always appealing to a Chinese audience.[15] Shih K'o-fa, according to the play, drowned himself in the Yangtze after the Manchu army had defeated him in Yang-chou 揚州 and crossed the river to attack Nanking.[16] The arrangement is such that the action is observed, then, by the old Master of Ceremonies, the nearly omniscient commentator of the play, and immediately made known to none other than Hou Fang-yü, Liu Ching-t'ing, and two other Revival Club scholars. The five join in a dirge for one of the last Ming martyrs in resistance of the Manchu invasion:

> Wandering by the river side,
> Anger in his bosom, to whom could he express it?
> Tears were scattered over this old man's face,
> Looking at the stretch of a lone city,
> Exhausted from expecting any rescue.
> He had fought in blood by commanding a reducing army;
> He had leapt out of the siege,
> To find that the old capital he loved so much
> Was empty with deserted feasts, songs vanished.
> The long Yangtze is a line,
> That links Wu and Ch'u three thousand *li* apart,
> Which, from here to there, have all fallen to an alien name.
> The rain whirls, the clouds change forms,
> And the chilly waves roll to the east—
> All the myriad things are just empty mists.
> We want your spirited soul to manifest,
> As this great summons follows you to the sea, under the distant sky!

走江邊，滿腔憤恨向誰言？
老淚風吹面，孤城一片，望救目穿。
使盡殘兵血戰，跳出重圍，
故國苦戀，誰知歌罷剩空筵！
長江一線，吳頭楚尾路三千，
盡歸別姓。
雨翻雲變，寒濤東捲──
萬事付空烟。
精魂顯，大招聲逐海天遠！

(Scene 38)

A minimal lament for the fall of Ming dynasty, finally, is implied in the personal mourning for a tragic hero. Shih K'o-fa superseded Tso Liang-yü in many respects, and one of them was his literary background which, unlike the way it had corrupted Ma Shih-ying and Juan Ta-ch'eng, sustained a Confucian personality to the last moment. The dirge is accentuated poetically with a comparison of the loyalist to Ch'u Yüan, whose death in the water was recognized as a heroic gesture affirming one's virtue against the menacing society.

All the characters in the three groups above are historical. By relating them privately or collectively, Hou Fang-yü enacts his life and, through him, the dramatist practices his *Ch'un Ch'iu* style of historical evaluation. The righteous generals are contrasted with the wicked civil officials, in a doubly antithetical parallelism, while they determine the fate of the hero and heroine. When the hero and heroine are not in direct contact with them or other characters in the rest of the two plots, Liu Ching-t'ing and Su K'un-sheng, the "aspects" of them, emerge to represent them and still function in the same manner as though they were the hero and heroine, through whose *separation* and *union* the dramatist evaluates the *rise* and *fall* of the political powers. This is the "decomposition" of Hou Fang-yü, and of Li Hsiang-chün. In decomposition, a person's character is "dissolved and replaced by several, each of whom possesses a different aspect of the character which in the simpler form of the myth is combined in one being." The technique makes the double plot proceed organically and functionally.[17] Why, then, would the dramatist choose to let Hou Fang-yü, the high-minded young Confucian scholar and poet, be "dissolved" into two popular artists of much lower cultural prestige? I should reiterate here that, in so doing, he not only justifies the employment of a vernacular genre in dealing with a momentous historical theme but also releases implicitly his regret that Confucian scholars such as Ma Shih-ying and Juan Ta-ch'eng did succumb to greed, and hints at his confidence that, fortunately, the so-called low culture would rise at any moment in place of the high culture to defy the foreign conqueror.

The story of Hou Fang-yü and Li Hsiang-chün, if we narrow it down to just the romantic relationship, is a simple, common one. However, as I have repeatedly tried to point out, it is not a simple, common story because it is one that cannot be appreciated without its political context, which displays simultaneously many other compelling elements always ready to afflict them. A modern scholar sums up in a good statement on that context: "The world of *The Peach Blossom Fan* is that late-Ming world of gross corruption, of callousness and cowardice and the breakdown of a long cherished order."[18] The play is more complex than those melodramatic pieces written in the early periods which sing of the love, separation, and reunion of a talented student, in the role of *sheng* 生 , and his theatrically required counterpart, be it a young lady from a wealthy family or a courtesan assuming the *tan* 旦 role. Nevertheless, the story of Hou Fang-yü and Li Hsiang-chün is concatenated with all the typical episodes known in such melodrama, including even a scene of lovesickness.[19] It transcends the convention, however, with that strongly deliberate reflection of morality against what happens in the political world.

The initiation of fondness for each other is a commonplace. The time is spring in a languorous ancient city, and the year falls in one that is full of rumors, about other places, regarding rampageous uprisings and how the imperial capital is under constant threats. Hou Fang-yü's first visit of the heroine is made in a purely pastoral atmosphere. While he and friends wait, Hsiang-chün stays upstairs playing music. Moved by all these, Hou tosses a pendant of his fan, which presumably is jade, to the loft, and, in response, cherries wrapped in a white handkerchief are thrown down presently. The gesture completes a classical method of showing the intention to love:

> You threw a quince to me,
> I requited you with a pretty jade pendant.
> But it was not just for requital.
> It means I'll love you forever![20]
> 投我以木瓜，報之以瓊琚。
> 匪報也，永以爲好也！

When she finally appears, Su K'un-sheng says: "Look, the fairy is descending from heaven to the mundane world!" Liu Ching-t'ing exclaims:

"Amitabha!" Again, since Su and Liu are the contributories to the hero, the first meeting of Hou and Hsiang-chün can be considered celebrated with Confucian, Taoist, and Buddhist approval.

The reference to Juan Ta-ch'eng in the hilarious feast, thereafter, indicates the unavoidable worldly context in which Hou and Hsiang-chün are going to experience sorrows (Scene 5). It anticipates, too, the conflicts between characters to be shown overtly later when Hsiang-chün rejects the trousseau sent by Juan as a token of friendship extended to the hero (Scene 7). Hsiang-chün's rejection of the trousseau, or wedding gift, from Juan is the dramatist's chosen technique to portray the heroine in terms of public spirit and personal temperament, an approach to characterization par excellence. It is, moreover, a perfect piece of evidence to identify K'ung Shang-jen as a conscious man of letters determined to participate in the perpetuation of the vernacular tradition, to promote the folk preference for the female power in resistance to hypocrisy and villainy, especially when man appears to be undecided. The image of a courageous, enlightened, far-sighted woman dominates the best of vernacular Chinese literature in early folk songs and narrative poems.[21] It enlivens the Yüan theatre with socio-political implications, as I indicated above, and directs a principal, tasteful pattern of characterization in major Ming drama. The same image proliferated during the Ch'ing period in such novels as *Hung-lou meng* 紅樓夢, *Ching-hua yüan* 鏡花緣, and the verse narrative *Tsai-sheng yüan* 再生緣. Like almost all the other women, Hsiang-chün rises higher in spiritual integrity and better in the judgment of what is true and false than all men, including her husband, in this particular scene.

Hsiang-chün's flawless integrity and judgment are reemphasized to the audience in Scenes 22–25, in which she resists all attempts to get her to remarry and subsequently, after a fierce verbal attack on the villains, is tricked into the Nanking imperial palace under a false identity. The two plots of *T'ao-hua shan* merge into one with the heroine deeply locked up in the palace, the season being early spring of 1645, when the snow is not entirely melted yet:

> The double gates are locked: dangling willows, dusky crows,
> Through the sparse screens reflect green pines and emerald tiles.
> My satin sleeves sough when the cold wind blows.
> And, in confusion, plum petals fall on my hair.
> 鎖重門垂楊暮鴉，
> 映疏簾蒼松碧瓦。

涼颼颼風吹羅袖，
亂紛紛梅落空髻。

(Scene 25)

By the next time Hsiang-chün appears, the Manchus have sacked Nanking.
The double plot is gradually directed toward a resolution far in the mountains. The political atmosphere vanishes measure by measure, when most of
the important characters in the left and right departments enter on the stage
as though a grand scene of reunion were in order. They have survived a
great catastrophe and have changed, each in his own way, but the hero and
heroine of the play remain very much the same in their affection for each
other. It is noteworthy that toward the denouement only Hou Fang-yü and
Li Hsiang-chün persist in their "modes," if just for a moment or two. Hou
produces the fan, when asked about the whereabouts of Hsiang-chün:
"Look at this peach-blossom fan, our token of wedlock; I always have it
with me" (Scene 39).

The last scene proper exhibits the highest passion expressed between a
man and woman in Chinese theatre, markedly so because it is shown amidst
a solemn, mournful, and horrible rite in a Taoist temple. As a congregation
of disillusioned Ming loyalists look on, the Priest performs the ceremony.
He makes sacrifices to Emperor Ch'ung-chen and his subjects who died in
the same cause and, subsequently, to the military men who died later yet for
another cause, defending the southern land against the Manchu armies. He
then consoles all the dead souls at large. The mourning ends in a triumphant
vision as the virtuous receive assignments in an announcement of deification. Then the rite turns into a horrible vision, showing the gory deaths of
the wicked. Amidst all of this, and the Priest's ceaseless preaching about the
vanity of mundane pursuits echoing in the temple, the hero, holding a fan
near his eyes, catches sight of the heroine and is astonished: "That's my
Hsiang-chün, the one standing over there! Why has she come to this place?"
He goes up to hold her. "You are my Master Hou," she cries. "O how I've
missed you!" The outright, loud exchange of passionate words is blasphe-
mous to the gods and spirits. The Priest, thereupon, intervenes and grabs the
fan from them, tears it in shreds, and throws it on the ground. With the thud,
their lasting search for pure love, through fire, flood, cold, hunger, and all
the mischievous schemes and insults, suddenly comes to an end. "Heaven
and earth are now turned upside down." The Priest screams: "Isn't it
ridiculous to cling to such love and desire?"[22]

As there is nothing to ensue in that plot about the fate of the Ming dynasty, in the desolate ruins of the "cherished order," whether it ever really existed at all, the romantic love loses a dependable context and the pastoral style of life is definitely deprived of its original meaning. This plot of mutual admiration, passionate love, and trust that once seemed to transcend the turmoil draws, naturally, to a conclusion because the context, in which all this attains significance for life eternal, is gone. The romantic is to be comprehended in the mythical interpretation which the Taoist may offer to the exhausted men and women in various modes, through the rest of their life, and to the dead ones remembered even today as both historical and dramatic in their individual moods. The pastoral is kept only for the fisherman and woodcutter, the impersonators of nonconformist reclusion.

K'ung Shang-jen wrote *T'ao-hua shan* not exactly for a living. He was an erudite scholar of the Confucian classics, specialized in such rare subjects as music and rite. The profound inclinations toward antiquity made him feel that, in writing a *ch'uan-ch'i* play, he was in practice "rectifying *ya* and *sung* music." This must be the reason why he made an effort to remark elaborately on the principles of musicality in the "fan-li."[23] His comments on Juan Ta-ch'eng's talent in *ch'uan-ch'i* are nonethelsss quite enthusiastic throughout the play. The depictions of Hsiang-chün being tutored by her music master on *Mu-tan t'ing* 牡丹亭 and later being audited before Hung-kuang for a role in that, instead of Juan's *Yen-tzu chien* 燕子箋, are charged with professional zeal, while the particular scene in which Su K'un-sheng improvises aloud in Wu-ch'ang at nightfall, in order to arouse General Tso's attention, is a straightforward applause for the power and charm of music. Lastly, in the Epilogue, entitled "Lingering Melodies" (餘韻), the dramatist introduces three different folk tunes, the *wu ch'iang* 巫腔, *t'an tz'u* 彈詞, and *I-yang ch'iang* 弋陽腔, to convey the poetry created in 1648 in the aftermath of the Manchu Conquest, through the form of reminiscences and laments by the old Master of Ceremonies, fisherman, and woodcutter respectively. As to his knowledge and interest in rites, the play shows abundant evidence too. While the old Master of Ceremonies is almost omnipresent, so much as that he is believed to be K'ung Shang-jen in dramatic disguise, the first elaboration on the rite is done in worship of Confucius (Scene 3). The second one is for mourning Ch'ung-chen on the first anniversary of his death (Scene 32). The last is the major one performed by the Taoist Priest in the White Cloud Monastery, again with the old Master of Ceremonies assisting in the sacrifices, despite any incongruity of ritualistic styles there may be (Scene 40).

It is true that, with the play, K'ung Shang-jen was able to exhibit his talent and erudition fully, but it is also true that most other subject matters would have provided him with similar opportunity. Indeed, he had once collaborated with Ku Ts'ai in the composition of a complicated play, *Hsiao Hu-lei*. Why, then, did he choose the story of the fan in the tragic frame of history this time, about the illusion of love, the vanity of literary fame, and the corruption of scholarship and military morale, as a Chinese throne was rapidly crumbling? K'ung Shang-jen never mentions the Manchus explicitly by name in the play. In the "Intercalary Scene," Chang Wei, who was once a Commander of the Imperial Guard in Peking, and would later become the Taoist Priest in the White Cloud Monastery, tells Lan Ying 藍瑛 the painter and Ts'ai I-so 蔡益所 the bookseller, under a beam trellis, about the death of Emperor Ch'ung-chen four months before. "Then early in the fifth month," he says, "the massive armies entered through the Great Wall, drove the bandits away, calmed down the people, and in that way avenged the Ming dynasty's great sorrows." The "massive armies" refer to the Manchus. The idea implied here is that, while Emperor Ch'ung-chen was forced by the bandits to kill himself that year in the third month, justice was returned to the Ming by the Manchus, an idea that confirmed the crime of Li Tzu-ch'eng 李自成 , as the Ch'ing court always maintained.[24] The Manchus are referred to in a neutral tone as the "northern armies" (北兵) and their political institution, the "northern court" (北朝).[25] On at least two occasions, the dramatist obviously asserts that the Manchus were passive about the conquest of China and that it was the Chinese traitors who encouraged them to make the moves (Scenes 26, 37), an idea confirming the crime of Wu San-kuei 吳三桂 which was, likewise, the official Ch'ing interpretation of the political transition. K'ung, furthermore, describes in good detail that on the eve of Manchus crossing the Yangtze, Nanking had been ruled by an illegitimate monarch and its politics unjustly manipulated by callous, greedy villains (Scenes 31–32). Through the lips of Juan Ta-ch'eng, in an improvization of poetry, China is even described as "the land without a lord" (無主江山) (Scene 14)—it is up for grabs.

No spectator or reader of *T'ao-hua shan* would suspect that the play was intended to justify the rule of China by the Manchus. Not even Emperor K'ang-hsi 康熙, I think, who was especially interested in the play and who would always comment on the follies of Hung-kuang as he watched it, could possibly imagine that K'ung Shang-jen had written it to please him, in spite of the list of "twelve auspicious omens" attributed to his reign in the

Prelude.[26] A genuine Confucian knows how to survive under the pressure of censorship, to avoid headlong confrontation with the imperial authority, and, still, to pass on his most critical view of events evanescent and eternal according to his conscience cultivated in the stalwart tradition. The play *T'ao-hua shan* is organized in a double plot, based on an antithetical parallel structure, which, K'ung Shang-jen obviously believes, is derived from classical metaphysics, and it purports to convey in this way, supported by the vernacular spirit, some important messages to the Chinese audience approximately half a century after the disgraceful submission to the aliens. Throughout Scene 20, we see how Kao Chieh is being relocated north to stop the "roaming bandits," meaning Li Tzu-ch'eng and his men, from crossing the Yellow River. Then in the poetic quatrain he and Hou Fang-yü chant before exit, the rash warrior calls himself:

> A general guarding against *autumn* in the bend of the Yellow River.
> 黃河曲裏防秋將。

To guard against *autumn* is the elliptical way of saying to defend the Tartars from invading and looting the Chinese homesteads in autumn, when their horses are fed strong. The objects are definitely the barbarians, but not the Chinese rebels; or, as a matter of philology, the nomadic Manchus can be construed as the roaming bandits. The Ch'ing Emperor and his able liege missed a ghastly mockery.

NOTES

1. *T'ao-hua shan*, edited by Wang Chi-ssu 王季思 *et al.* (Peking, 1982), p. 1. All references to the play (*THS* hereafter in the notes) are made to this edition. Translations of passages, sentences, phrases and terms are mine.
2. Liang Ch'i-ch'ao 梁啓超 praises *THS* for its "complete maturity." See his edition of the *T'ao-hua shan*, 2 vols. (rept. Peking, 1954), I, p. 7. Richard E. Strassberg calls it "China's greatest historical drama"; see *The World of K'ung Shang-jen: A Man of Letters in Early Ch'ing China* (New York, 1983), p. xi.
3. *THS hsiao-yin* 小引, p. 1.
4. As the namesake of the play, this fan is presented to her by Hou Fang-yü in Scene 6. When he produced the fan Hou remarks that it is a "palace fan" too, usually meaning a round one. However, based on the stage directions related to the handling of the fan in Scene 23, it is more likely a folding fan than anything else. "Palace fan" (*kung-shan* 宮扇) may just be a theatrical stockphrase for it, though

the one tossed to her in Scene 25 may reasonably be a round one.

5. *THS*, p. 13. The Wang edition does not present the play in two parts, though the editors were certainly aware of the arrangement, but in four *chuan*. Liang Ch'i-ch'ao makes it very clear in his edition that the play is conceived in two parts.

6. For a good study of K'ung and his unique intellectual background, see Strassberg, *The World of K'ung Shang-jen.*

7. Quoted from the "Additional Act," *THS*, p. 133.

8. K'ung Shang-jen was born in 1648, four years after the fall of Peking to the rebels. He completed the play in 1699. The year of his death is uncertain. Liang Ch'i-ch'ao, op. cit., conjectures it sometime after 1708, as does Aoki Masaru, *Shina kinsei gikyoku shi* 支那近世戲曲史, translated into Chinese by Wang Ku-lu 王古魯, *Chung-kuo chin-shih hsi-ch'u shih* 中國近世戲曲史, 2 vols. (rept. Taipei, 1965), I, p. 383. Wang Chi-ssu, op. cit., dates it in 1718.

9. An example of the former is T'ao Ch'ien's 陶潛 preface (記) to his "T'ao-hua yüan shih" 桃花源詩, which is documented with a rough dating in the beginning and a reference to a hermit-scholar at the end. See *T'ao Yüan-ming chuan* 陶淵明卷, 2 vols. (Peking, 1961), II, p. 338. I use the term "fiction" here in the sense Ernst Robert Curtius uses it in *European Literature and the Latin Middle Ages*, translated by Willard R. Trask (New York, 1953), especially in Chapter 1.

10. *THS*, p. 268.

11. For an excellent discussion on Liu Ching-t'ing in history and in the play, see H. C. Chang, *Chinese Literature: Popular Fiction and Drama* (Edinburg, 1973), pp. 303–11.

12. For a biography of Ma and Juan, see *Ming shih* 明史 (Peking, 1974). 308.7937–45.

13. The image that shows Juan killed by the mountain spirits agrees with the historian's writing in *Ming shih*, 308.7945. The one about Ma does not.

14. The dramatist's recounting of the last days of Kao Chieh appears to be more critical than the historian's; see *Ming shih*, 273.7005–6.

15. This interpretation is different from what is found in *Ming shih*. The latter specifies that Tso was by then quite senile and ill and that the sudden death had nothing to do with his son, Meng-keng 夢庚; *Ming shih*, 273.6997–98. K'ung, however, may have in mind a passage in the biography of Ma Shih-ying and Juan Ta-ch'eng; see *Ming shih*, 308.7944.

16. Historically, Shih was killed by the Manchu soldiers in Yang-chou; see *Ming shih*, 274.7022–23.

17. Cf. William Empson's comment on the double-plot methods, *Some Versions of Pastoral* (New York, 1960), p. 64. He points out that the term and its explanation belong to Ernest Jones, a major critic of *Hamlet* and *Oedipus*.

18. Cyril Birch, "Introduction" to *The Peach Blossom Fan*, translated by Chen Shih-hsiang and Harold Acton, with the collaboration of Cyril Birch (Berkeley, 1976), p. xvii.

19. The term "melodrama," as defined by Robert Bechtold Heilmann, is a vital concept in the modern study of drama; see, for example, his *Tragedy and Melodrama: Versions of Experience* (Seattle, 1968). An application of the concept to the study of Chinese drama is found in Ping Cheung Cheung, "Melodrama and Tragedy in Yüan *tsa-chu*" (unpublished Ph.D. dissertation, University of Washington, 1980), esp. Chapters II, IV.

20. *Shih Ching* 詩經 64/1.

21. For a related topic discussed along these lines, see C. H. Wang, "The Nature of Narrative in T'ang Poetry," in *The Vitality of the Lyric Verse: Shih Poetry from the Late Han to the T'ang*, edited by Shuen-fu Lin and Stephen Owen (Princeton, 1986), esp. pp. 246–50.

22. Wang Kuo-wei 王國維 criticizes the scene, but mainly it is because he finds a lack of voluntarism in the deliverance of the hero and heroine. See "*Hung-lou meng p'ing-lun*" 紅樓夢評論, *Wang Kuan-t'ang hsien-sheng ch'uan-chi* 王觀堂先生全集, 16 vols. (Taipei, 1968), V, pp. 1646–47.

23. Five out of the sixteen principles are about music, see *THS*, pp. 11–12. Cf. Liu Ching-t'ing's penetrating telling of Confucius' rectification of music in Scene 2.

24. Cf. Scene 13, *THS*, p. 87.

25. *THS*, pp. 169, 209, 222, 228, 232, 234.

26. For K'ang-hsi's comment on Hung-kuang, see, Wu Mei 吳梅, *Ku ch'u ch'en t'an* 顧曲塵談 (rept. Taipei, 1969), p. 184.

5. *Tsa-chü* as a Lyrical Form

Sai-shing Yung

Introduction

In this paper, the term *tsa-chü* 雜劇 will refer to the Yüan *tsa-chü*, the representative dramatic form of the Yüan dynasty (1279–1368). Yüan *tsa-chü* is a musical drama which consists of four acts. In each act there is a set of arias in the same musical mode and with the same rhyme. Two kinds of language, namely, the *pin-pai* 賓白 and *ch'ang-tz'u* 唱詞 , are used alternatively in the play. *Ch'ang-tz'u* is the language used in the arias. It is usually more literary and is put into verse form. When compared with the *ch'ang-tz'u*, the *pin-pai* is more vernacular and is closer to the daily language. Although there are exceptions, all the arias in a Yüan *tsa-chü* are sung by only one singer: the leading male or female player. However, the *pin-pai* part can be uttered by all actors in the play. These are some of the formal characteristics of the Yüan *tsa-chü* related to the following discussion.

In the following analysis, I will try to show how the formal structure of the Yüan *tsa-chü* supports an aesthetics of lyricism in the genre. Special attention will be paid to the two main categories of language and their relationships to the narrative and lyrical acts in the play. In the second half of this paper, I will try to argue that the generic convention of one singing role in Yüan *tsa-chü* is not necessarily a limitation as understood by many scholars of Chinese literature. Rather, when we relate this formal feature to the structuring principle of the genre, that is, the co-operation of the narrative and lyrical acts, we can recognize that this generic rule provides a favourable condition for the realization of lyricism in a Yüan *tsa-chü*.

Tsa-chü is a generic concept. It embraces different texts with a broad range of stylistic variation. Moreover, the primary aim of the *tsa-chü* is to provide entertainment. Thus, when we discuss Yüan *tsa-chü* from a lyrical point of view, there is no implication that all Yüan *tsa-chü* are necessary lyrical by nature. What we may try to illustrate is how the formal rules of the *tsa-chü* drama help to provide an ideal medium when this dramatic form is used by an author to achieve the lyrical purpose.

Two Types of Language and Their Different Functions

A *tsa-chü* basically consists of two sets of utterances: *pin-pai* and *ch'ang-tz'u*.[1] Their differences, in a general sense, can be put into the dichotomies of daily language versus poetic language, vernacular versus literary and non-musical versus musical.[2] These two linguistic forms intersperse within a text and fulfill different functions. Although the functions of the *pin-pai* and *ch'ang-tz'u* are multiple, and the ways of using these two categories of language vary according to different authors, their usages in the Yüan *tsa-chü* are generally tied to narrative and lyrical acts in the text respectively. It would be too simplistic and mechanical to say that all *pin-pai* are used exclusively to serve a narrative purpose and all *ch'ang-tz'u* are necessarily lyrical. However, the distinction serves to highlight their separate functions and the existence of two different types of uttering subjects in the text of a Yüan *tsa-chü*.

In a *tsa-chü* drama, there are events and actions which assume the existence of an objective world where characters interact. Nonetheless, unlike in a novel, this objective world is not presented to the reader through a narrator. Rather, the physical setting in the play is unfolded mainly through the speech acts in the text. The background of the drama, the succession of events, and even the actors' actions are made known to the reader through the utterances in the text. These utterances include both the *pin-pai* and the *ch'ang-tz'u*. However, among these two, it is mainly the *pin-pai* which is responsible for informing the readers of the events and actions in a play. To use Tomashevsky's term, *pin-pai* is the part of utterance in the Yüan *tsa-chü* where we can find dynamic motifs.[3] For example, in the *hsieh-tzu* 楔子 of the *Wu-t'ung yü* 梧桐雨 (Rain on the Wu-t'ung Tree), monologues and dialogues among Chang Shou-kuei 張守珪 , An Lu-shan 安祿山 and T'ang Hsüan-tsung 唐玄宗 etc., which are uttered through the *pin-pai* form, are used to introduce the reader to the setting as well as to the interrelationships among the characters in the beginning of the play. Moreover, in Act Two, it is also through the utterances of Li Lin-fu 李林甫 and the dialogue between Li and Hsüan-tsung that the author informs the reader of the riot of An Lu-shan.

In Yüan *tsa-chü*, the *pin-pai* language is closely tied to the narrative code which is responsible for motivating the narrative progression of the play. This code is used to signify an imitative world which has time and space. All actors deliver *pin-pai*. They all are qualified to use this code in order to weave the relational and interactional web of the play. When an actor speaks *pin-pai*, he in fact participates in the work of a multi-voiced narrative team to unfold the actions of the play. In other words, all actors work together to form a collective addresser to tell the reader about events and happenings in the play. Since the duty of this narrative team is to develop an objective world, *pin-pai*, the relatively less stylized language, becomes an appropriate form for achieving this effect of verisimilitude.

On the other end of the scale, we find the *ch'ang-tz'u* language, which is tied to the lyrical act of the dramatic work. *Ch'ang-tz'u* is the language used in the arias. On the rhetorical level, it is the place where the images, metaphors and allusions converge. When compared with the *pin-pai*, it is more poetic. Moreover, all verses within an act are in the same rhyme. This special rule of rhyming ensures a consistency of rhyme among verses in the same song-set. In addition, all arias of this song-set are also in the same musical mode. Thus, although the performing reality of the Yüan *tsa-chü* is unclear to us, we can still imagine that the artistic language, the music and the dancing performed by the actor work together to achieve a continuous lyrical effect in the play. The linguistic code combines with the musical, kinesics and other codes to form a lyrical code.[4]

When this lyrical code is used in the text, the movement of events is temporarily frozen and the narrative progression is suspended. When the progression of the *pin-pai* and, at the same time, the progression of actions are interrupted by the *ch'ang-tz'u*, the lyrical subject seems to detach himself from the flux of time, practising the lyrical act in a realm of timelessness. For example, in Act Four of the *Tan-tao hui* 單刀會 (Lord Kuan Goes to the Feast), after the monologue of Lu Su 魯肅, the Lord Kuan (Kuan Yü 關羽) and Chou Ts'ang 周倉 enter and say:

Lord: Where are we now, Chou Ts'ang?
Chou: We are in the middle of the stream.
Lord: This great river is a noble sight!

(sings) [*Hsin-shui ling*]

A thousand billows flow eastwards,

A few dozen rowers are with me in this small craft

I go to nine-storeyed dragon-and-phoenix place,

But a lair, ten thousand feet deep, of tiger and wolves.

A stout fellow is never afraid,

I go to this feast as if to a country fair.

What a magnificent river!

(sings) [*Chu ma t'ing*]

Tossing waves, hill after hill—

Where is the young Chou Yü today?

He has turned to dust.

General Huang Kai suffered much

The warships that conquered Ts'ao Ts'ao are no more,

But the waves are still warm from past Battles—

This wrings my heart!

This is no river water,

(sings)

But the blood of heroes

Shed for these twenty years!

Here we are. Announce my arrival.[5]

〔正末關公引周倉上云〕周倉，將到那裏也？〔周云〕來到大江中流也。
〔正末云〕看了這大江是一派好水呵。〔唱〕

【雙調新水令】大江東去浪千疊。引着這數十人駕着這小舟一葉，又不
比九重龍鳳闕。可正是千丈虎狼穴。大夫心別，我覷這單刀會似賽村
社。

〔云〕好一派江景也呵。〔唱〕

【駐馬聽】水湧山疊。年少周郎何處也？不覺的灰飛煙滅。可憐黃蓋轉
傷嗟。破曹的檣櫓一時絕。鏖兵的江水猶然熱。好教我情慘切。

〔云〕這也不是江水。〔唱〕

二十年流不盡的英雄血。

〔云〕卻早來到也。報伏去。

It is interesting to find that this set of arias is embedded in *pin-pai* utterances in which spatial markers are located. The quotation starts with the question asked by Kuan Yü: "Where are we now?" And Chou Ts'ang answers: "We are in the middle of the stream." Then Kuan discloses the spatial setting, that is, the river, and begins to sing. Instead of encountering spatial or temporal markers, we now find a series of images converging in these *ch'ü*-songs. In fact, the language of these *ch'ü*-songs alludes to the *tz'u*-poem *Nien-nu-chiao* 念奴嬌, written by Su Shih 蘇軾 (1037–1101). The title of this famous *tz'u*-poem is *Ch'ih-pi huai ku* 赤壁懷古 (Reflecting on the Past at the Red Cliffs). In this poem, Su Shih thinks back on the San-kuo 三國 heroes at the battle of the Red Cliffs. He expresses his Taoist vision that life is transitory and that all the glories of the San-kuo heroes have passed away. Kuan Yü in real history is considered to be one of these past figures in this period.

But these verses are recited by Kuan Yü himself in the dramatic text. This intertextual reference makes the temporal status of this original *ch'ü*-song more complex and ironic. However, it will suffice here to point out that the images and allusions in this piece of *ch'ang-tz'u* reveal the internal feelings of Kuan Yü at the present moment. It is only when the *ch'ang-tz'u* utterances end and Kuan Yü utters the *pin-pai*: "Here we are. Announce my arrival!", that he returns to a world of reality which assumes a spatio-temporal setting. From then on the narrative process resumes again.

This dominance of lyrical expansion which leads to a timeless self-expression is more obvious in the last act of *Wu-t'ung yü*. In this act, T'ang Hsüan-tsung is awakened by the rain at night. He sings a set of arias: *Man-ku-erh* 蠻姑兒, *Tao-tao-ling* 叨叨令, *T'ang-hsiu-ts'ai* 倘秀才, *San-sha* 三煞, *Erh-sha* 二煞, *Huang-chung-sha* 黃鍾煞. All of these verses are elaborations of one theme: rain. The image of rain and its variations are repeated and juxtaposed throughout these *ch'ü*-songs to intensify the sadness and loneliness of the lyrical subject, Hsüan-tsung. For example, in *Tao-tao-ling*, we read:

> In one moment, it rains so intense that it is like ten thousand pearls
>   falling from a jade plate.
> In another moment, it is so loud that it is like music played at a feast.
> In another moment, it is so clear that it is like a waterfall coming down
>   by a jade cliff.
> In another moment, it is so fierce that it is like the battle drums sound
>   beneath embroidered banners.
> Oh, it depresses me so much!
> Oh, it saddens me so much!
> The sounds of the rain have annoyed me so much.[6]

一會價緊呵似玉盤中萬顆珍珠落。
一會價響呵似玳筵前幾簇笙歌鬧。

一會價清呵似翠岩頭一派寒泉瀑。
一會價猛呵似繡旗下數面征鼙操。
兀的不惱殺人也麼哥。
兀的不惱殺人也麼哥。
則被他諸般兒雨聲相聒噪。

In this moment of timelessness, the progression of narrative is replaced by
the "lyrical progression," which "[acts] through variation and expansion of
themes, changes in rhythm and elaborations of images to reach a point of
greatest intensity at which the poet's vision is realised."[7] Like the layers of
an onion, layers of imagery are juxtaposed so as to express the subjective
feelings of this main character at this present moment. The impression of
timelessness and detachment is explained by the alternating use of the
lyrical code and the narrative code in the play.

The main function of *ch'ang-tz'u* is not informational. Even though it is
possible for *pin-pai* and *ch'ang-tz'u* to be used separately by two characters
in the form of a dialogue, the dominant function of *ch'ang-tz'u* is still not to
provide information. For example, in the third act of *Tou O yüan* 竇娥冤
(Injustice to Tou O), the main character Tou O is about to be executed. She
makes three wishes before the execution. Dialogues occur between Tou O,
the executioner, and the officer in charge of the execution. Tou O says, in a
pin-pai utterance, that since she has truly been wronged, after her death
Heaven will send down three feet of auspicious snow to cover her corpse.
The execution officer says it is nonsense. Then Tou O sings:

[*Erh-sha*]
You say that hot summer is not a time for snow.
Have you heard that frost formed in June because of Tsou Yen?
If I have a chestful of wronged feelings that spurt like fire,
It will move snow to tumble down like cotton,
And keep my corpse from exposure.
What need is there of white horses and a white carriage,
To escort my funeral through the ancient path and wild trail?[8]

【二煞】你道是暑氣暄不是那下雪天。
豈不聞飛霜六月因鄒衍？
若果有一腔怨氣噴如火，
定要感的六出冰花滾似綿，
免着我屍骸現。
要甚麼素車白馬，
斷送出古陌荒阡。

This piece of *ch'ü*-song repeats the sense of a preceding *pin-pai*. However, the differences between these two utterances, rest on the varied functions performed in the text. In discussing the difference between standard and poetic language, Jan Mukarovsky says:

> The function of poetic language consists in the maximum of foregrounding of the utterance.[9]

and

> In poetic language foregrounding achieves maximum intensity to the extent of pushing communication into the background as the object of expression and of being used for its own sake; it is not used in the services of communication, but in order to place in the foreground the act of expression, the act of speech itself.[10]

As we have mentioned, *pin-pai* is the language in the Yüan *tsa-chü* where dynamic motifs can be identified. It is the main medium used by characters in the dialogues and monologues through which the dramatic events unfold. Thus, we can maintain that the function of the *pin-pai* is communicative. I would like to repeat that all actors in a text participate in the *pin-pai* utterance. This means that all the actors work together to form a collective addresser to convey messages to the reader. However, the emphasis of *ch'ang-tz'u* is not on the message, but on the expressive act itself. To use Mukarovsky's words, the function of communication in *ch'ang-tz'u* is pushed to the background and the expressive form itself is foregrounded. The semantic content of this *ch'ü*-song repeats what Tou O has said previously in a *pin-pai* utterance. But in the *ch'ang-tz'u* part, the expression is codified into a particular form. The use of imagery, a prescribed tonal, rhyming pattern and rhythmic skeleton, and so on, are manifestations of this foregrounding and self-focusing. This is where the difference between *pin-pai* and *ch'ang-tz'u* lies.

Inwardness and the Significance of One Singing Role

We have mentioned that the aesthetics of the Yüan *tsa-chü* are realized by two kinds of creative acts, namely, the narrative act and lyrical act. It is interesting to observe that at times, corresponding to these two acts, we find two layers of structure manifested in a text. On the level of narration, we find the story structure, which is constituted of events in the play. Its main structuring principles are causal relationships, sequential ordering, conflicts and tensions and so on. Based on these principles, events are linked into a unified whole on the horizontal axis, to borrow a term from structural narratology. On the lyrical level, we find the structure of images. Motifs and imagery in a play reflect and echo each other within the four acts and form a cohesive whole. Its main organizing principle is recurrence. A vertical reading is required from the reader in order to identify its structural form.

The plot structure of the *Wu-t'ung yü*, for example, can easily be grasped by all readers. Events are organized on the basis of causal relations and temporal sequence, and a physical world is accordingly established. However, various images in the four acts of the play are repeated so as to form another layer of structure.

Flowers and winds are the two obvious examples.[11] In the first act, before the outbreak of An Lu-shan turmoil, T'ang Hsüan-tsung lives a joyful and luxurious life. The motif of wind here is accompanied by music, dance, feather robes and jade pendants. In this act, we read: "In a good mood at night, I [T'ang Hsüan-tsung] was awakened by a gentle breeze. Loosening my dragon robe buttons, and throwing aside the red ribbons and belt" (晚來乘興，一襟爽氣酒初醒，鬆開了龍袍羅扣，偏斜了鳳帶紅鞓) (p. 2b), "I listen and with the wind comes the sound of music" (順風聽，一派簫韶令) (p. 2b), "The wind rustles in the feather dress, light. Fragrance has stirred the jade pendants to sound 'ding-dong'" (風掠得羽衣輕，香惹丁東環珮聲) (p. 3b). Moreover, the legend of the Cowherd and the Weaving Damsel and the statements: "With tears shed as cold as rain. At the early dawn [they will heave] a long sigh, For [their] one-night love is too short" (別淚雨冷冷，五更長嘆息，則是一夜短恩情) (p. 3b) already foreshadows the melancholy scene in the last act.

Flower motifs appear in the second act. Flowers are commonly used as a metaphor for a pretty woman both in Chinese and in Western literary convention. In this act, we read: "Willows take on a yellow hue, and the lotus has lost its green. The autumn lilies have shed their petals" (柳添黃，荷減翠，秋蓮脫瓣) (p. 4b). The images of withering flowers are used to foreshadow the death of Yang Kuei-fei 楊貴妃. At the end of this act, when Hsüan-tsung has to escape from the turmoil and is forced to leave Ch'ang-an, the capital, the motif of the wind appears again as: "My heart is broken for my old gardens. For the river Wei in the west wind, and the setting sun at Ch'ang-an" (傷心故園，西風渭水落日長安) (p. 6a). In the beginning of Act Three, the images of wind, willows and flowers are used instead to reflect the bleak atmosphere and miserable situation of Hsüan-tsung. They are: "Five-cornered banners are fluttering in the setting sun. Cold and lonely is the Imperial Chariot" (五方旗招颭日邊霞，冷清清半張鸞駕) (p. 6a), "Along River Ch'in, the remote trees and flowers are blurry in fog. By the Pa-ling Bridge witherèd willows are weak in the chilly wind" (秦川遠樹霧昏花，灞橋衰柳風瀟灑) (p. 6b). At the climax of this act, the author uses the images of flowers and wind to depict the death of Yang Kuei-fei and the sadness of Hsüan-tsung: "I [T'ang Hsüan-tsung] hate the ruthless wind blowing from the ground, Which has blown down the famous flower in my royal garden" (恨無情捲地狂風刮，可怎生偏吹落我御苑名花) (p. 8a) and "The yellow dust is blowing and the sad wind is cold. The dark cloud is gloomy and the sun has set" (黃埃散漫悲風颯，碧雲黯淡斜陽下) (p. 8b).

In the last act, the lyrical intensity in the play is pushed to a climax. (On the narrative level, this act appears to be redundant.) All the motifs appear again. Crabapple, willow and mimosa are used to describe the beauty of Yang Kuei-fei. Also the image of wind has been elaborated and developed in two songs, *Pan-tu-shu* and *Hsiao-ho-shang*, to reveal the deep sorrow of Hsüan-tsung.

These images reflect each other in the text. On the one hand, they resonate to form a system of imagery. On the other hand, since these images are always located in the *ch'ang-tz'u* part, and the main character is its only addresser, all these images are linked to the particular situations and experience of the main character.

By using the narrative code, the "narrative we"—that is, all the uttering subjects—in the Yüan *tsa-chü* conveys a message, that is, the events and actions of the play to the reader. Since there is only one singer in a play, the whole chain of song is sung by the same actor. On the verbal level, it means that all verses in the text share the same "lyrical I." During the lyrical moments, the main character is at once the only perceiver and addresser, the experiencing subject of the surroundings as well as the only speaker of the verse's utterances. In these moments of timelessness, myriad external scenes and views are reduced to a single perspective, that of the lyrical subject. They all refer to the sensory experience of the subject's here-and-now.

For example, in the second act of *Ch'ien-nü li hun* 倩女離魂 (Ch'ien-nü's Soul Leaves Her Body), the soul of the main character, Ch'ien-nü, follows Wang Wen-chü 王文舉 her lover, and reaches the river. She sings:

[*Hsiao-t'ao-hung*]

Suddenly I hear horses whinnying and people chattering, too much noise
All hidden in the shade of the weeping willows.
So frightened, my heart beats rapidly in fear
Actually, it was the sound of fishing boards for catching fish and shrimp.
Here, following the west wind, I quietly listen.
Accompanied by the lazy dew on flowers,
Under the bright crystal clear moonlight,
A cold frightened goose flies over the smooth sand, "Yah-yah."

【小桃紅】我驀聽得馬嘶人語鬧喧譁。掩映在垂楊下。諕的我心頭丕丕
那驚怕。原來是響瑠瑠鳴榔板捕魚蝦。我這裏順西風悄悄聽沉罷。趁
着這厭厭露華。對着這澄澄月下。驚的那呀呀呀寒雁起平沙。

and

[*T'ao-hsiao-ling*]

Gently I step on the sandy dike.
The wild grass is slippery with dew.
It has dampened my silk skirt
Like green moss, with cold dew, it has chilled my thin silk stockings.
Look! The river scene at dusk is worth painting.
The bright moon, like a crystal pot, shines above and below.
Like a piece of jade, without a flaw.[12]

【調笑令】向沙堤款踏。莎草帶霜滑。掠濕湘裙翡翠紗。抵多少蒼苔露
冷凌波襪。看江上晚來堪畫。玩冰壺瀲灩天上下。似一片碧玉無瑕。

The sounds made by people, horses and geese, the dampness of the flowers
and grass, the brightness of the moonlight, the coldness of the dew, all are
observed and sensed by Ch'ien-nü. Everything seen and felt is directly tied
to the consciousness of the subject. Most importantly, since the intended
world of the subject and the world of scenes and imagery are unified, the
images in the chain of verse always refer to the movement of the inner mind
of this lyrical I. With this perception and consciousness as a referential
centre, fragments of images throughout the play are linked together. This
network of imagery and scene in turn illuminates the internal self of the
main character. All images in the *ch'ang-tz'u* rotate around this character.
Accordingly, the lyrical I becomes the centre of the whole play.

I have pointed out that the generic principles of a consistent pattern of
rhyme and musical mode in an act of the *tsa-chü* work with the poetic
language of the *ch'ang-tz'u* and the stylized body movements of dance to
form a lyrical code. The main emphasis of this code is a continuous,

timeless expression. Under the convention of one singing role, only the leading character can use this well-designed lyrical code. That convention helps to maintain a consistent and continuous lyrical voice in the text and further intensifies the emotional impact. This advantage has already been observed by Chin Sheng-t'an 金聖嘆 (1608–1661). He says:

> As I have observed, the *tsa-chü* of the Yüan people consist of four acts, with only one singer in each act. Other actors, who use *k'o-pai*, only play a secondary role of provoking and connecting [actions]. This is because people in the past had pieces of extremely marvellous writing in their minds. These pieces are independent, each with its own meaning. Each has its own beginning and end, expansion and restraint, crying and echoing, pause and caesura. They cannot be expressed without a context, and therefore must be attached to and be shown in the form of a story about ancient people.... After the decline of the generic principles of the *tsa-chü*, it became permissible to include more than forty acts in a play. Several singers sing in each act. Consequently, like the croaking of a frog, the language became tedious, while the rhythms degenerated. Sentences and words broke down. They sounded like a sick person.[13]
>
> 吾觀元人雜劇，每一篇爲四折，每折止用一人獨唱，而同場諸人，僅以科白從旁挑動承接之。此無他，蓋昔者之人，其胸中自有一篇一篇絕妙文字，篇各成文，文各有意，有起有結，有開有闔，有呼有應，有頓有跌，特無所附麗，則不能以空中抒寫，故不得已旁托古人生死離合之事，借題作文……自雜劇之法壞，而一篇之事乃有四十餘折，一折之辭乃用數人同唱，於是辭煩節促，比於蛙鼓，句斷字歇，有如病夫。

The formal design of the one singing role sustains a lyrical continuity in the text and strengthens its emotive intensity. The entire series of arias, which mirrors the internal mind of the main character, constitutes a continuous lyrical act realized by the same actor. These all ensure that the lyrical code will be used in the most effective way, and maximize the emotional impact of the lyrical act.

Conclusion

The aesthetics of the Yüan *tsa-chü* are constituted by two forces. While the narrative act motivates the movement of events in the text, the lyrical act unfolds the movement of mind of its main character. These two acts are realized and are made known to the reader (or spectator) through different codes. The lyrical code of the Yüan *tsa-chü* emphasizes the inwardness, oneness, timelessness and consistency. It works centripetally to signify the internal world of the main character in the here-and-now. On the other hand, the narrative code works centrifugally to establish the spatio-temporal frame of the work. These two main codes work together to realize the signification of the Yüan *tsa-chü*.[14]

Finally, as the only character in a play allowed to use the lyrical code, the main character is always located at the centre of the play. This main character is thus foregrounded and is placed at the apex of the performance hierarchy on the theatrical level.[15]

NOTES

1. In fact, three kinds of language can be identified in a text of Yüan *tsa-chü*. Besides the two mentioned here, we also find *k'o-chieh* 科介, the stage directions attached to the script. For the time being, we may put it aside and concentrate on the utterances in the text.

2. Concerning the different categories of language and their different functions in the Yüan *tsa-chü*, refer to Helmut Martin, "Lyricism in Yüan Drama," in *Etudes d'histoire et de littérature chinoises offertes au Professeur Jaroslav Prusek* (Paris: Institut des Hautes Etudes Chinoises, 1976), pp. 247–58; Ching-hsi Perng, "Language as Discovery," *Renditions*, 9 (Spring 1978), 92–101; Yu Chih-ch'eng 游志誠, "Lun Yüan *tsa-chü* yü-yen ti liang yüan tui-pi" 論元雜劇語言的兩元對比, *Chung-wai Literary Monthly*, Vol. 15, No. 8 (1987), 110–21. In the following analysis, I emphasize the functional differences between *pin-pai* and *ch'ang-tz'u* based on the extent to which they are separately tied to the narrative and lyrical acts in the play and on the existence of two sorts of speaking subject who participate in these two kinds of utterance. I will explain these points further in the following analysis.

3. According to Tomashevsky, "A story may be thought of as a journey from one situation to another. During the journey a new character may be introduced [complicating the situation] ... or the prevailing relationships changed. Motifs which change the situation are dynamic motifs; those which do not are static." See his "Thematics," in *Russian Formalist Criticism: Four Essays*, ed. Lee T. Lemon and Marion J. Reis (Lincoln/London: University of Nebraska Press, 1965), p. 70. This concept parallels Roland Barthes' idea of the functional unit. For Barthes' discussion on the functional and indexical units, see his "Structural Analysis of Narratives," in *Image-Music-Text*, trans. Stephen Heath (London: Fontana, 1977), pp. 91–97.

4. Here I borrow the terms from K. Elam. See his *Semiotics of Theatre and Drama*

(London & New York: Methuen, 1980), Ch. 3, pp. 32–97.

5. *Yüan ch'ü hsüan wai pien* 元曲選外編, ed. Sui Shu-sen 隋樹森 (Peking: Chung-hua shu-chü, 1959), pp. 67–68. I have used the translation of Yang Xianyi and Gladys Yang. See *Selected Plays of Guan Hanqing* (1958; rpt. Peking: Foreign Languages Press, 1979), pp. 179–80. In quoting the text, I have changed the romanization system from *pin-yin* to Wade-Giles for the sake of consistency of the paper.

6. *Yüan ch'ü hsüan* 元曲選 (*Ssu-pu pei-yao* 四部備要 ed.; rpt. Taipei: Chung-hua shu-chü, 1965), I, *Wu-t'ung yü*, 10b. When quoting the *Wu-t'ung yü* and, later in this paper, *Ch'ien-nü li hun*, I have used, with some revisions, Richard Yang's translations. See his *Four Plays of the Yuan Drama* (Taipei: The China Post, 1972).

7. Ralph Freedman, *The Lyrical Novel* (Princeton: Princeton University Press, 1961), p. 7.

8. *Yüan ch'ü hsüan*, IV, *Tou O yüan*, 8b. I have used the translation of Shih Chung-wen. See *Injustice to Tou O (Tou O Yüan)* (London: Cambridge University Press, 1972), p. 217.

9. "Standard Language and Poetic Language," in *A Prague School Reader on Esthetics, Literary Structure and Style*, ed. Paul Garvin (Washington: Georgetown University Press, 1964), p. 19.

10. Ibid.

11. In the following discussion on the motif of wind in *Wu-t'ung yü*, I have consulted Huang Ching-ch'in 黃敬欽, "Lun *Han kung ch'iu* yü *Wu-t'ung yü* ti chieh-tsou su-lü" 論漢宮秋與梧桐雨的節奏速率, *Yüan chü p'ing lun* 元劇評論 (Taipei: Feng-ch'eng ch'u-pan-she, 1979), pp. 36–43.

12. *Yüan ch'ü hsüan*, II, *Ch'ien-nü li hun*, 4a and 4a–b.

13. Chin Sheng-t'an's criticism on Chapter 33 of *Shui-hu chuan*. Refer to *Shui-hu chuan hui-ping pen* 水滸傳會評本, ed. Ch'en Hsi-chung 陳曦鍾 et al. (Peking: Pei-ching ta-hsüeh ch'u-pan-she, 1981), I, 622.

14. It should be recalled that there are various types of Yüan *tsa-chü* with different thematic and stylistic emphases. Some of them appeal to the reader through enchanting plots, while there are also some in which the lyrical acts are emphasized at the expense of the stories and events.

15. The concept of performance hierarchy is used by the Prague theorists to denote the dynamic hierarchy of the performance structure. Here we can see that the idea of "foregrounding" which we have discussed is used to analyze a performance text. See Elam, *The Semiotics of Theatre and Drama*, pp. 16–19.

6. Mimetic Desire/Dramatic Structure: Racine's *Phaedra* and Ma Chih-yüan's *Han-kung ch'iu*

Han-liang Chang

"What?" "'Dramatic structure'?" "Structuralism again?" "Linguistic fetishism!" Well, given language's metaphoricity, it's never too late (or too early) to talk about "structure." All versions of structure are readers' metaphorical configurations of the text, or to appropriate Paul de Man, they are "allegories" of their own readings. Within the closure of *découpage classique*, there are always people untiringly rehearsing Aristotelian exposition, complication, simple or complex plot with or without reversal and recognition, or musing on the Freytagian pyramid where action rises and falls.

The myth of rise and fall reminds us that during and after the Structuralist Controversy there are other metaphors added to the list of "organizing principles." To mention only a few: the *scene* (i.e., the entrance and exit of players) as the basic structural unit; the related typology of point of attack and plotting in the wake of the Formalist distinction between plot and story; the pattern of "exchange" derived from economic transactions; the "displacement" of linguistic, phenomenological time and space; and various kinds of actual or hypothetical world models based on other frames of reference, such as communication and information theories and possible-world philosophy.[1] All these and many other conceptualizations of dramatic structure are shaped by individual critics' beliefs and they in turn govern the production and consumption of the critical discourses that pester us.

What, then, is the metaphor in this essay? It can be explained by the term before the paralinguistic slash "/" in the title. Dramatic structure is produced, defined, but also questioned by "mimetic desire." The relationship between the two is one of reciprocity rather than differentiation. As is commonly asserted nowadays, desire is language and the other way around, and who else but Aristotle first points out drama as mimesis? "But whose desire are you talking about?" For one thing, it is characters' or the "subject's" desire if structure is restricted to the text's enclosed semantic universe. Therefore, dramatic structure in light of mimetic desire refers to the structure of *actants invested by desire*. For another, I have also in mind the desire of the producer and consumer, which realizes the dramatic text. In this latter case, desire is inevitably involved with dramatic pragmatics.

It has become trendy to talk about desire in language after Lacan's sophisticated misreading of Freud in terms of "linguistic fetishism."[2] One could easily evoke such luminaries as Barthes, Kristeva, Greimas and Todorov.[3] The term "mimetic desire," however, is coined by René Girard, a critic who finds himself curiously uncomfortable with people of the structuralist and psychoanalytic persuasions.

1. Mimetic Desire

The psychological model of mimetic desire postulated by Girard can be appropriated as a strategy for the reader to perceive a basic actantial pattern in complex literary texts widely separated in genre. It has been applied to texts ranging from Athenian tragedies to nineteenth-century narratives. Unlike most anthropological and psychological "projections"[4] which are oriented towards the author's creative process or the reader's reception, the Girardian model has the merit of covering at once the text's semantic and pragmatic aspects.

The basic idea of Girard's argument is as follows. Since one's desire is never one's own choice, but aroused and determined by a mediator, the mediator, the subject and the object form a triple, triangular and intersubjective relationship.[5] Examples can be found in Cervantes's *Don Quixote*. Don Quixote's desire for chivalric existence is from the very beginning mediated by Amadis of Gaul, but Don Quixote in turn mediates Sancho Panza for the latter's desire for the imaginary island. The effects of triangular desire are the same in the two characters: Desire is defined according to Another rather to Oneself. Thus Girard's argument echoes Lacan's well-known formula: "Man's desire is the desire of the Other."[6] Both Don Quixote and Sancho Panza are, in Girard's term, *vaniteux*, who cannot draw their desires from their own resources, but have to borrow them from others. "A *vaniteux* will desire any object so long as he is convinced that it is already desired by another person whom he admires. The mediator here is a *rival*, brought into existence as a rival by vanity, and the same vanity demands his defeat."[7] The rivalry shows the conflict nature of mimesis, and often gives rise to reciprocal violence. The triangular relationship can be shown in the following diagram.

desired object (Lacan's Other)

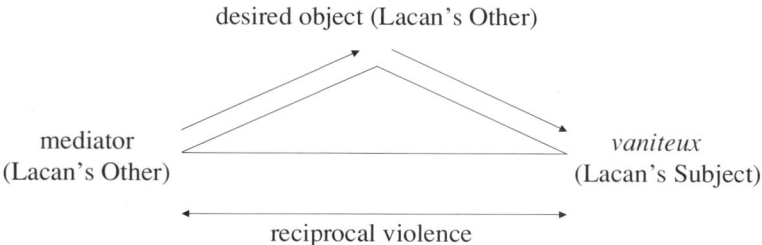

mediator
(Lacan's Other)

vaniteux
(Lacan's Subject)

reciprocal violence

Girard further distinguishes between two types of mediation according to the accessibility or inaccessibility of the mediator. As in the case of Don Quixote and Amadis, if there is such a long distance between the subject and the mediator as to eliminate any possibility of contact, the mediation is external. But if the distance between the two is small enough to permit the rivalry of desires, then the mediation is internal,[8] such as the relationship between Julien and Mathilde in Stendhal's *The Red and the Black*.

Girard applies his triangular model to the "romantic" narrative texts of Cervantes, Flaubert, Stendhal, Proust and Dostoevsky in his monumental *Mensonge romantique et vérité romanesque* (1961), a book whose witty title fails to appear in the English translation (1965). His subsequent studies also extend to the dramatic texts, including works by Shakespeare.[9]

A critique can be levelled at Girard's formula, or for that matter, any other critical models, namely, the circularity of interpretation. A critic who projects his model onto the text would find it sufficiently confirmed by the text, without realizing that it is his model that produces the text, and that other models can also be confirmed by the "same" text. Textual confirmation does not ensure validity in interpretation and the model's truth claim. In this post-structuralist era, it is almost a commonplace that any attempt at explicit formalization runs the risk of reductionism and is futile in search of *logos*. For various reasons, Girard criticizes structuralism,[10] but his model of mimetic desire reveals affinity with some structuralist approaches to narrative semantics concerning human desire.

2. Actantial Matrix

Desire, as Todorov puts it, is a basic predicate which serves to define characters' relations and to form the sequence of action. Subordinate to the axis of *desire* are the axes of *communication* and *participation*. With the rules of derivation and passive, the three basic predicates can be multiplied, such as to love/to hate, to confide/to reveal secret, to confide/not to confide, to help/to hinder, to be loved/to be hated, to be confided/to be publicized, to be helped/to be hindered, etc.[11] We notice how a series of narrative syntagms can be generated through different semantic investment. Todorov's categories correspond to A.-J. Greimas's actantial matrix formed by three categories of human relations postulated in his *Structural Semantics* (1966, English 1983). Modifying Propp's spheres of action, Greimas identifies six actants in three binary pairs: (1) subject/object, (2) sender/receiver, and (3) helper/opponent.[12] Three semantic areas (functions) are invested on them. The relation between subject and object can be defined in terms of *desire*; that between sender and receiver *communication*; and that between helper and opponent *power*.[13] The syntagmatic and thematic relations of the six actants can be diagramed as follows:

sender ⟶ object ⟶ receiver [*communication*]

↑ [*desire*]

helper ⟶ subject ⟵ opponent [*power*]

Greimas argues that this model's

> simplicity lies in the fact that it is entirely centered on the object of desire aimed at by the subject and situated, as object of communication, between the sender and the receiver—the desire of the subject being, in its part, modulated in projections [i.e., *power* or Todorov's *participation*] from the helper and opponent.[14]

The diagram shows how desire of the subject creates the space of discourse and the possibility of dialogue among the actants.

From Girard's point of view, several criticisms can be launched against Greimas's project. First, the actantial matrix is based on the linguistic notion that signification starts with binary opposition, whereas to Girard mimesis desire admits of no differentiation. Second, the two critics would accord different value to the desired object. While Greimas asserts that the "semantic investment" of the desired object "particularizes the symbolic universe of the subject,"[15] Girard considers the object only secondary in importance but holds "the rival ... should be accorded the dominant role."[16] However, in Greimas's system, the function of an actant can be performed by several acteurs just as one acteur can perform the functions of more than one actant. This is made possible by the distributional schemas of the actants and the typology of the relationships between actants and acteurs, such as syncretism, hyponymic and hypotactic divisions, and instances of absence.[17] Therefore, the rival which serves as a model for the subject can be seen as the subject's sender and opponent joined in one arche-actant. Third, Girard would question the autonomy of the subject's desire because it is already mediated by an Other, as in the case of the external mediation between Don Quixote and Amadis. Thus every actant is motivated by another actant and no desire is self-generated. Although in Greimas the "subject" is the subject of desire, it is not necessarily the generator of it. He can be a composite acteur of subject and receiver, initiated and mediated by the sender. Under these circumstances, the subject becomes the *vaniteux* whose desired object is possessed by the mediator-sender.

Defined in the realm of language, the subject of the signifier is preceded by the Other that holds the master position. If language is desire and desire language, then the subject's locus of speech can only be found elsewhere, that is, in the Other. As Lacan says, "One can speak of code only if it is already the code of the Other ... since it is from this code that the subject is constituted, which means it is from the Other that the subject receives even the message that he emits."[18] This "linguistic fetishism," as Girard describes it, not only sheds light on characters' verbal relations in the dramatic discourse, but also accounts for the relationship between the playwright and his precursors, as in the case of Racine and Euripides.

In the pages that follow, I shall attempt to coordinate Girard's triangular model with Greimas's actantial matrix and apply them to two dramatic texts that are as distant and unmediated as Racine's *Phaedra* and Ma Chih-yüan's 馬致遠 *Han-kung ch'iu* 漢宮秋 (Autumn in the Han Palace). The only possible mediation is probably the desire of myself as a much abused comparatist. My choice of the two plays is purely arbitrary because I believe the applicability of a model has little, if anything, to do with the empirically visible or verifiable "facts" of the text onto which the model is projected. Nor do I intend to establish the two texts as analogues because any texts can be analogous via a single, consistent critical discourse. After a second thought of the choice, however, I have found it rather acceptable.

Girard has been criticized for his theory's inability to account for feminine desire and, as such, its lack of universality.[19] The criticism is not "empirically" true because Girard has done good analyses of female characters in *A Midsummer Night's Dream* and *The Waves*. As to the theoretical aspect of the criticism, such as the absence of mother in Oedipus Complex, I shall put it aside for the present. My analysis will show how in the chosen texts the female can be both the desiring subject and the desired object.

3. Phaedra and Hippolytus: Desiring Subject or Desired Object?

The plot of Racine's tragedy is developed along two lines: Phaedra's illicit desire for her stepson Hippolytus and the latter's forbidden desire for Aricia, his father Theseus's sworn enemy. I shall deal with their desires respectively. Phaedra's desire, as the heroine sees it, is the result of Venus's curse.

> Venus I felt in all my fever'd frame,
> Where fury had so many of my race
> Pursued.   (ll. 277–78)[20]

Just as in Greimas's account of the quest for the Holy Grail, where the sender is God and the receiver humanity, here Venus plays the actantial role of sender, and Phaedra the role of receiver. We notice too Phaedra's desire is mediated by an external mediator, her mother Pasiphaë, who was once driven by Venus to fall in love with a bull to beget the monstrous Minotaur. Though Phaedra in her conscious mind has been trying to fight against this incestuous desire for her stepson, she is not unaware of the existence of an immediate opponent, her husband Theseus. Shortly after Phaedra's confession to Oenone, Panope enters in Act I, scene iv to announce Theseus's supposed death. It seems that the opponent has been eliminated. Taking the advantage of this newly reversed situation, the nurse persuades Phaedra:

> … but this new misfortune
> Alters the aspect of affairs, and prompts
> Fresh measures. Madam, Theseus is no more,
> You must supply his place.
> ....
> Live, your guilt is gone,

No blame attaches to your passion now.
The king's decease has freed you from the bonds
That made the crime and horror of your love.
Hippolytus no longer need to be dreaded,
Him you may see henceforth without reproach.   (ll. 340–42, 349–54)

Apparently, Oenone and Theseus assume respectively the functions of
helper and opponent, though the latter does not consciously participate in
the subject's pursuit of desire. As Greimas says, "[I]t is well understood
that helper and opponent are only projections of the will to act and the
imaginary resistance of the subject itself, judged beneficial or harmful in
relationship to its desire."[21] Thus the relations of actants defined by
Phaedra's desire can be diagramed as follows:

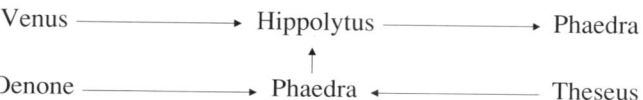

To be sure, Theseus is not the only opponent. Phaedra later discovers that
she has an actual rival, Aricia, whose relationship with Hippolytus constitutes the second plot line.

   In Euripides's version of the tragedy, which serves as the mediator of
Racine's mimetic desire, Hippolytus is portrayed as a devoted follower of
Artemis, the goddess of chastity. It is precisely this excess of austerity, the
classical hubris, that arouses Aphrodite's implacable resentfulness and
leads to Hippolytus's downfall. Racine says in the Preface that he intends to
portray Hippolytus with "some weakness which would make him slightly
culpable in his relations with his father." Since in this play Venus is not
represented onstage, as she is in Euripides's text, to reveal her scheme
against the hero, Theseus becomes the unaware syncretic acteur that subsumes the actant-sender and actant-opponent.

   In the opening scene, Hippolytus addresses Theramenes that he is leaving Troezen, to the latter's great surprise. After an exchange of questions
and answers, Hippolytus confides to his tutor his secret love for Aricia.

It is not her [Phaedra's] vain enmity I fear;
Another foe alarms Hippolytus.
I fly, it must be own'd, from young Aricia,   (ll. 49–51)

The only visible obstacle to his desire is his father:

... By my father's stern command
Her brethren's blood must ne'er be reinforced
By sons of hers; he dreads a single shoot
From stocks so guilty, and would fain with her
Bury their name, that, even to the tomb
Content to be his ward, for her no torch
of Hymen may be lit. Shall I espouse
Her rights against my sire, rashly provoke
His wrath ...?   (ll. 105–11)

It is Theramenes who points out the opponent Theseus is rather the sender
of Hippolytus's desire and who urges the young prince to love in spite of his
father:

Wishing to shut your eyes, Theseus unseals them;
His hatred, stirring a rebellious flame
Within you, lends his enemy new charms.   (ll. 116–18)

Late having learned of Theseus's "death," Hippolytus believes the obstacle
is gone, so he announces Aricia's freedom. The relationships among the
four characters regarding Hippolytus's desire are as follows:

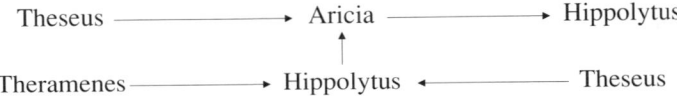

Ironically, Theseus the arche-actant sender and opponent survives both
Phaedra's and Hippolytus's death and gains belated wisdom through suffering.

The parallelism of Phaedra's and Hippolytus's desires helps identify the
two acteurs in their common passion that violates the moral and ethical
code: the former being disloyal to her husband, the latter to his father. Both
suffer from the conflict between repressed desire and repression, which is
signified by opposing semantic elements, such as darkness versus light,
animality versus divinity, and death versus life. Phaedra alludes now and
then to her mother's monstrous love for the bull and her blood relation with
the Minotaur, and compares herself often to a monster:

And rid the world of an offensive monster!
Does Theseus' widow dare to love his son?
The frightful monster!
Let her not escape you!   (ll. 701–3)

But on other occasions, she accuses Hippolytus of being a monster: "The rudeness of the forests/ Where he was bred, inured to rigorous laws,/Clings to him still" (l. 782) and "[I see him] As on a monster frightful to mine eyes" (l. 884). It seems that Hippolytus's "flaw" is not only a violation of filial piety, but a violation of a taboo against desire, which puts him on an equal footing with Phaedra.

Although Phaedra and Hippolytus are identical in their disloyalty to Theseus the immediate opponent, Theseus's significance to them is different. To Phaedra, her husband is only an opponent, not a rival; to Hippolytus, his father is at once an opponent and rival. The real rival, as Phaedra sees it, is Aricia. After Theseus's return, Hippolytus, to defend himself and to show his honesty, reveals his desire for Aricia to his father, which Theseus in turn informs Phaedra. Although Phaedra has long been aware that her desire is in vain, she now regards Aricia as the opponent-rival. She bursts into anger and despair: "Hippolytus can feel, but not for me!/ Aricia has his heart, his plighted troth" (ll. 1203–4). But this apparent rivalry to Phaedra is not in the Girardian sense, for Phaedra's desire is not aroused and mediated by Aricia, nor the other way around.

4. Rivalry and Mimesis

The word "rival" has appeared several times before Phaedra comes to realize Hippolytus's secret. In the opening scene, the prince dismisses as irrelevant Theramenes's allusion to his father's philandering, saying: "Phaedra long has fix'd a heart/ Inconstant once, nor need she fear a rival [*rivale*]" (ll. 25–26). Hippolytus's words prove eventually an ironic foreshadowing: Phaedra fears no rival for her love for Theseus, but not for that for Hippolytus. This casual remark accidentally strikes the note of discord in the tragedy and suggests a potential rivalry between the father and the son. If, as Girard puts it, the subject desires an object so long as the mediator desires or owns it, then this mediator can be regarded as an arche-actant of sender-opponent. Theseus as mediator and rival does not exist in Phaedra's case since he does not desire Hippolytus, unless we bring forth the essential homosexuality of mimetic desire. Phaedra's sender is Venus and Theseus's role as opponent is later replaced by Aricia. But the mimetic desire does exist between Hippolytus and Theseus and in a unique way.

The object of Hippolytus's mimetic desire is two-fold: love and conquest, or in the Freudian vocabulary, Eros and Thanatos. His desire for love and conquest has been aroused by his father. In Act I, scene i, Hippolytus describes how when young his soul blazed up when he was told Theseus's heroic feats, and how he felt disgusted at his love affairs. Born to the great warrior Theseus and the Amazon Antiope (Hippolyta) and skilled in horsemanship (Etymology: Hippolytus-stampeding horses) and martial arts, Hippolytus has an inclination to match his model-mediator of a father in conquests and slaughters. But his aversion to Theseus's love history might not be a genuine one, as is betrayed by his confession to Theramenes. When the young prince says he has never been interested in his father's love affairs, he is resorting to the Freudian mechanism of repression, according to which his repressed desire is ironically expressed through negation.[22] This verbal negation not only accounts for the psychology of Hippolytus and two other main acteurs, Phaedra and Aricia, but also serves as a structural principle of the text noted for its epistemic modality. If, as Laplanche points out in his study of Freud, "What is accepted is repression but what is repressed is ... sexuality,"[23] then Hippolytus cannot be averted to love, neither in Racine's nor in Euripides's text. His expressed aversion only reveals his repressed desire. This desire is already expressed when he makes confession to Theramenes, but under the excuse of lack of justification.

> ... The more contemptible
> That no renown is mine such as exalts
> The name of Theseus, that no monsters quell'd
> Have given me a right to shake his weakness.   (ll. 98–100)

Later in the text, after Theseus's return, Hippolytus asks leave to sail abroad under the same pretext of the desire for conquest. This request for permission to follow in his father's footsteps to slay a monster that has escaped Theseus is rather another verbal negation that serves a double function: not to disclose himself as the subject and object of desires in connection with Aricia and Phaedra. But on the other hand, the excuse contains a partial truth, namely, the son's desire to identify himself with his father.

It is Freud who first points out that identification is the original form of emotional tie with an object.[24] However, he fails to push his argument further but moves in his later writings to a different assumption that the boy's choice of object is instinctive rather than mimetic. It is Girard's insight to show that filial desire undergoes the influence of mimesis, and that the father-son relationship is but a filial variation of the model-disciple relationhip. To be sure, this does not imply that the model-disciple relationship precedes or is not based on the father-son relationship. The point is that there is a clear resemblance between identification with the father and mimetic desire, and such identification puts into question the anterior and autonomous existence of object. According to Girard, "the identification is a desire *to be* the model that seeks fulfillment, naturally enough, by means of appropriation; that is, by taking over the things that belong to his father."[25] This model-disciple relationship precludes the disciple's sense of equality to see himself as a possible rival to his model. Furthermore, while mimetic desire usually gives rise to reciprocal violence between the subject and the mediator, especially in a mythical world order as in *Phaedra*, the son is incapable of meeting violence with violence.

Hippolytus's confession reveals how Theseus's heroic adventures have aroused his own mimetic desire for similar experience since childhood. The adventures that are violent in nature, including the slaughters of Phaedra's half brother the Minotaur and Aricia's brothers, have turned out to be Hippolytus's obssession: to slay a monster in order to live up to his father's reputation, for both conquest and love. Throughout the Racinian text, signs of monsters keep haunting Hippolytus, until he meets his violent death by a monster evoked by his mediator father. The mimetic desire of Hippolytus manifests itself, perhaps more importantly, in his forbidden desire for Aricia, his father's sworn enemy. It would be curious to say that Aricia is desired by Theseus. But Theseus desires her barrenness, as Aricia says, "[What severe law] How thro' all Greece no heart has been allow'd / To sigh for me, lest by a sister's flame/ The brothers' ashes be perchance rekindled" (ll. 427–30). This severe law made by Theseus after the massacre to maintain the political order ironically provokes Hippolytus's rebellious flame, a desire for transgression. As Hippolytus's confidant Theramenes rightly observes, it is Theseus who ironically sets fire to his son's desire. Here as elsewhere, desire is repressed by the verbal negation of law. This situation reminds us of Lacan: "It is in *the name of the father* that we must recognize the support of the symbolic function which, from the dawn of history, has identified his person with the figure of the law."[26] By means of language, i.e., to confide one's forbidden desire, transgression of law assumes another form of verbal negation, a negation of negation enacted in language. Herein lie the force of tragedy and its "ontological" rupture from reality.

If Hippolytus's desire is mimetic, resulting at once from his identification with his father and transgression of paternal authority, Phaedra's desire is no less mimetic. For one thing, her illicit desire, as I said in the beginning, is mediated, though distantly and only alluded to, by her mother Pasiphaë, a victim of Venus, who fell in love with a bull, to give birth to the Minotaur. This family romance has turned out for Phaedra to be not only a mediation, but also a prohibition. She is urged in the opening scene to forget the myth, the monster in her labyranthine mind. When she comes out from three-days' hiding, she makes her confession, and brings her repressed desire to light, whereby the prohibition is verbally transgressed. While Hippolytus's mediator is internal, Phaedra's is external, if we recall Girard's distinction. Such a distinction seems at this point superficial and arbitrary, for both mediations are symbolic negations of poetry. But what really matters is perhaps this: If repressed rationality had prevailed over the repressed, there would have been only silence and no drama. Language, in which tragedy is encoded and enacted, is itself mimetic desire. This accounts not only for the tragedies of Phaedra and Hippolytus, but also for Racine's relations to Euripides and Seneca, and Girard's relation to Freud.

5. Mimesis and Sacrifice: A Chinese Variation

Han-kung ch'iu, a "closet play" written by Ma Chih-yüan in the mid or late thirteenth century, is based on a well-known narrative from Hsi-ching tsa-chi 西京雜記 (Miscellaneous Tales from Ch'ang-an) in the third century. The story relates how Wang Chao-chün, a beloved consort of the Han Emperor Yüan, is given to the Tartar Khan Hu-yen Yeh as propitiation but finally drowns herself in the Amur River. The villainous go-between is the court painter Mao Yen-shou whose portrait of Wang first beguiles the Emperor and then the Tartar Khan. Mao is commissioned by the Emperor to recruit consorts for his palace when Wang is then an eighteen-year-old peasant girl of extreme beauty. Having been declined his request for bribery, Mao disfigured Wang's portrait. So Wang is relegated to "the palace of neglected ladies," where she suffers from the Emperor's neglect for ten years. The Emperor comes across her by accident, discovers Mao's wicked scheme, and orders Mao to be beheaded, but the latter manages to flee the country. Wang now enjoys the Emperor's favor, but only briefly. Mao presents Wang's portrait, the unblemished one, to the Tartar Khan. The

Khan then sends a messenger to the Han court for Wang's hand, and threatens to invade China if refused. Urged by the Minister, Emperor Yüan reluctantly gives her away. Towards the end of Ma's text, the Emperor has a brief reunion with Wang in a dream, but is soon awakened by the warbling of autumn geese. The play ends with Mao's execution.

The above synopsis is sufficient to establish Wang as the desired object of both the Han Emperor and the Tartar Khan, and the rivalry between the two rulers takes place on the background of the age-old military conflict between the Han Chinese and the Tartars. The desired woman finally falls a surrogate-victim to the sacrificial violence so powerfully depicted in Girard's *Violence and the Sacred* (1977, French 1972). A closer examination would make one reconsider the nature of both male acteurs' desire regarding Wang.

In the *hsieh-tzu* 楔子 (prologue) the Emperor is seen lamenting over the emptiness of his imperial harem, a deprivation not worthy of his position:

> It was he [the first Han emperor] who established the imperial authority passed down to me through ten reigns ... The palace ladies were all dismissed after my father's death, and now the women's palace is lonely and deserted. What would be best for me to do?[27]

It is clear that the Emperor's desire for palace concubines is mediated by an ancestral tradition and more importantly, by his immediate predecessor. This desire to live up to the image of his father is further strengthened by the sycophantic painter Mao, who comments on the Emperor's observation:

> Your majesty, even a country fellow, when he harvests ten more loads of wheat than he had expected, will want to change his wife. Why should your majesty, whose rank is supreme, and whose riches encompass the nation, not enjoy as much? Would it not be wise to send an official throughout the empire to select maidens for the palace?

Now Mao acts as the helper turned opponent regarding the Emperor's pursuit of the yet unspecified desired object. Thus the relationships among actants can be diagrammed as:

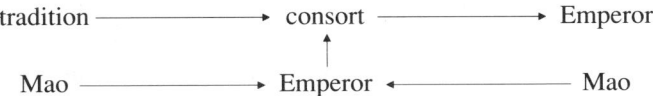

Here the sender of the object is performed by the Emperor's ancestors who were each in possession of a large harem; the receiver as well as the subject of the object is the Emperor himself; and the desired object is only a rather vague female sexuality that signifies imperial power. In Emperor Yüan's quest for the desired object, Mao plays the ambivalent *acteur* that subsumes both actant-helper and actant-opponent, because his primary intention is to build up a fortune by selecting beauties on behalf of the Emperor. The same relationships among the six actants, of which four are syncretic, can be simplified by the triangular model of Girard:

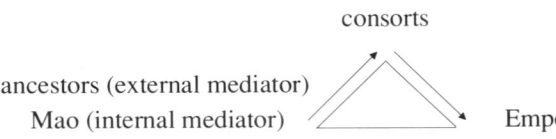

consorts

ancestors (external mediator)
Mao (internal mediator)   Emperor (*vaniteux*)

The rivals of the *vaniteux* Emperor Yüan are his external mediators because of their distance. The role of Mao as the internal mediator requires clarification. He is not a rival that owns female sexuality, but he does intend to corrupt the Emperor through fleshly pleasures in order to secure a solid position in the court in addition to amassing wealth. As he admits in his self-exposition, characteristic of the Yüan stage convention,

> ... I have employed a hundred arts of deceit and steady flattery to dupe that old man, the emperor, and I keep him in sufficiently good spirits. My words are heeded; my plans are followed. Within and without the court, is there a man who does not respect me, does not fear me?
>
> I have been studying a new plan: if I can persuade the emperor to devote as little time as possible to his learned ministers, and to give himself instead to fleshly pleasures, my command over the imperial favor will truly be secure.

For his own part, Mao's desire for imperial favor is also mediated by the other courtiers who serve the throne, and his desire for power and wealth is aroused by the Emperor himself, who owns what he lacks.

Now the "dupe" Emperor is at the disposal of the sycophant Mao whose power derives from his arts of deceit and, above all, from art itself. The portrait of Wang Chao-chün that can be disfigured freely controls the action of the play, questions the immediacy of sexuality, and comments reflexively on art's essential rupture from reality. As the reader perceives in the course of action, both the Han Emperor and the Tartar Khan are duped by the distorting power of art, whose mimesis of reality is problematic from the beginning. This mediating power of art, into which Girard never bothers exploring, is of no small importance in the text of *Han-kung ch'iu*. It interacts with the other signs, such as Wang Chao-chün's lute music, and the many theatrical conventions that join to make drama possible.

As the synopsis shows, the "tragic" (pathetic) outcome of Consort Wang the desired object results from the rivalry between Emperor Yüan and Khan Hu-yen, with Mao serving as the pander. I have analyzed how Emperor Yüan's desire in the beginning is but an abstract femininity, a property indeed, of which his ancestors have been proud of. This femininity becomes incarnate in the body of Wang only after the triple mediation of rivalry, portrait, and music, but it can be sacrificed when reciprocal violence looms up. The sacrificial crisis emerges in the wake of the rivalry and mimesis of the acteur Tartar Khan. This time, the mediator manifests itself internally rather than externally. To Khan Hu-yen, his immediate mediator-rival is the Han Emperor whose supremacy he now challenges. Internal mediation put aside, Khan Hu-yen and Emperor Yüan are almost identical in their pursuit of desire.

It is no accident that the play is launched into action by the *vaniteux* Hu-yen. In his self-exposition, the khan relates the rivalry history of the two peoples.

> … My ancestor, the Khan Mao-tun, besieged the Han Emperor Kao at Po-teng for seven days. The emperor, adopting the policy proposed by Lou Ching, sued for peace between our two nations, and a Chinese princess was sent in marriage to our khan. This practice has been followed in every generation since the time of the Emperor Hui and the Dowager Empress Lü.

Now it is Hu-yen's duty to resume the once interrupted tradition of marrying a Han princess, whoever she might be. Thus Hu-yen's desire is also externally mediated by his ancestors, like the internal mediator he challenges. The presence of an internal mediator renders the external mediation secondary and eventually replaces it. Khan Hu-yen says in Act II (折 *che*, fold):

> … Recently I sent envoys to offer my allegiance to the Han and to ask in return for a Han princess. The Chinese emperor refused, claiming that the princesses of his palace are still too young for marriage. I am most annoyed. I am sure that the Chinese court holds countless palace ladies, and it would by no means embarrass the emperor to give me one. I shall recall my envoys at once. I intend to raise troops and invade the Han lands to the south …

At this juncture, the exiled Mao appears in the Tartar land, with a portrait of Wang to "induce" the khan to demand her. Seeing the portrait, the khan says admiringly:

Is it possible that the world contains such a woman? My wishes would all be fulfilled if I could have her for my queen. I shall dispatch an official and some retainers with a letter to the Chinese emperor asking for Wang Chao-chün. In exchange for the princess, I shall offer peace between our two nations. If the emperor refuses, I shall invade his domains without delay, and he will not find it easy to defend his rivers and mountains …

In popularized Chinese historiography, the figures of "rivers and mountains" and female sexuality maintain a curiously dialectic relationship, both being the emperor's properties. Hu-yen Yeh desires the Han princess as much as he desires Han's territories because both are metonymies for his rival, Emperor Yüan. The crisis that confronts Emperor Yüan forces him to make a choice between his desire for "rivers and mountains" and that for his favored consort, the two properties which are subject to substitution and hence metaphorical one to another. When mimetic desire gives rise to violence, the Emperor has another resort to take: to meet violence with violence. Since he is incapable of so doing, he has to renounce his desired woman to save his kingdom from captivity. Between sexuality and power, only sexuality can be repressed. Otherwise, the emperor would be like King Chou, observes the Minister, "who, for the love of Ta-chi, destroyed his kingdom and lost his life." Interestingly, the story of King Chou happens to be the subject matter of a play popular in the author's time, to which the emperor alludes in one of his arias. The profusion of allusions in the text and its high conventionality suggest another dimension of mimetic desire that the playwright is involved in.

What, then, is the force of Girard's triangular model based on mimetic desire and Greimas's actantial pattern invested by desire? On the semantic level, they help clarify actantial relationships in the macro-universe of the dramatic text, but only to a limited extent. That is, when all characters are dealt with in the abstract, whether binary or reciprocal, having been deprived of their sexual difference and individuating qualities to be mutually identifiable. While Girard's model claims to be universally valid, Greimas's syntagm of desire, being one of the three syntagms, is open to modal transformation. There could be virtual transformations among different modalities in paradigmatic oppositions. This enables Greimas's actantial matrix to account for the role of the classical *confidant(e)* that mediates between the repressed and repression. This is an aspect which Girard's model fails to deal with.

Going beyond the enclosed textual semantic universe, the Girardian model could perhaps explain the mechanism of artistic creation that helps shape literary history. Euripides the mediator inspires Racine's desire for composing a tragedy of his own. The strong precursor plays the formidable acteur that syncretizes sender, helper and opponent; whereas, the ephebe Racine in turn subsumes receiver and subject in his quest for the object of tragedy. The rivalry between the ephebe and his precursor in the case of Racine is replaced by that between Ma Chih-yüan and his contemporaries Kuan Han-ch'ing 關漢卿 and Chao Wen-yin 趙文殷, whose texts the emperor alludes to in Act II: "And why speak only of a wicked king, / Not of a loyal minister like Yi Yin?" (不說他伊尹扶湯，則說那武王伐紂).[28] A literary history that shows the relationship between writing and desire is worth exploring in terms of both Girard's and Greimas's models.

NOTES

1. See, for example, Paul M. Levitt, *A Structural Approach to the Analysis of Drama* (The Hague: Mouton, 1971); Jacques Ehrmann, "Structures of Exchange in *Cinna*," in *Structuralism*, edited by Jacques Ehrmann (New York: Doubleday Anchor, 1966), pp. 158–88; Jacques Ehrmann, "The Tragic/Utopian Meaning of History," *Yale French Studies*, 58 (1979), pp. 15–30; O. G. Karpinskaja and I. I. Revzin, "A Semiotic Analysis of Early Plays by Ionesco (*The Bald Soprano, The Lesson*)," in *Soviet Semiotics*, translated and edited by Daniel P. Lucid (Baltimore: Johns Hopkins University Press, 1977), pp. 199–202; Keir Elam, *The Semiotics of Theatre and Drama* (London: Methuen, 1980).
2. René Girard, *Violence and the Sacred*, translated by Patrick Gregory (Baltimore: Johns Hopkins University Press, 1977), p. 185.
3. Roland Barthes, *A Lover's Discourse: Fragments*, translated by Richard Howard (New York: Hill and Wang, 1978); Julia Kristeva, *Desire in Language: A Semiotic Approach to Literature and Art*, translated by Thomas Gora, Alice Jardine and Leon S. Roudiez, edited by Leon S. Roudiez (New York: Columbia University Press, 1980); A.-J. Greimas, *Structural Semantics: An Attempt at a Method*, translated by Daniele McDowell, Ronald Schleifer and Alan Velie, edited by Ronald Schleifer (Lincoln: University of Nebraska Press, 1983); Tzvetan Todorov, "Les catégories du récit littéraire," *Communications*, 8 (1966), pp. 125–51.
4. Tzvetan Todorov, *Poetics of Prose*, translated by Richard Howard (Ithaca: Cornell University Press, 1977), p. 235.
5. René Girard, *Deceit, Desire, and the Novel: Self and Other in Literary Structure*, translated by Yvonne Freccero (Baltimore: Johns Hopkins University Press, 1965), p. 2.

6. Jacques Lacan, *The Four Fundamental Concepts of Psycho-Analysis*, translated by Alan Sheridan, edited by Jacques-Alain Miller (New York: Norton, 1978), p. 38; *idem, Ecrits: A Selection*, translated by Alan Sheridan (New York: Norton, 1977), pp. 58, 301.

7. Girard, *Deceit, Desire, and the Novel*, p. 7.

8. Ibid., p. 9.

9. René Girard, *Des Choses cachées depuis la fondation du monde: Recherches avec Jean-Marie Oughourlian et Guy Lefort* (Paris: Grasset, 1978); *To Double Business Bound: Essays on Literature, Mimesis, and Anthopology* (Baltimore: Johns Hopkins University Press, 1979).

10. Girard criticizes structural models to the effect: "All types of structural thinking assume that human reality is intelligible; it is a *logos* and, as such, it is an incipient *logic*, or it degrades itself into a logic. It can thus be systematized, at least up to a point, however unsystematic, irrational, and chaotic it may appear even to those, or rather especially to those who operate the system." See *Deceit, Desire, and the Novel*, p. 3.

11. Todorov, "Les catégories," p. 134.

12. Greimas, *Structural Semantics*, p. 207.

13. Ibid., pp. 203, 205, 242.

14. Ibid., p. 207.

15. Ibid., p. 215.

16. Girard, *Violence and the Sacred*, p. 145.

17. Greimas, *Structural Semantics*, pp. 211–31.

18. Lacan, *Ecrits*, p. 305.

19. See Toril Moi, "The Missing Mother: The Oedipal Rivalries of René Girard," *Diacritics*, 12.2 (1982), pp. 21–31.

20. All quotations from *Phaedra* are from Robert Bruce Boswell, *Dramatic Works of Jean Racine*, Bohn's Classic Library (London: G. Bell & Sons, 1890). "Six *Phaedra*s in search of a *Phèdre*" is a commonplace in traductology. The line numbers throughout the text refer to Jean Racine, *Œvres complètes*, Bibliothèque de la Pléiade (Paris: Gallimard, 1965), Vol. 1, pp. 763–821. This French edition has no act and scene divisions.

21. Greimas, *Structural Semantics*, p. 206.

22. Francesco Orlando, *Toward a Freudian Theory of Literature*, translated by Charmaine Lee (Baltimore: Johns Hopkins University Press, 1978).

23. Jean Laplanche, *Life and Death in Psychoanalysis*, translated by Jeffrey Mehlman (Baltimore: Johns Hopkins University Press, 1976), p. 27.

24. Sigmund Freud, *Group Psychology and the Analysis of the Ego*, translated and edited by James Strachey (New York: Norton, 1959), p. 39.

25. Girard, *Violence and the Sacred*, p. 170.

26. Lacan, *Ecrits*, p. 67.

27. All quotations of *Han-kung ch'iu* are from Donald Keene's translation in *Anthology of Chinese Literature: From Early Times to the Fourteenth Century*, edited by Cyril Birch (New York: Grove, 1965), pp. 422–48. The Chinese text is from *Yüan-ch'ü hsüan*元曲選, edited by Tsang Chin-shu 臧晉叔, *Ssu-pu pei-yao* 四部備要 edition (Taipei: Chung-hua shu-chü 中華書局, 1974), 4 vols.

28. Wang Kuo-wei 王國維, *Sung Yüan hsi-chü shih*宋元戲曲史(A History of Sung and Yüan Drama) (Taipei: Shang-wu yin-shu kuan 商務印書館, 1968), p. 90.

7. English Renaissance Acting: With Reference to Peking Opera

Shu-chu Wei

English Renaissance acting style has been a topic of scholarly concern since the 1930s; despite the appearance of numerous articles discussing and debating such possible styles as the "natural" or the "formal," we have to admit that we know very little for sure and that the terms "natural" or "formal" remain problematic.[1] This result can be derived from at least two causes. First, the theatres were closed for eighteen years after 1642, a period long enough for traces of convention to be lost to later generations. Second, when theatres reopened, the stage and auditorium the audience saw was no longer that of the open-stage theatres but of the Caroline court masque "with its proscenium arch and curtain that 'flew up suddenly' to show the painted scene."[2] The use of the proscenium stage, as Professor Bradbrook points out, "completely altered the relation of actors and audience and also the presentation of scenes" as a result.[3] When modern scholars started to pay attention to English Renaissance acting, the dominant, and almost the only kind of theatre available as a model for these scholars was the proscenium stage theatre, the illusionistic kind that tried to present a life as close to the real as possible in an indoor theatre with fourth-wall staging. Because the proscenium stage did not function the same way as the open-stage theatres would have functioned in Renaissance England, it was difficult for scholars to imagine that English Renaissance acting might be very different from the only style they were familiar with. However, the situation gradually changed through continued scholarly discussion of the English Renaissance theatres and other theatres in the world. New theatres were built to provide more lively presentations with multiple purposes. By 1976, the four hundredth anniversary of the founding of England's first theatre, Professor Bradbrook claimed that the modern theatres "now provide stages nearer to the Elizabethan model than anything known since the mid-seventeenth century."[4] Many of the plays of Shakespeare and his contemporaries were given new productions in the hope of catching their Renaissance essence. Scholars who were familiar with other theatrical traditions tried to draw connections between those theatres of Renaissance England and those of other times and places. French critics and directors in the 1950s were inspired by the techniques of Peking Opera for staging Shakespeare's war scenes. Professor Pronko, in his 1967 publication *Theater East and West*, applies the theatrical spirit and techniques of the Orient, particularly the Japanese Kabuki, the Chinese Peking Opera and the Balinese Dance, to Western theatrical productions. Mr. Tao-ching Hsu's 700-page book, *The Chinese Conception of the Theater*, which contains three long chapters on "The Chinese and the Elizabethan Theater," written in the 1950s and revised in the 1970s, was finally published in 1985, a clear indication that today's theatrical concern is moving towards multiple dimensions.[5]

Since no film recordings are available to give us a living documentation of English Renaissance acting and written descriptions, if available and reliable, are open to different interpretations no matter how detailed and vivid the descriptions are, we try to turn to the still-living classical theatres for reference. If we can document some similarities between English Renaissance theatre and a still-living classical theatre, we can use the still-living one as a hypothetical model for the former.

Peking Opera, one of the still-living classical theatres in the world, has been carefully studied and compared with the English Renaissance theatre by Tao-ching Hsu. His comparison reveals that the two theatres, though not without minor differences, are fundamentally similar with regard to theatre buildings, staging and dramatic conventions.[6] He does not, however, have much to say about specific acting techniques in the Elizabethan theatres and his presentation of the historical development of the Peking Opera theatres is not clear in dating different periods of development. Therefore, I have found it necessary to present a clearer picture of the shaping of Peking Opera theatres here.

Today, because of a lack of traditional theatre buildings, Peking Opera performs mostly on modern proscenium stages, yet with traditional methods of presentation, which, according to Professor Pronko, cancel out the disadvantages of the proscenium stage.[7] The theatrical structures that shaped the conventions of Peking Opera are definitely unlike those of the proscenium stage. Peking Opera slowly became popular around the 1850s, replacing the dominant K'un Drama of the Ming dynasty (1368–1643) and the first half of the Ch'ing dynasty (1644–1911) by performing in the same theatre buildings with different music, dialect and musical accompaniment.[8] The oldest Peking Opera theatre building in today's Peking, Kuang-He-Lou, is a reconstruction of the theatre building which belonged to a certain Cha family in the Ming dynasty. This "Cha Theatre" was burnt during the reign of Emperor Ch'ien-lung (1736–1796) of the Ch'ing dynasty and rebuilt with the name Kuang-He-Cha-Lou. Emperor Ch'ien-lung was recorded to have attended performances at this theatre.[9] We are unable to compare the two theatres; all traces of the original theatre have been erased. The only document we have is an 1805 Japanese reprint of a picture of the Kuang-He-Cha-Lou during a performance. The two copies of this picture (Fig. 1) that appear in two books available to me are quite blurred.[10] Tao-ching Hsu has a diagrammatic representation of this picture (Fig. 2) that gives us a better idea what this theatre looks like.[11] From two descriptions about this picture we can get some information about the theatre building and performance. The entrance as shown in the picture is a gate with the sign Kuang-He-Cha-Lou. "Lou" is a term meaning "storeyed building" or "tower," one of the popular terms used for theatres at the time. Two people behind a bench at the theatre entrance are selling tickets or collecting money. Two separate booths for women spectators can be seen near the ticket collectors and facing the stage. Another booth near the entrance to the right might be a snack bar. Further, to the right side of the stage is a wine shop with six or seven people watching the performance while drinking wine. Between these booths and the stage and on three sides of the stage is an open ground for the standing audience. The audience is approximately two hundred in number, quite a few of whom are women. One of the audience members on the open ground is riding on a horse. The stage is an elevated, roofed permanent building. On the two posts supporting stage front a couplet is written. The square, jutting stage with railings on three sides is decorated as for festivals. The two doors connecting to the back stage which should have been used as stage entrance and exit are covered with curtains but the properties and costumes in the rear of the stage are slightly visible. The play being performed can be identified as "Drunken Lu Chih-shen Fights at Mountain Entrance" (魯智深醉打山門). A musician can be seen accompanying the performance with a flute.[12] It is stated that during Emperor Ch'ien-lung's reign women were forbidden to watch theatre performances.[13] Judging from the number of women watching the performance in a picture reprinted in 1805, we may conclude that

Figure 1. A modern sketch of Kuang-He-Cha-Lou without audience or players.

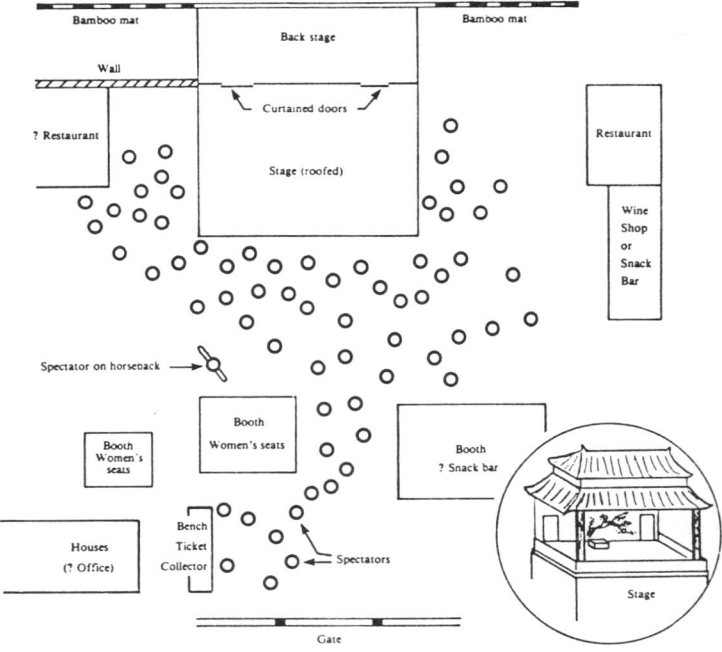

Figure 2. A diagrammatic representation of Kuang-He-Cha-Lou in Tao-ching
Hsu, *The Chinese Conception of the Theater*, p. 317. Reproduced by kind
permission of the University of Washington Press.

the Kuang-He-Cha-Lou in this picture might be the original theatre building before the fire.

The theatre construction and performing conditions as illustrated above bear striking similarities to the "temple stages" which had been in existence since at least the Sung and Chin dynasties. Detailed descriptions of temporary and permanent temple stages became available in the late eighteenth and early nineteenth centuries.[14] By 1888, we find both descriptions and drawings of a temple stage performance, as quoted in William Dolby's *A History of Chinese Drama* from Mrs. Gordon Cummings' book, *Wanderings in China*:

> ... It is a strange sight to look down upon that densely packed yet ever-restless throng, almost all dressed in blue.... The stage is always a separate building facing the temple—a sort of kiosque, open on three sides—its beautifully carved, curly roof being supported on carved pillars. The court is enclosed by open corridors with galleries, in which seats are provided for the mandarins and principal citizens.
>
> In the lower corridors many barbers ply their trade diligently, for skull-scraping and hair-plaiting is a business which must not be neglected, and which can be successfully combined with the enjoyment of the play. Vendors of refreshments find a good market for their wares....[15]

Gordon Cummings' drawing (Fig. 3)[16] and a plan of an early nineteenth century permanent temple stage (Fig. 4)[17] are supplied here to show the basic structure of this kind of theatre.

Another kind of public theatre popular in the Ch'ing dynasty showing resemblances to the temple stage theatre is the tea house theatre. The entire building of the tea house theatre is roofed over,[18] and ventilation is a problem.[19] But the interior arrangement does not show much difference from the other public theatres in Ch'ing China. The earliest reliable record and the most frequently quoted description of a tea house theatre is found in Yang Mao-chien's *Meng hua so pu* 夢華瑣簿, written in 1843.[20] Here is an excerpt from Yang's description of a tea house theatre:

> In the theatre the audience seats are divided into two parts: upstairs and downstairs. Upstairs, the two ends nearest the stage are divided into three or four boxes, called Aristocratic Seats (官座), gathering place of the rich.... Next to the Aristocratic Seats are rows of small tables (with chairs), called the Tables (桌子), prices for which decrease according to their distance from the stage. The box directly facing the stage, called Main Tower (正樓), is not for sale probably because customarily it has to be always ready for officials of high ranks. Downstairs, long tables (with long benches) are arranged around the wall so that the audience sits shoulder to shoulder

Figure 3. Temple theatre. Drawing by Gordon Cummings, 1888.

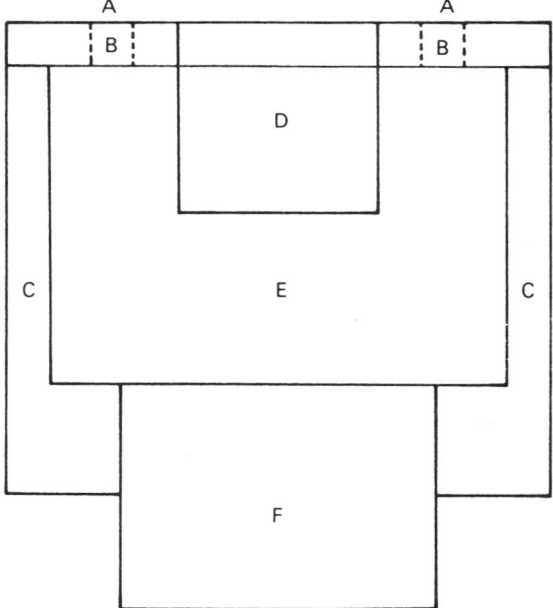

A: gate;   B: passage;   C: storeyed building;   D: stage;
E: central courtyard;   F: main temple

Figure 4. Plan of stage and surroundings.

in semi-circular shape. This is called Ordinary Seats (散座). Behind these, against the wall, are High Seats (高座), from which spectators can watch from a higher position. In the inner court long tables (with long benches) are arranged like the Ordinary Seats downstairs. These seats are in what is called the Pit (池子) and the occupants are usually workers and servants....[21]

Other generalizations about the tea house theatre conditions include explanations of the stage and the audience. The square, bare stage, protruding into the centre of the theatre, is, depending on the size of the theatre, approximately three or four feet off the ground and seventeen to twenty square feet in area size. On the two corners at stage front there are two supporting posts rising up to the roof which could hinder some spectators' view. Descriptions of the audience tell us that they could sip their tea and chat freely in the theatre and the vendors, in loud voices, sold snacks.[22] As for the number of the audience, between the tea house theatres and the temple stage theatres lies a considerable range:

> Roughly speaking, the capacity of the majority of tea-house theaters is from two hundred to a thousand and that of most of the temple theaters, owing to the dense crowd of standing audience, one to five thousand.[23]

As described above, the overall condition of nineteenth-century public theatres, including those temple and tea house theatres that shaped the making of Peking Opera, bears striking similarities to the condition of English Renaissance theatres. The general structure of the public theatres, according to Andrew Gurr's careful study of the English Renaissance theatres based on a sketch (Fig. 5) of the Swan in 1596[24] and materials and research on other English Renaissance public theatres, is summed up as follows:

> The public playhouses were usually round or polygonal buildings, at least on the inside of the amphitheater, built on a timber frame with plaster infilling, on brick and pile foundations, with thatch or tile roofing for the galleries.... There were ... lords' rooms ... partitioned off from the galleries closest to the stage.... The stage was a platform measuring as much as 40 feet across and extending out from one side to the middle of the yard. At the rear of the stage was a "tiring-house" or players' changing-room, the front face of which had two or more openings on to the stage. At the first gallery level in the tiring-house façade was a balcony or gallery ... which was occasionally used as a supplementary playing area in conjunction with the stage itself. Near the front of the stage in some play-houses was a large trap-door. Over the stage, extending out from the tiring-house above the balcony or tarras was a cover or "heavens" supported by two pillars rising from the stage. This was to shelter the

stage from the weather and to provide a place from which things could be let down on to the stage.... Set on top of the heavens or cover was a "hut" or huts, within which stage-hands operated the machinery for "flights" or descents on to the stage, and where they produced thunder and lightning effects. Alongside the hut was a small platform, level with the gallery roof, from which a trumpeter announced the beginning of a performance....[25]

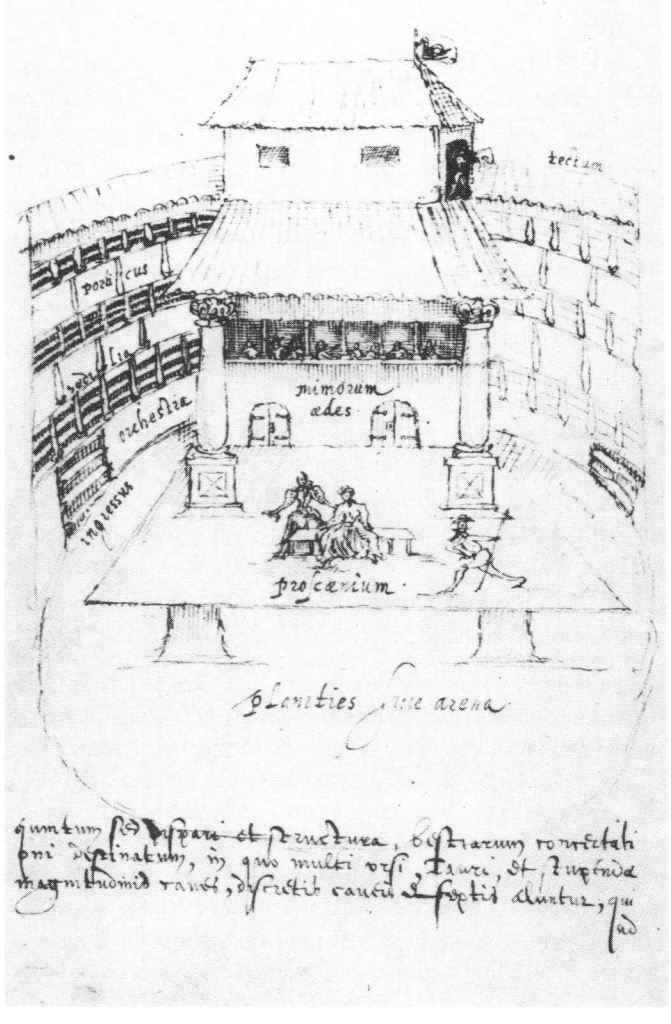

Figure 5. De Witt's drawing of the Swan, c. 1596.

By contemporary estimates, these public theatres had a capacity of 3,000.[26] The plays were presented in the afternoon in the broad daylight with simple staging, "chiefly ... a bare stage with portable properties."[27] During the performances the audience drank and ate as "beer was sold ... along with bread and fruit."[28]

The later development of English Renaissance theatres led to the establishment of indoor private theatres with a much smaller capacity than the public ones, "perhaps no more than 500 or 600," and their performances were candle lit.[29] The auditorium was paved, and the pit and galleries equipped with benches.[30] However, the stage, smaller in comparison with the public theatre stage, protrudes into the centre of the auditorium and is like the public ones surrounded by the audience on three sides;[31] the staging of plays at the private theatres appears to have followed the conventions of the earlier English Renaissance open stage.[32]

Comparatively speaking, conditions and conventions of the English Renaissance public theatres are pretty much like those of the Chinese Ch'ing dynasty temple stage theatres; likewise, conventions of the English Renaissance indoor private theatres are similar to those of the Chinese indoor tea house theatres. The difference lies mainly in the nature of the performing area. The English Renaissance stage, public or private, had an "above" area, whether it be the music room above the stage or one of the lords' rooms upstairs, and if one cannot be sure of the existence of a "discovery space" or "inner stage," at least a "trap-door" for ghosts to arise from near the front of the stage is clearly marked in contemporary sketches.[33] The Chinese temple stage theatres and tea house theatres have none of these performing areas. However, this minor difference does not affect the fact that both the English Renaissance and the Peking Opera actors have to perform on a bare, open stage to entertain a large, noisy crowd. This basic convention could have demanded similar acting styles in these two theatres. The stage structure alone could have decided ways of acting and performing as can be concluded from Oscar Brockett's discussion of theatre architecture in general:

> There are three basic stage forms: proscenium, open (or thrust or platform), and arena (or in-the-round). Each creates a different audience-actor relationship, each has different facilities, and each promotes a different approach to production.... With an open or thrust stage, the seats are usually arranged around three sides of a raised platform that juts into the auditorium.... Most open stages permit only a restricted use of scenery.... The basic purposes of the open stage are to bring the

audience and the actors into more intimate relationship and to do away with the
trappings of realism. Since three sides of the stage are usually surrounded by seats,
even if the auditorium is large audience members are closer to the actors than in a
proscenium theater with the same seating capacity. Because the open stage is usually
seen from three sides, it is in most respects more three-dimensional than the
proscenium stage; acting and other elements of theatrical production must project in
three directions simultaneously.[34]

The other background fact that the actors in both theatres had to entertain
a large, noisy crowd also influenced the acting technique. Professor Bradbrook points out that for English Renaissance actors to maintain attention
"it would be necessary to exaggerate movement or statuesqueness, to use
inflated delivery and conventional posture."[35] On the Chinese temple stage,
the actors have to compete with all sorts of noise made by the audience,
vendors, barbers, children and dogs; therefore, as Lin Yu-tang points out,
"only a thin falsetto keyed in a high pitch could have been heard, as
anybody may verify for himself."[36] Here, we find it possible to argue that a
certain kind of theatrical background will very likely shape a certain kind
of acting and performing convention. It becomes meaningful for us to use
Peking Opera as a reference to a better understanding of English Renaissance acting, just as Professor Pronko's use of Japanese Kabuki to experiment ways of presenting Elizabethan plays:

> The juxtaposition of Kabuki with Elizabethan ... serves as a fruitful approach to
> the problem of style in the production of Elizabethan plays.... Kabuki offers a
> still-living theatrical tradition which exhibits astonishing similarities to much of
> what we are told took place on the English stage three or four hundred years ago.[37]

What I am going to do in this article is to replace Professor Pronko's
"Kabuki" with "Peking Opera" to serve the same purpose for exactly the
same reason.

The basic element that constitutes the parallel quality between English
Renaissance and Peking Opera theatres is the use of the open stage with
simple, portable properties, which allows the continuity of story lines
taking up to six or seven different locations without the problem of having
to change stage sceneries, thus enabling the actions to move swiftly without
interruption. This continuous process requires a good deal of imagination
from the actors and the audience. Understandably, simple, portable properties cannot sufficiently present a realistic scene. The Peking Opera convention takes it for granted that a part or some parts can be made to represent

the whole in a symbolic way, and in the English Renaissance theatre, we hear the Prologue in Shakespeare's *Henry V* ask the audience to "piece out our imperfection with your thoughts," inviting somewhat apologetically the audience's participation with imagination to make the performance whole. Both theatres stress that imagination is the magic power that functions on the open stage.

With the understanding of the function of imaginative capacity as the basic spirit on the open stage, we will proceed to see what specific acting techniques used in Peking Opera could shed light upon English Renaissance acting. Let's begin with the portable properties. What happens on the Peking Opera stage is that a property man or two will walk in and out of the performing area to set up, rearrange or move away the portable properties such as tables and chairs. Sometimes the property man will appear on the stage to wait on a leading actor or actress to take off an outer garment or throw a cushion to an actor who must kneel a long time. The appearance of the property man does not seem to bother the Peking Opera audience because verisimilitude is not sought for in this theatre. On the English Renaissance open stage, because of the ambiguity of stage directions, scholars have a hard time trying to decide whether the portable properties were discovered for display or brought on to the stage. Andrew Gurr's speculation goes as follows:

> ... The portable nature of most properties means that somebody or some bodies had to be employed to bring on those properties that were not actually worn or carried on and off the stage by players.... It seems logical to assume that a four-poster bed "put out" for a bedroom scene would be put back again afterwards. But would the same thing have happened to trees, mossy banks and similar less obtrusive objects? Some scholars think they could have been on stage throughout the play. I should think the stage-keepers were kept busier than that.... If tables, chairs, benches, beds and thrones could be shifted, so could every other object.[38]

We can see that Andrew Gurr's speculation on the use of portable properties on the English Renaissance stage is a centuries-old actuality on another similar stage in China. If Peking Opera can use a property man without causing any problem, so could English Renaissance theatre.

Tables and chairs, the most frequently used portable properties on the Peking Opera stage, are used not only to represent living rooms and court rooms where there is actual existence of such furniture but also to symbolize outdoor objects or space. A table and two chairs together can be made to stand for a mountain. When an actor climbs up on a chair, steps across the table and down onto the other chair the action is understood as someone having crossed a mountain. Or, in front of this design of a table and two chairs if two soldiers display a piece of cloth with walls painted, then a city wall is created. A general can then mount the table to signify that he is climbing onto the city wall. In the English Renaissance theatre, because of a performing area "above," the Peking Opera design of a city wall might not be necessary.

When portable properties such as a door to indicate the exterior and interior of a house cannot be used, Peking Opera actors create one by using mimetic gestures. The gesture of opening the bolt on a traditional door would signify the existence of the door; another gesture which suggests stepping over a high threshold would create two spaces, the inside and outside of a house or a room, and make the activities inside visible to the audience without having the door or posts or wall to block their view. In *Romeo and Juliet*, Act V, scene i, Romeo goes from his dwelling place to the apothecary's shop for poison. The shop cannot have been set up on the stage as there are swift shifts of many different localities among these scenes and the shop exists only for a very short scene. Of course the "inner" space behind the backstage curtain could have been used in Renaissance England; however, it would be easier for the apothecary to mime a gesture of door opening as Romeo says that the shop is shut. The conversation between Romeo and the apothecary must have taken place inside the shop because there is no indication that the apothecary would go into the "inner" space to fetch the poison and it is impossible to assume that the apothecary would carry such mortal drugs with him. It is safe to assume that the apothecary would make gestures of fetching poison from one of the imaginary shelves in his imaginary shop. After Romeo would pay his gold and the two leave the stage for their different ways, the imaginary shop would disappear automatically, leaving the bare stage for Friar John and Friar Laurence to create another scene.

In *A Midsummer Night's Dream*, the craftsmen cannot bring a wall and moon into Theseus' court for their play. Quince, the naïve playwright/director, without an assumption that the audience can imagine such things as the wall and the moon and that he can ask the audience to "piece out our imperfection ..." as Shakespeare does, has to use one actor for the presentation of the wall and another actor for the moon. For a Peking Opera actor to follow the conventional gesture of stepping over the threshold of a door on an illusionistic stage with full scenery is considered ridiculous by people acquainted with Peking Opera, just as for an actor to represent the wall and another to represent the moon with explanations were considered ridiculous by the courtiers and the English Renaissance audience. The experienced Globe and Swan visitors must have been more accustomed to watching Pyramus and Thisby talk through the chink of an imaginary wall created by the actors' gesture. Shakespeare would have easily rendered the existence of the moon by having it mentioned in a speech which could have been performed with an indicative gesture by one of the actors.

In Peking Opera, outdoor scenery is mostly presented with actors' verbal description plus gesture, especially when the scene, one on the river or the ocean, for example, cannot be staged with adequate properties. In the famous Peking Opera play *The White Snake*,[39] part of the action of the opening scene is a journey over the scenic West Lake. When a boat is called for to ferry the three main characters home, it suffices that a boatman moves an oar in such a skilful way that it looks as if he were really rowing a boat towards the three characters (of course the boatman earns a bravo). The boarding activities are presented with mimetic gestures. The imaginary boat is presented to be first swaying up and down violently because of the boarding activities and then slowly getting back to its normal sway on water—all in the gestures and movements of the four actors. As the four actors and actresses move together as if on the same boat, the stage is turned into a lake and the beauty of the scenery is introduced through the descriptive lyric. The specific details of all these gestures and movements can be viewed in actual performances and video tapes as well, so these acting techniques are readily available as reference models for similar scenes in the English Renaissance theatre. In the opening scene of Shakespeare's *The Tempest*, for instance, a ship is about to be wrecked in a storm. Other than two mariners who appear "wet" to provide stage realism, we see no ship nor indication of ocean. We hear noises of lightning and storm "off" stage. We are not sure whether the mariners or the boatswain carry any portable properties onto the stage to indicate they are on board a ship. What we can be sure of is that all the actors in this scene must have acted in such a way as to show that they are on the verge of a shipwreck. Their movements must have followed the movements of the violent waves. The acting of the boating scene in *The White Snake* can serve as a good reference for the tempest scene.

Presentation of the "night scenes" is another area where Peking Opera and English Renaissance theatre might have shown similarities. Both theatres had their performance in the daytime without modern artificial lighting facilities. Even today, the Peking Opera performances do not make use of electric equipment to change lighting for the indication of night scenes; lanterns are the night indicators. The actors also use dialogue, gestures and movements to show they are in the dark. The actors, who in reality see one another very well, pretend that they cannot see anyone and act accordingly. The gestures and movements in the night scenes are highly mimetic and are usually interesting to watch in the Peking Opera theatre, *San ch'a k'ou* (Encounters at the Fork Roads) being one famous example. In the English Renaissance theatre, dialogue and properties such as torches and lamps are used to indicate night time, but we do not know how the actors move, especially in scenes where no lamps or torches are used. In *A Midsummer Night's Dream*, a play with four successive scenes enacted at night, Warren Smith counted the number of times the word "night" was used in the dialogue,[40] but if we are interested in knowing how the four lovers have played their game of hide-and-seek in the dark, the Peking Opera technique may be instructive, especially as it aids in producing a comic effect.

To stage a war scene is problematic if verisimilitude is the goal; however, "the Chinese and Elizabethan conventions of indicating an army are similar and the text always calls for individual combats rather than mass action." [41] In Peking Opera, a single actor carrying a banner indicates that there are a thousand soldiers. The way the banner is carried and handled shows the movement of the whole army and turns out to be a marvellous acrobatic show. In English Renaissance plays war scenes for staging are abundant. Surely it was impossible to put the whole army on the stage, so actors in the English Renaissance must have had their solutions. To have single combats was certainly one solution, but it did not solve all the problems. Modern Western critics and directors have found Peking Opera a meaningful source for inspiration. In the following passage Leonard Pronko recorded one Western response to a Chinese acrobatic performance:

> M. Georges Lerminier, a leading Paris critic, was over-whelmed by the performance of Chinese acrobats, but in 1955 he hesitated to admit that such athletic prowess belonged in the theater. When the troupe returned in 1958, however, he was most enthusiastic: "The fight of the heavenly warriors and the warriors of the water, and the single combat of the woman rebel and the heavenly general are ... Shakespearean. For three years I have been thinking of what a Western director might do

with the battles in *Julius Caesar, King John,* or *Richard III,* calling on the acrobats from the Medrano Circus." [42]

Jean-Louis Barrault, "a spiritual heir of Coupeau and Dullin, both of whom expressed their admiration time and again for the suggestive, poetic, highly controlled dramatic arts of the East," [43] actually designed the battle scenes of *Richard III, Julius Caesar* and *Anthony and Cleopatra* as stylized dances, believing that to stylize a battle "was to move quite naturally in the direction of Chinese opera without necessarily imitating it." [44]

Peter Brook, a director of the Royal Shakespeare Company, when praising the Berliner Ensemble's production of *Cariolanus* as "a triumph," pointed out that in this production "the battles used ancient Chinese techniques to carry modern meanings." [45]

The stylized acting tends to be considered by many Westerners as rigid and lifeless. Marvin Rosenberg's article "Elizabethan Actors: Men or Marionettes?" [46] is a good example of this opinion. Rosenberg believes that the stylized actors are trained to become "graceful, mannered mouthpieces" who recite the dramatic poetry without emotions, act formally instead of naturally and symbolize character instead of portraying it.[47] He assumes that stylized acting cannot achieve the uniqueness that all great actors and artists would like to achieve because individual emotions cannot be expressed in this kind of acting. To him, if an actor is seen to have expressed emotions this actor is certainly not acting in a stylized manner. He therefore uses Geoffrey Tillotson's description of Desdemona in a performance of *Othello* by the King's Men at Oxford in 1610 as evidence of natural acting. The fact that the boy actor played Desdemona to convey emotion and to implore the pity of the audience "simply through facial expression" is evidence for him that English Renaissance actors could act anything "without the need to formalize or symbolize their actions." [48]

Is it true that stylized actors cannot express emotions to move their audience? Peking Opera uses highly stylized acting techniques and is still living for us to make close studies. I once saw a film production of a Peking Opera play, *The White Snake,* the names of the producer and the acting company of which I have forgotten. The film production made it possible for me to clearly see, just as the front row audience in an open stage theatre would have seen, the facial expressions of the leading actress. She followed the conventional, stylized method of acting, but I could see that she portrays the leading character truthfully. Her expressions of anxiety and sorrow through the movements of her eye-brows, eyes, lips, the whole face and the head were particularly touching to me.

Chinese scholars and play-goers often write articles to record or comment on important performances. Professor Yü Ta-gang, a specialist in Peking Opera, comments on the performance of an actress in *Meng Chiang Nü* as follows: "Her powerful and shining eyes and her facial portrayal of the inner pathos are clear, vivid and truthful." [49] Professor Yü also quotes from a Ming dynasty book by Chang Tai in which there are discussions on the acting skill of a famous actor P'eng Tien-hsi, who is good at playing evil characters:

> Mr. Chang Tai praised him, saying, "Historical villains became more vicious through his heart, more knavish by his face and more devilish out of his mouth …" The word "heart" indicates his psychological portrayal of the character; "face" indicates image; and "mouth" indicates speech. An actor with these three capacities is doubtless the most successful. [50]

Westerners who have taken an interest in Peking Opera have also observed that Peking Opera actors are capable of expressing emotions. In 1838, M. Bazin Aine published a volume of four Chinese plays in France. In the introduction he points out that "the theatre moves the Chinese to be ethical not only through moral stories but also through a strong appeal to the emotions; even the most ignorant … weep and groan during the sad scenes …" [51]

An American performance of the Peking Opera production *The Butterfly Dream* reveals more about the secret of stylized acting. Here a group of American actors were trained to do stylized performance. In 1961 Mr. A. C. Scott was asked to direct a production of a Peking Opera for the Institute for Advanced Studies in Theater Arts (IASTA). In the fall of 1962 Scott wrote an article in *Drama Survey* as a record of the entire experience. In this article the actors are reported to have learned something important:

> The actors learned to use the entire body within a rigidly fixed system of acting, and yet succeeded in imprinting their own personalities on the roles they performed.... [52]

Facial expressions are not the only techniques used in Peking Opera to express emotions because facial expressions cannot be viewed by the audience far away from the stage. Broader and more visible gestures are used to convey strong emotions to the large crowd. In *Ssu-lang Visits His Mother*, there is a scene in which Ssu-lang, after a ten minute visit, has to bid farewell to his wife who, believing that her long lost husband was already dead, holds on to his leg and refuses to let him go back to the enemy camp. Ssu-lang is torn between staying home with his mother and his wife and keeping his promise to go back within a certain hour. Such a tremendous inner conflict is presented by the actor's broad and violent physical movements: he pushes his wife away with great strength; horrified by his own violence, he raises his hands and shakes them with his head; he then attempts to stride away, but, seeing his wife lying on the floor, he jumps up with a loud cry and a loud clapping of his hands and then rushes back to hold up his wife.[53] The scene is powerfully moving. The whole process for the acting of this scene could have happened in English Renaissance theatre for the purpose of presenting strong emotions to a large audience. Some cases in point could include the final scene in Marlowe's *Dr. Faustus*, Hamlet after meeting his father's ghost and Hamlet in his mother's chamber in *Hamlet*, Edgar's first encounter with his blinded father in *King Lear*, etc.

My discussion of the parallelism between Peking Opera and English Renaissance theatres is not intended to turn English Renaissance plays into Peking Opera. Though the two theatres are similar in many crucial aspects, they are two unique theatres, just as Peking Opera and Kabuki are two unique theatres though they are both still-living classical theatres that share many similar conventions. Using Peking Opera acting convention as a reference model for the English Renaissance theatre may simply add another dimension to our understanding of potential acting techniques and of our response to them.

NOTES

1. Alfred Harbage and Bertram Joseph are the two representatives of the debate between "formal" and "natural" styles of English Renaissance acting. After his publication of the article on "Elizabethan Acting" in 1939 establishing the idea of formal Elizabethan acting, Harbage wrote one more article in 1951 to review Joseph's *Elizabethan Acting*, still in support of his own idea. But then he started to shift his standpoint by announcing in his *Theater for Shakespeare* in 1955 that these two terms tended to be misleading and therefore should not go on being subjects for discussions. By 1966 when his *Conceptions of Shakespeare* was published, he seemed to have realized where the problem lay and set on explaining what the Elizabethans meant by praising their finest actors as "natural." Joseph

went the other way, almost the opposite. His *Elizabethan Acting* (1951) related Renaissance rhetoric and oratory to acting. Although he did not emphasize the terms "formal" or "natural," many of his points could be easily interpreted as supporting elements for "formal" acting, at least Marvin Rosenberg, in his "Elizabethan Actors: Men or Marionettes?" (see Note 46 below), read him as a formalist. However, in his *The Tragic Actor* (1959) and *Acting Shakespeare* (1960), Joseph started to argue with Harbage by stating that Elizabethan acting style should have been "natural." Then in 1964 his second edition of the 1951 *Elizabethan Acting* showed him a firm believer in "natural" style of Elizabethan acting. He based his argument on almost the same materials he used in the first edition—another evidence of Harbage's realization of the problem with the terms "natural" and "formal," the problem being that the two terms could be interpreted almost any way and thus cause confusion. Anthony Caputi, in his *John Marston, Satirist*, tried to use a different term to avoid confusion. Andrew Gurr's "Elizabethan Action," published in 1966, was the only article in this debate that explained the misinterpretations of these two terms in the linguistic context. In the whole process of discussions concerning Elizabethan acting styles, we can see that no one seemed to believe in "formal acting only" any more after 1951. Most scholars either tried to shun the terms or, if they did use the terms, believed that a mixture of the two styles would have been more probable.

2. M. C. Bradbrook, *The Living Monument: Shakespeare and the Theater of His Time* (N.Y.: Cambridge University Press, 1976), p. viii.

3. Ibid., p. 106.

4 Ibid., p. vii.

5. Also, searching for references from other similar theatres for a better understanding of the English Renaissance production becomes more comprehensible to the Western mind.

6. Tao-ching Hsu, *The Chinese Conception of the Theater* (Seattle: University of Washington Press, 1985), pp. 455–563.

7. Leonard Pronko, *Theater East and West: Perspectives toward a Total Theater* (Berkeley: University of California Press, 1967), p. 35.

8. Hsu, pp. 272–80. Also in Ch'en Wan-nai 陳萬鼐 , *History of the Yüan, Ming and Ch'ing Drama* (元明清戲曲史) (Taipei: Ting-wen 鼎文 , 1980), pp. 617–19.

9. Ch'en, pp. 614–15.

10. Ibid., p. 613. Figure 1 is a modern sketch of the picture which appears in *Collected Essays on Fiction and Drama* by Chou Yi-pai (Shantung: Ch'i-Lu 齊魯 , 1986), p. 471.

11. Hsu, p. 317.

12. Ch'en, pp. 613–14.

13. *Developmental History of Chinese Drama* (中國戲劇發展史). (Tainan: Min-mian 僶勉 , 1975), p. 737. Although name of the author is not given, this reprint must be

made from Chou Yi-pai's *Developmental History of Chinese Drama*.

14. William Dolby, *A History of Chinese Drama* (London: P. Elek, 1976), pp. 186–88.

15. Ibid., p. 188. The source comes originally from Gordon Cummings, *Wanderings in China* (1888), pp. 187–91, "Temple Theater."

16. The drawing is taken from Dolby, illustration 11, between pp. 196–97.

17. Ibid., p. 187.

18. Hsu, p. 22.

19. Dolby, p. 191.

20. This book and *Chin-t'ai ts'an lei chi* 金台殘淚記 (1829) are collected in *Ch'ing Dynasty Theatrical Resources at the Capital* (清代燕都梨園史料) edited by Chang Chiang-ts'ai 張江裁 (Taipei: Student Bookstore, 1964).

21. Ch'en, pp. 615–16; Dolby, p. 190; Hsu, pp. 24–25.

22. Ch'en, p. 616. Original sources are from *Meng hua so pu* 夢華瑣簿 and *Chin-t'ai ts'an lei chi*.

23. Hsu, p. 23.

24. Andrew Gurr, *The Shakespearean Stage, 1574–1642* (N.Y.: Cambridge University Press, 1980), p. 123.

25. Ibid., pp. 120–21.

26. Ibid., p. 114.

27. Ibid., p. 156.

28. Ibid., p. 119.

29. Ibid., p. 114.

30. Ibid., p. 145.

31. Ibid., p. 139.

32. Ibid., p. 156.

33. Ibid., pp. 120–39.

34. Oscar G. Brockett, *The Essential Theater* (San Francisco: Holt, Rinehart & Winston, 1976), pp. 309–11.

35. M. C. Bradbrook, *Themes and Conventions of Elizabethan Tragedy* (Cambridge: Cambridge University Press, 1969), p. 21.

36. Dolby, p. 277, Ch. 9, Note 15. Originally from Lin Yu-tang, *My Country and My People*, p. 249.

37. Pronko, p. 161.

38. Gurr, pp. 172–73.

39. *The White Snake* (白蛇與許仙), videotape by Taiwan TV Culture Co. (台視文化公司). The leading actress is Kuo Hsiao-chuang (郭小莊).

40. Warren D. Smith, *Shakespeare's Playhouse Practice: A Handbook* (Hanover, New Hampshire: University Press of New England, 1975).

41. George Freedley and John A. Reeves, *A History of the Theater* (N.Y.: Crown Publishers, 1941), p. 192.

42. Pronko, p. 45.

43. Ibid., p. 46.

44. Ibid.

45. Peter Brook, *The Empty Space* (N.Y.: Atheneum, 1968), p. 81.

46. Marvin Rosenberg, "Elizabethan Actors: Men or Marionettes?" *PMLA*, Vol. 69 (1954), pp. 915–27.

47. Ibid., p. 915.

48. Ibid., p. 918.

49. Yü Ta-kang 兪大綱, *Random Talks on Drama* (戲劇縱橫談) (Taipei: Chuan-chi wen-hsüeh-she 傳記文學社, 1969), p. 119. My translation.

50. Ibid., pp. 237–38. My translation.

51. Pronko, p. 39.

52. Ibid., pp. 48–51.

53. *Ssu-lang Visits His Mother* (四郎探母), videotape by Taiwan TV Culture Co. The leading actress is Hsü Lu 徐露.

8. The Structuring of Spontaneity:
An Assessment and Documentation of Improvisational Creative Methods in the Modern Taiwan Theatre

Sheng-chuan Lai

The late seventies to the present has witnessed a new flourishing of theatrical creativity in Taiwan. In what has become a reshaping of the modern Chinese theatre, many innovations in actor training and the making of plays have come through the driving inspiration to create new theatre in accordance with native, organic needs and impulses. A new theatre is being created for a new audience, and in many ways this new theatre is a product of the willingness to begin explorations from point zero and discover the new potentials behind all theatrical aspects involved. The Lan Ling Theatre Workshop (蘭陵劇坊), Taiwan's seminal experimental theatre group, the Performance Workshop (表演工作坊), and many avant-garde groups such as the Notebook Theatre (筆記劇場), the Circular Ruins Theatre (環墟劇場), and the Left Bank Theatre (河左岸劇場) are performing original works that have brought audiences into the theatre in unprecedented numbers, and have greatly enlarged the vocabulary and possibilities of theatre in Taiwan. All of these groups work with experimental methods of making and performing theatre, the most important being the use of improvisation as a creative tool. This study focuses on the use of improvisation in eight plays supervised by the author in his work with the Performance Workshop and the National Institute of the Arts (國立藝術學院), in the period covering 1983 to 1987. The theory and methods of using spontaneity in the creation of theatre will be dealt with in detail.

I

In our industrialized and post-industrialized age, the spontaneous and intuitive faculties of the human psyche have become less and less emphasized, while logical and ordered perception and expression have become more and more important and functional. Jacques Moreno, one of the pioneers of theory and practice concerning the use of spontaneity in theatrical performance and in psychotherapy, has noted that

> When compared with many other mental functions of individuals [who underwent laboratory testing], such as intelligence and memory, the sense for spontaneity is seen to be far less developed. This may perhaps be so because, in the civilization of conserves which we have developed, spontaneity is far less used and trained than, for instance, intelligence and memory.[1]

Running counter to this current in our "civilization of conserves" is the radical urge to express oneself through spontaneous actions of various kinds. The development of jazz into a highly sophisticated art form, the deployment of techniques that, in effect, parallel trance states in abstract expressionist painting, and the reliance on chance in various modern dance choreography and avant-garde performance, all belie the acknowledgement that the rational consciousness plays a small, if not minimal part, in the perception of reality, and that the unconscious is in touch with currents that work below the façade of consciously perceived experience, currents that in significance are seen to dwarf the meaning of the experience and symbols that are processed by the consciousness.

As in the case of the accomplished jazz musician, intuitive gesture becomes a direct connection with deeper urges, and that the intuitive, spontaneous act itself engenders a form that in itself is a whole, organic entity, regardless of outer appearance. C. G. Jung, in speaking of intuition, says:

> Intuition is an unconscious process in that its result is the irruption into consciousness of an unconscious content, a sudden idea or "hunch." It resembles a process of perception, but unlike the conscious activity of the senses and introspection the perception is unconscious. That is why we speak of intuition as an "instinctive" act of comprehension. It is a process analogous to instinct, with the difference that whereas instinct is a purposive impulse to carry out some highly complicated action, intuition is the unconscious, purposive apprehension of a highly complicated situation.[2]

In these terms, the form that is engendered by intuition is in fact an apprehension that is in itself complete. The use of spontaneity towards the specific conscious goal of artistic creation involves both Jung's "unconscious, purposive apprehension of a highly complicated situation," and the conscious acknowledgement that such apprehension is to be used towards specific expressive purposes. Thus the accomplished jazz musician realizes that the art of improvisation is a subtle combination of the conscious and the unconscious, where the conscious is suspended to allow for the intuitions and energies of the unconscious to expand spontaneously through the musician's instrument, and yet the conscious is also retained, to allow for the expanding energies to be shaped in accordance with the structure of the piece being played.

II

Since late 1983, I have supervised the creation and performance of eight full-length pieces for the theatre, through the use of improvisation as the basic tool in a collective process of playmaking. Explorations began in October 1983, when at the National Institute of the Arts in Taipei, I began using improvisational exercises as prelude to the collective creation of a theatre piece. Fresh from theatre training in the United States, I had on one hand observed the uncertainties of the cultural environment and the lack of production resources in Taiwan, and on the other hand what I had seen to be serious deficiencies in the American way of producing mainstream, "professional" theatre that had made for technically efficient performances that seemed to lack organic wholeness and creative sincerity.

In 1982 and 1983, as a doctorate student in Dramatic Art at the University of California, Berkeley, I had the opportunity to observe and work with Shireen Strooker of Amsterdam Werkteater, particularly on the 1983 production of *Ondine* at Berkeley. Like the Open Theatre in the United States and the Théâtre du Soleil in France, the Amsterdam Werkteater grew in the radical cultural climate of sixties and early seventies, where the traditional hierarchical structure of theatrical production, and indeed, the whole purpose and practice of the theatre had been put into question. Groups such as these responded with communal efforts towards the creation of theatre, in which playwright/director/producer/actor hierarchies were abolished in favour of a process of collective creation and production. Much of the creative energy of the West in the sixties and seventies was channelled into the theatre, where, during the development of a "genuine aesthetic radicalism," C.W.E. Bigsby notes that

The counter-cultural fascination with communes and a renewed sense of group identity, in process of being asserted by various sub-groups, found a paradigm in the theatre group.[3]

The development of a theatre alternative to that of the conventional theatre in the West marked a deep re-evaluation of political, social and subsequently aesthetic values. The creation of the rich body of "alternative" theatre that includes the work of Grotowski, the Open Theatre, the Performance Group, the Living Theatre and Robert Wilson, to name but a few, can be related to new views in the role that theatre plays in society and life. To adjust to these new views, the whole concept of the theatre event underwent radical reconsideration and restructuring.

Improvisation became a natural tool under the circumstances, where the creative potential of each individual was emphasized. In speaking of the collective creations of French theatre groups after the May 1968 unrest, Lenora Champagne notes common characteristics:

The personal creativity of the actor was the basis of the work. The conventions of a linear narrative dramatic structure and psychological characterization were rejected along with the playwright. Instead, actor's improvisations shaped the creative process. A collage or montage structure suitable for showing different points of view was developed to include the contributions by the actors.[4]

These were basically the features I observed in Strooker's work, in which a highly sophisticated method of organizing improvisational activities in the rehearsal room led to the development of theatrical moments or images which might then be shaped into scenes, and hence might be developed into larger works. The use of improvisation proved to me to free spontaneous energies and concerns in the actors participating, and coupled with the subjective, individual artistic sensibility of the leader of the project (Strooker), led to exciting creative possibilities that drew deeply on the intuition of the actor, and communicated deeply to the intuition of the audience.

Writing of my observations in Dunbar Ogden's *Actor Training and Audience Response*, I noted:

What drew me to Shireen's work was precisely the process of "making" a play that was radically opposed to conventional methods of approaching theatrical production. In a nutshell, I see conventional practice in America, in general, to be an attempt to assemble the divided pieces of production—acting, lighting, scene design, sound, etc.—into a final, cohesive whole. This process involves lots of unknown factors and chance—can an actor attain the certain quality for a certain role? Is the "chemistry" right? Will the scenic designer's idea conflict with the director's? How will the actors adjust to makeup and costumes? The Amsterdam Werkteater's techniques employed by Shireen Strooker invert this process: Instead of pieces towards a whole, she takes the essence—some guiding thought or emotion—first, and from this genuinely heartfelt essence, the form and pieces of production begin to take shape. Though the end product is never predictable, this process eliminates much of the chance factors of conventional means. From the standpoint of the actors, they are not asked to "inhabit" a role, but rather to use themselves to create a role. From the standpoint of the designers and technicians, the ideas come by necessity, from the process itself.[5]

At the National Institute of the Arts in 1983, I was faced with serious choices concerning the training of actors and theatre practitioners. The theatrical environment, basically beginning to burgeon under the efforts of Lan Ling and the annual Experimental Theatre Festival but still in a state of infancy and uncertainty, was receiving a strong injection from American-trained teachers, who in technical fields were teaching American methods of production, methods employed on Broadway, to be specific, to students at the Institute and at other training centres such as the Cloud Gate Dance Theatre (雲門舞集). These new methods would ensure production efficiency, but I feared the repercussions of such industrial-age methods on the still-fertile grounds of creative possibilities. To break the theatrical event into specialized pieces, like that of an assembly line, was a path that I feared, for such specialization could easily lead, in my mind, to the loss of organic unity that I had witnessed in the American theatre.

In terms of actor training, I was equipped with the skills to teach Stanislavski-type theories and methods. Yet there was a serious lack of contemporary scripts on which to use such methods, as well as an insufficiency of Western plays in translation. The point, to me, was not to import foreign methods to be used in foreign modes of theatre, but to see how creativity could be channelled out of natural means, into whatever form suited such natural output. Such creativity, in my mind, would reflect on the sensibilities of the particular time and place, and become a building block on which to begin to shape a theatre that would suit the particular needs of the society. The improvisational methods used in making plays by Shireen Strooker and the Amsterdam Werkteater seemed to me a safe place to begin, for the methods involved were not concerned specifically with what final form creative processes took, but rather in the processes themselves, in which the fundamental building blocks were the intuitions and emotions of the actors, channelled through highly disciplined exercises that drew on spontaneous, improvised actions. In using the emotions and experiences of the actors as a starting point, I felt that what would evolve might be specific actor training techniques for use in the contemporary Taiwan theatre, and methods of making plays that would reflect on the concerns of the times. In effect, though different in socio-political background, this was essentially what alternative groups like the Werkteater and the Open Theatre were doing in the cultural environment of the sixties and seventies in the West.

What occurred was the creation of an organic form of playmaking, through improvisational work of actors supervised by a director. This new process of making theatre created new theatrical forms that, in spite of their odd shapes and structures, addressed the needs and concerns of the society. Beginning from point zero, a playmaking process evolved in 1983 and 1984 where free improvisations on specific situations gave birth to freely-structured, collage-type forms that made their impact on the Taiwan theatre. Having asserted its influence on creativity, this new method, which gained popular support, began to assert itself on production methods. Whereas the original efforts drew freely from spontaneous energies on both the parts of the actors and director, the making of plays through these methods after 1985 began to evolve into a more traditional relationship between "playwright/director" (in place of playwright alone) and actors. The ensuing pages document this evolution, and attempt to put it in perspective in view of current and future trends in Taiwan theatre.

1. Initial Explorations

We All Grew Up This Way (我們都是這樣長大的)
   (developed 10/1983–1/1984; performed 1/1984 and 7/1984)
Plucking Stars (摘星)
   (developed 1/1984–3/1984; performed 3/1984–4/1984)

We All Grew Up This Way was the first product of these explorations, performed 11 and 12 January 1984 at the Tien Educational Center in Taipei. The work grew out of improvisatory exercises based on significant experiences in the lives of the fifteen student actors who were at the time attending Second Year Acting class at the National Institute. In form, the piece was structured as a collage of ten scenes broken up into seventeen short segments. Creative development took place from October to December 1983, in which the collage structure developed organically from the nature of the subject matter and the improvisational rehearsals. The result was a collage of scenes of growing up in contemporary Taiwan, which we called *We All Grew Up This Way*. Though disjointed in outer structure, the scenes worked together in an organic, inner structure that held the piece together. The performance, which Dr. Shen Ma (馬森) called "the birth of a new theatre form on the Chinese stage,"[6] marked the new use of personal experience as subject matter, and the method of improvisational rehearsals to explore and expand the subject matter, creating, as it was, a form that grew out of and with the subject matter as it expanded organically.

Plucking Stars, the next play created through the improvisational process, focused on the lives of the mentally retarded. Working with the Lan Ling Theatre Workshop, the creative process emphasized field work and interviews of the mentally retarded and their families. We accumulated much material, images, physical actions and ideas for improvisational development.

In assimilating the material, my work was to set up well-defined situations and offer directives to the actors, who would then proceed spontaneously. Actors began developing mentally retarded characters as well as characters who were not mentally retarded. Structure was not set, nor was it a priority to set one. With the experience of *We All Grew Up This Way*, I enjoyed the way the structure of a work grew organically from the ensemble and its work. I was not to interfere with the growth of the structure of this work, but rather aid the work along in its development, while at the same time stimulate it into new directions and possibilities. Thus original situations or images related by the actors from their observations were often altered, or given added dimensions, by me, in the exploratory spirit of seeing where the new directives would take us.

By late February 1984, it became clear that we were working with a series of loosely connected scenes, and my job became to identify the criteria by which the scenes would be selected and arranged. We began classifying two types of scenes: verbal and non-verbal, the non-verbal scenes being set to the music of Bach's Solo Flute Partitas. In all, over eighty situations were explored, of which were selected sixteen scenes that were developed and arranged for final performance in late March. The process of selection and arrangement was done privately, by myself, and continued until a week before the opening. The sequence of scenes, in fact, continued to be altered after opening, as the order of some key scenes was shifted during the tour of central Taiwan in May.

The performance was noted for its social function, as well as creative innovation. The *Min Sheng News* (民生報) headline was "Lan Ling Drills into a Corner of Society to Pluck Stars,"[7] while the poet Yang Mu 楊牧 called the play "a poetic theatrical parable ... [that is] almost religious in its ritual qualities."[8] The idea of beginning without a text or structure, progressing towards a performance through the use of improvisational rehearsals, and arriving organically at a collage structure of short scenes and theatrical images was radical for Taiwan, and opened up new possibilities for creativity within the stagnant creative climate. Several college theatre clubs began experimenting with the methods, and from the Lan Ling group that performed *Plucking Stars*, Huang Ch'eng-huang 黃承晃 and Lao Chia-hua 老嘉華 went on later in the year to form Notebook Theatre, an influential group that experimented essentially with improvisation. Li Kuo-hsiu 李國修 also worked with improvisation with a group he supervised, the Screens Acting Class (屏風表演班).

In analyzing the influence of *Plucking Stars* on the theatrical scene in Taiwan, Chang Chia-ju 張嘉茹 saw the work as combining and refining the efforts of Lan Ling, up to Actor's Experimental Studio, and the National Institute of the Arts' *We All Grew Up This Way* into

> a model of collective/improvisational creation, not only asserting the collective/ improvisational creative method as a legitimate method, but at the same time laying the foundation for the development of collective/improvisational creativity in Taiwan's experimental theatre.[9]

During this initial period of using improvisational methods, it became clear to me that the use of improvisation was a swift way to tap the genuine depths of the actors. Though I agree with the American artist Robert Rauschenberg who denounced the use of improvisation in creative work "because, trusted to improvise, people rarely move out of their own particular clichés and habits,"[10] the particular methods of improvisation that were being developed in the Taiwan environment from the basis of Amsterdam Werkteater methods were very restrictive and clear in laying down the boundaries for spontaneous freedom, letting the actor react spontaneously in an environment and character that he was already very knowledgeable about. In other words, what was being practised was not "anarchic," but rather "controlled" spontaneity. When clichés and idiosyncracies arose, they were either discouraged or used for the further development of character or staging possibilities. The actor became the medium and the material towards theatrical creation, and I found, like the eighteenth-century Italian *commedia dell-arte* actor Riccoboni, that

The actor who improvises plays in a much livelier and more natural manner than one who learns his role by heart. People feel better, and therefore say better, what they invent than what they borrow from others with the aid of memory.[11]

2. Transition

The Passer-By (過客)

(developed 4/1984–6/1984; performed 6/1984 and 9/1985)

The Other Evening, We Put on a Show of Hsiang-sheng (那一夜，我們 說相聲)

(developed 8/1984–2/1985; performed 3/1985–4/1985)

Completed in June 1984, *The Passer-By* was the most swiftly created work through improvisation that I had taken part in, and marked the end of a period of nine straight months of conducting improvisational rehearsals that had led towards the creation of three plays. Differing from the two previous works, developmental rehearsals for *The Passer-By* were instigated with the clear purpose to create a play with a traditional narrative structure, not the disjointed collage structure that had been previously used.

Second year students of the National Institute of the Arts were again chosen to form an ensemble, and we decided to develop a play on mental stress of the young generation by exploring a character whom we named Lin Wei (林未).

In effect, what we did was create an environment, complete with people, and then throw in a catalyst to trigger off a chemical reaction: the students' apartment became a reactor where Lin Wei, in improvisational sessions, gave them wave after wave of weird but logical actions to which they had to react.

The play grew quickly, so quickly that I was amazed at the process. After four weeks, the work was completed, and a fluid narrative structure had been formed. Each of the actors reacted to the various situations with wit, insight and a strong communal sense of purpose. The clearer their characters, the more spontaneous and inspiring were the improvisations. The rehearsal room resembled in my mind a basketball court, with the ball being fired from player to player. Myself, as coach, sent in set plays, sometimes at "time outs," where the whole group was assembled and given directives, and more often through directives to single actors, who on the "sidelines," were whispered instructions, after which they would go on to the "court" at a selected moment to carry out the "play." In basketball, "plays" are drawn up on the sidelines, but there is never any guarantee that what is planned will actually occur. In our case, there was never intent for specific things to happen, that is to say, *events* were never planned, only psychological motivations or isolated actions. These were the things that were sent into the "court," where the improvised "game" was in progress, and from these "plays," new action arose, as the "game" developed into further and more complex stages. An assistant was employed to take note of all that transpired during rehearsal, and it was to these notes that we constantly turned for reference when we wanted to re-develop certain things that had been attempted before, things that needed new development due to new events that had arisen out of subsequent improvisational sessions.

During the process, as director, I often worked in what I would call a state of spontaneity, detaching myself from rational functions and flowing with the fluid improvisational action. Directives thus would be given under these circumstances, often in the midst of improvisations, and the actors would pause momentarily to digest the directive, then continue the improvisation. My rational faculties were put to work after rehearsal, while going over notes, reviewing the day's new input, and putting down ideas and structures into writing.

Though the play had a distinct narrative structure, it was not shaped the way a conventional narrative-structure theatrical work was, for the story meandered and took turns in ways that were not orthodox. This was due to the improvisational process that had given shape to the various unexpected incidental and structural twists. Though not at all orthodox in narrative structure, *The Passer-By* suggested new possibilities for narrative structure that could be attained through the free-form shapes that collective creation through improvisation could provide.

The possibilities in improvising on a pre-meditated structure were carried one step further in the making of *The Other Evening, We Put on a Show of Hsiang-sheng*, the première work of the new theatre group the Performance Workshop, which was formed by the actors Li Li-chün 李立群, Li Kuo-hsiu and myself in late 1984. This work did not consist of a narrative structure *per se*, and in fact the subject matter was taken exclusively from improvisational sessions, but unlike the earlier works, the form of the piece was not allowed to grow and develop with the process, but was rather set at the inception of the work period. In many ways, this move was a maturing in method from the earlier work, in which more conscious calculation was involved to create a theatrical piece. This consciousness, however, inadvertantly limited the freedom of allowing the structure to grow through the process.

At the outset, the task was clear: I had resolved to use the traditional Chinese stand-up comedy routine art form *hsiang-sheng* to comment on the actual decline of this very form. In other words, this well-loved but now neglected folk art was to serve as the vehicle for its own elegy, and hopefully, as a vehicle for the ensemble's feelings towards the loss of traditions in general.

Pre-determined structure was a starting point, and not the result of exploratory improvisations. What was to be said, and how it was to be said, was the objective of the improvisational sessions. The sessions were a strange combination of rational analysis and spontaneous action, with either activity coming in spurts. Like in the creation of *The Passer-By*, I worked privately on the actual selecting and arranging of content, after rehearsals, and would usually walk into the next day's rehearsals with new directions for scenes that had already been developed. Like *The Passer-By*, goals were set at the outset, and in this case, a structure was imposed on yet-to-be-developed contents. Like *Plucking Stars*, new developments through improvisational inspiration directly influenced the shaping of the contents, but in this case such shaping was to take place, unlike in *Plucking Stars*, within a pre-determined structure.

On a level unattained by any of the previous performances, and, indeed, by any performance since Lan Ling's *Ho Chu's New Match* (荷珠新配), *The Other Evening, We Put on a Show of Hsiang-sheng* was an immense popular success, so much so that the producers, New Aspect, added as many performances as they could, and U.F.O. records hastened to sign a contract with us to record the performance and issue it as an audio recording. The popularity was due in part from the unusual and appealing subject matter and its treatment, and in part from the popularity and performance of the two actors. In a truly unexpected twist, an experimental theatre piece created collectively through improvisational rehearsals had suddenly become a popular hit, through what analysts in the *Min Sheng News* of 8 March 1985 called "multi layers" of meaning, through which "the initiated see the subtleties; the uninitiated watch the festivities." Paul Shackman, writing in the *Asian Wall Street Journal*, commented:

> Buoyed by the original, often startling humor and swept along by the play's energetic pace, the audience doesn't think about the essentially serious messages embedded

within the piece's tight, meticulous structure until later, and then more likely than
not with an irrepressible smile.[12]

The task of using tradition to comment on tradition, doubled by the task of
using a comic form to create what in effect constituted an elegy, was carried
forth through the benefits of collective creation through improvisation,
through which the combination of "original" and "startling" humour was
made possible.

3. Return to Free-Form
Bach Variations (變奏巴哈)
(developed 3/1985–6/1985; performed 6/1985)

The Taiwan performances of the avant-garde Hong Kong group Zuni
Isocahedron (進念二十面體) in the summer of 1984 inspired me to incorporate post-modern aesthetics in a future improvisationally created work.
The work, *Bach Variations*, was conceived during the rehearsal period of
The Other Evening, We Put on a Show of Hsiang-sheng, and rehearsals
began with an ensemble of twenty-four National Institute students immediately after the opening of *The Other Evening*. In many ways, the influence
of having just worked with pre-meditated structure was still felt, but in spite
of this, this work can be seen as a return, or a relapse, into a modified
method of letting form through process, as in the earlier works.

Whereas the initial impetus for previous works came through inspiration
provided by people, characters, or thematic concerns, the impetus for *Bach
Variations* was to come from a body of music, Bach's *The Well-Tempered
Clavier*, to be specific. Though I did not pre-designate a structure for the
piece, the ensemble explored the fugues in *The Well-Tempered Clavier*, and
I decided at an early point that the play would be built on the structure of a
Bach fugue, though how this was to be done was as free a choice as had
Bach when he composed his fugues. Subject matter was not specified. All
was to come through a communal sense of direction, inspired by the music,
by the ensemble as a whole.

The final product was a complex performance piece in which, like in a
fugue, there seemed to always be something different happening some-
where at any given point in time, verbally, physically, visually, spatially.
Like a slow, unfolding, metamorphosizing display, *Bach Variations* had
specific images and motifs that recurred and intensified, but had no narrative structure or specific thematic objective. If there was an objective, it was

to create a theatre piece that was like a piece of Bach's music. The improvisational process proved to be particularly fruitful under the circumstances.

4. The Assertation of Director as "Playwright"

Secret Love for the Peach Blossom Fount (暗戀桃花源)
   (developed 10/1985–2/1986; performed 3/1986–4/1986)
Pastoral (田園生活)
   (developed 3/1986–6/1986; performed 6/1986)
Circle Monogatari (圓環物語)
   (developed 11/1986–2/1987; performed 3/1987–4/1987)

The creative process of *Secret Love for the Peach Blossom Fount*, the Performance Workshop's second production, solidified the practices that began with the attempt at narrative structure in *The Passer-By* and the pre-designation of structure in *The Other Night, We Put on a Show of Hsiang-sheng*. Within a pre-determined narrative structure that was actually a piecing together of fragments of two separate narrative structures, the actors executed improvisational exercises aimed at filling in specific material for specific scenes in the overall structure. This was the maturing of the process that had actually begun in the making of *The Other Evening*, and in practice it sought to retain the intuitive input of spontaneity attainable through improvisation, while at the same time be more efficient in giving exact placement to improvisational segments. It could be said that I produced the "bones," while the actors, in collaboration with myself, filled in the "meat." Such a process did not rule out the possibility that, like in the earlier plays, the blossoming of subject matter through improvisation would in effect dictate growth of the overall structure, for though in this case the structure itself was scrutinized at the outset much more closely than had been before, I remained open to letting spontaneous stimulation affect the building of the whole work.

The whole work was based on a complex situation: two theatre groups would be found in the same theatre, each having booked the theatre to exercise their final dress rehearsals. One is playing a tragic modern-day work about an old mainland man, living in Taiwan since 1949, who is obsessed with memories of his first love in Shanghai. The other is a farcical treatment of the utopian tale *The Peach Blossom Fount*. Conflicts and interruptions served the basis for fragmenting both rehearsals, as the audience sees fragment pieces of the two plays in an order that is not necessarily sequential.

As rehearsal progressed, the pieces of the play became to take shape. I compare the making of the play to the building of a complex that includes two buildings—one classical, one modern. Yet the two, when considered together, are in fact one work. If the modern building was, for instance, originally scheduled in the architect's blue-prints to have seven floors, then perhaps as we worked on the fourth floor, the unexpected would occur through improvisation, and the architect would alter the blue-print to let the building accommodate eight floors. Then, on considering the two buildings as a whole, the adding of a floor on the top of the modern building would seem to necessitate the taking out of a floor on the classical, then expanding the floor space on another floor. This is how the whole play grew, from the original "blue-print" into the final, mature shape. While much energy was expended in improvisational rehearsals, my work after rehearsals proved to be more taxing. With the material expanding daily, I would restructure and re-evaluate the whole "blue-print" on paper, and prepare new directives for the coming rehearsal session. Once the two subgroups combined, new alterations were made, and the final form was achieved.

The performance was enthusiastically received by audience and critics, and the dynamics of seeing a comic scene after a tragic, and then have another tragic scene follow, created a special theatrical experience. The popularity of the play gave it a longer run than even *The Other Evening*, and collective creation through improvisation had solidified its position in Taipei's artistic and popular culture.

The creative methods laid down in the making of *Secret Love* were further refined in the following endeavour *Pastoral*, which, in fact, was a direct continuation and natural expansion of the methods used in *Secret Love*.

Whereas *Secret Love* used fragments from what were conceived to be two whole pieces, *Pastoral* expanded the count to four, using the visual pun on the Chinese character for "field" (田) to construct a two-storey apartment building on stage, and let the four compartments, in which lived four different families, live independent of each other, an independence that, considered as a whole, created an interdependent, whole work.

Like with *Secret Love*, I took the initiative at the outset and outlined not only the characters in each apartment, but the situations as well. I went one step further, designating also what was eventually to happen in each situation.

In *Pastoral*, improvisational sessions were only the beginning of a much more complex process of fitting the four units together, editing the events and dialogue so that the action flowed freely from unit to unit without interruption. In many ways, the use of spatial and temporal elements, like in *Bach Variations*, was more poetic than narrative, though in *Pastoral* the overall framework was definitely narrative. Privately, I faced the enormous task of editing the daily input that came from rehearsals into a structure that reflected my original blue-print. As the date of performance drew nearer, I slowly found myself reverting more and more to the traditional role of the "director," as I had already decided on the final form of the play and finished what was in effect a "playwriting" task. Whereas original explorations using improvisation were in part aimed at breaking up the traditional relationship between playwright, script, director and actors, the process of creating *Pastoral* actually served to differentiate between two distinct processes of "playwriting" and "directing," with both jobs being taken simultaneously by the same person.

Circle Monogatari, the Performance Workshop's third play, basically continued the methods of *Pastoral*, refining them in terms of cutting the cast into a small nucleus of seven actors, and working with the greatest amount of pre-determined structure and subject matter ever. In the play's inception in October 1986, not only was the *La Ronde* structure decided upon, but the characters were sharply defined in terms of occupation and characteristics, and the events in the circle progression were clearly laid out. More than ever, the actors felt that the improvisational sessions were a means to add "meat" on to "bones," and that the "bones" had indeed grown more and more substantial with each new endeavour.

Room was still present for alterations in structure through inspiration gathered in rehearsal, but in this case, the alterations were few.

The production met with popular success, and the longest run in recent Taiwan theatrical history, thirty-six performances. Critical reaction, however, was mixed, as to many, the comic façade did not reveal the serious overtones as well as the previous endeavours *The Other Evening* and *Secret Love*. In creative terms, *Circle Monogatari* marked a movement towards greater control on the part of the director, who, in assuming the role of "playwright," had fashioned the new role "director/playwright" in the process, seriously limiting the spontaneous outgrowth of form, as well as content, through improvisational rehearsals. In many ways, after completing the production, I felt that the end of a period in improvisational theatrical creation had come.

III

The graph had been used in different ways as an essential aid in my private work in structuring plays in progress. The progression of the graphs used in the various stages of improvisatory creation reveals a clear movement towards more sophisticated graphs that represents a marked change in the structuring procedures of the spontaneity that arises in improvisational rehearsals. The early work forms itself, with conscious help from the designated supervisor of the project, the "director," whose job, in Amsterdam Werkteater terminology, is referred to as "stimulator."[13] The later work begins as a conscious structure in the "stimulator's" mind, and in rehearsal the directives are not meant to channel ensemble energy any more, but to channel individual or small group inspiration and genuine emotion, towards the goal of filling in the needs of the structure. Freedom is still allowed for the natural outgrowth of structural elements, as in *Secret Love*, which witnessed the organic growth of the whole business of the strange woman and the man she was looking for, yet in *Circle Monogatari* this freedom has been cut to the minimum, by necessity of the tight, geometrical structure.

The analogy of a spider's web can be used to illustrate this essential difference: In conventional European and American theatre practice, where the producer selects a playscript, finds a director, who casts the play and begins rehearsing it, meeting with designers outside of rehearsal, the whole process begins with all parties involved standing, it may seem, at the outer parameters of a gigantic spider's web. At the centre of the web, unseeable, is the nucleus, the guiding spirit behind the original creation of the playscript. The director, actors and designers begin moving towards the centre from these outer parameters, through the various lines that give access to smaller rings in the chain of concentric circles. Whether or not the whole group arrives at the nucleus in time for opening night is questionable, and indeed hazardous, and although any given member of the group may have intuitive access to the nucleus, there is no guarantee that he can bring the others in.

With the use of improvisation as a tool in a process of collective creation, as in early work such as *Plucking Stars*, this whole process is inverted. All members involved begin together, within the nucleus, and then being a process of moving outward, towards the outer parameters and the establishment of a performance text. Whatever is developed comes from the nucleus, and yet since there is so little criteria to guide the movement of the group as it ventures out from the centre, often the shape of the spider's web is irregular. It tends to meander, forming odd shapes that nevertheless create unified pieces on the strength that everything comes from the core.

These are two radically different approaches to the making of the theatrical event. In the experiments of the past four years, what has happened in Taiwan seems to be a combination of various aspects of the both forms:

The early work of *We All Grew Up This Way* and *Plucking Stars* sets the model for the meandering, irregular spider's web. In practice beginning with *The Other Evening* and reaching its heights in *Circle Monogatari*, all involved still begin at the centre, in the nucleus of the yet-to-be-formed spider's web. Yet while in the centre, "poles" are erected at the parameters that all can clearly see, and as the ensemble moves out from the centre, the direction is clearly marked. If actors move in directions other than set by the poles, either the poles are re-marked, or the actor is asked to conform with the existing structure. Ideally, the ensemble reaches the poles at the outer parameters naturally, and thus the inner structure, designated at the outset, is given an outer display that is totally in harmony with it.

In many ways, this revised use of improvisation bears the marks of conventional theatre production, the difference being that there is not a dramatic text *per se* to begin with, but rather the structure of a dramatic text. The revised practices gain conscious clarity of purpose and, when used properly, are very efficient. On the other hand, they threaten to restrict the very inherent charms of the improvisational process itself, making it a tool towards preconceived, conventional means of theatre.

The use of improvisation is never easy, for either the actor or director. When it works, deep and genuine emotions that reflect common concerns are freely channelled, surprising all with their "apprehensive" intuition. When it fails to work, it is particularly frustrating and depressing for all concerned. In writing of the Amsterdam Werkteater, Dunbar Ogden says:

> Nothing is certain. Chaos can result. The only condition that makes possible a group of this nature rests in enormous mutual trust. Each individual has to make extreme demands on himself, involving self-criticism and personal responsibility, as well as long term acceptance of others.[14]

As improvisational techniques are difficult to master, actors are often frustrated when they find obstacles to letting their emotions flow spontaneously, and even when they can function spontaneously, they often are

frustrated because they cannot know whether their work is really contribut-
ing to the whole piece or not. An actor with America's Open Theatre sums
up emotions that are common to all actors who have worked in similar
situations:

> It's a fog, a huge fog that I'm squinting into trying to join in with. Joe [Chaikin,
> director] seems to have the clearest picture because he can say yes this, not that....
> But I don't feel I'm creating a thing in which I'm consciously going about to say
> what I want to say. I feel like a blind person trying to learn to dance. It's hard for me
> to come up with ideas. It's too big for me to grasp. I can chew on my little corner but
> I can't see the whole thing.[15]

For me, the essential question remains, and always has been, the question of
exactly what the "whole thing" is, and how it can be structured through the
use of spontaneity.

NOTES

1. J. L. Moreno, *The Theatre of Spontaneity* (Ambler, Pa.: Beacon House, 1983),
   p. 40.
2. C. G. Jung, "Instinct and the Unconscious," in *The Portable Jung*, edited by Joseph
   Campbell (New York: Viking, 1971), p. 51.
3. C.W.E. Bigsby, *A Critical Introduction to Twentieth Century American Drama*,
   Vol. 3 (Cambridge: Cambridge University Press, 1985), p. 25.
4. Lenora Champagne, *French Theatre Experiment since 1968* (Ann Arbor: UMI
   Research Press, 1984), p. 23.
5. Dunbar H. Ogden, *Actor Training and Audience Response* (Berkeley: Oak House,
   1984), p. 25.
6. *China Times*, 15 January 1984.
7. *Min Sheng News*, 30 March 1984.
8. *United Daily News*, 31 March 1984.
9. Chang Chia-ju, "The Development of Collective/Improvisational Creation in
   Taiwan's Experimental Theatre" (B.F.A. thesis, National Institute of the Arts,
   Taipei, 1987).
10. Quoted in Richard Kostelanetz, *Theatre of Mixed Means* (London, 1970), p. viii.
11. Quoted in Pierre Louis Duchartre, *The Italian Comedy* (New York: Dover, 1966),
    p. 32.
12. *Asian Wall Street Journal*, 17–18 May 1985.
13. Dunbar H. Ogden, *Toward "Sunset": A Collective Working Process (1973–75)*,
    manuscript, 1E.

14. Ogden, *Toward "Sunset,"* p. 2.
15. Quoted in Eileen Blumenthal, *Joseph Chaikin: Exploring at the Boundaries of Theatre* (Cambridge: Cambridge University Press, 1984), p. 143.

9. Blurring Line between Stage and Life: "Poor Theatre" in China

William Hui-zhu Sun

Long before Jerzy Grotowski's poor theatre and Richard Schechner's environmental theatre ever came into being, in Ting Hsien 定縣 of northern China between 1932 and 1937, thousands of peasants, including hundreds of active performers, had their experimental theatre, literally poor and environmental. It was not traditional Chinese opera, which is originally environmental as Schechner asserts, but spoken drama, a brand new theatre genre introduced by intellectuals influenced by Western culture. Hsiung Fu-hsi 熊佛西, the leader of the theatre experiment, a M.A. graduate of Columbia University, disliked the traditional operas of the time because he thought they had become stagnant and definitely unsuitable for the peasants who were to be cultivated by modern civilization.

This might be one of the poorest experimental theatres in the world. Most participants were really poor peasants. Their theatre activities were in open air, on dirt ground; they acted, watched and participated without a "curtain line" between stage and life. This line was blurred not only because of the method of performances, but because the content of the plays they did was so closely related to their own lives that they were simply expressing themselves in the performances. Furthermore, what initially and ultimately broke the boundary between stage and life was the social context of the experiment.

This peasants' theatre experiment was not just an aesthetic theatre movement but part of an overall social reform project conducted by the Chinese National Association of Mass Education. This project was politically independent of both the Nationalists and Communists, and financially sponsored by Rockefeller Foundation and other institutions in the United States. Ting Hsien was chosen as a model county for the Association's experiments in four areas: literacy, economy, sanitation and arts. The whole project was to improve peasants' life in all these aspects through education. There were three types of education programmes: family, school and community. Overlapping school and community education in the arts and literacy, theatre therefore was intended to be one means of helping educate and organize the poor peasants.

As the head of the Association's theatre division, Hsiung together with his colleagues tried to provide the peasants with "spiritual nutrition," i.e., new drama with appropriate content and ways of presentation. Besides writing new plays about peasants, the most radical thing they did in Ting Hsien was to remove the "curtain line" between performers and spectators, so that the peasants could more easily identify themselves with the situation and people in the plays. Thus the most important advantage of the new spoken drama as reflection of daily life, in contrast to the old traditional operas, was developed not only to its extreme but beyond. The invisible fourth wall was simply uprooted entirely.

The first attempt to remove the "curtain line" was initiated by peasants' spontaneous reaction while watching some relatively naturalistic performances of spoken drama. During the last act of one performance of Wang Szu 王四 when the innocent Wang Szu was taken by the police for trial, some peasants in the audience stood up to defend Wang Szu out loud. The whole theatre became the court; the audience became involved in the trial. When the judge on stage asked for bail, people really came up and consoled Wang Szu.

Inspired by the peasants' touching spontaneity, the professional theatre people tried deliberately to remove the curtain line. During the production of *Trumpet* (喇叭), Hsiung set several actors' entrances and exits in the audience. Therefore, spectators often acted along with the actors, and even followed them onto the stage. A play worth a cast of twenty would have seventy or eighty people on "stage."

The peasants' immediate and great enthusiasm for the new theatre genre, spoken drama, was a pleasant surprise to the theatre professionals and mass educators. The even greater surprise was the fact that the peasants wanted to create theatre themselves. Soon they organized their own village theatre groups and asked the professionals to teach and direct.

The poorness of the peasants' theatre seems to coincide with Grotowski's later poor theatre in that only the actor and audience are the crucial elements of the theatre. Their music was songs sung with their own voices; their costumes were their own clothing; their settings were minimal and often made from grain stalks. Besides the professionally written scripts based on peasants' life, and the untrained bodies of the peasant actors, the only other means they could explore was the performer-spectator relationship. Working with the peasants, Hsiung and his colleagues developed a series of "poor theatre" performance patterns:

1. Linking stage and audience: walking up and down, conversation between performers and audience.
2. Audience surrounding performers: circus-like low ground or stage.
3. Performers surrounding audience: taking audience into theatrical action, or simultaneously using the stage on the opposite end of the open theatre.
4. Moving theatre: ... or street theatre, carriage theatre, etc.[1]

In addition to the Greek-style and Roman-style performances Hsiung mentioned in another article about the same theatre experiment, these spatial performance patterns prefigures most of the possibilities of the poor theatre and environmental theatre introduced over thirty years later by Grotowski and Schechner. And practically most of these devices were used in *Cross the River* (過渡), one of the most influential theatre productions in China in the 1930s.

Hsiung wrote *Cross the River*, an "open air play for peasant performers," particularly for the peasants' poor and environmental theatre. It was about the class struggle between a tyrannical ferry owner and many peasants building a bridge on a construction site, which was to be set up easily in the open air theatre with scaffold on dirt terrace. The cast of dozens of performers is a combination of briefly trained peasants and mostly untrained peasants. During the performances many spectators, who were treated as passengers and by-standers at the ferry, spontaneously joined the struggle against the ferry owner, who conspired to destroy the half-completed bridge.

As one of the earliest modern Chinese playwrights to have studied in the West, Hsiung was inevitably influenced by some of the new trends in Western theatre, especially by the innovative works of Reinhardt and Meyerhold. But in general the Ting Hsien theatre experiment went far beyond the mainstream Western theatre Hsiung had mainly studied. Alexander Dean, a Yale professor of drama visiting Ting Hsien, said that the Ting Hsien experiment had moved beyond the theatre in any other country: "It is not artificial; it is life itself."[2]

Hsiung and his colleagues pointed out that the major impetus for the peasants' poor and environmental theatre was from the peasants' own enthusiasm for participation, part of the precipitated cultural tradition in the rural China. As Yang Ts'un-pin 楊村彬 , Hsiung's chief assistant, said:

> Even if there had not been those Westerners (Such as Reinhardt and Meyerhold who inspired Hsiung — Note) who advocated new performing methods, certainly we would still have invented our own new performing methods, because we have learned from the peasants. Our new methods are from the heritage of our traditions. We came to the country, at first we invited the peasants to see the pictures in the frame, so to speak. Though beautiful, they could not satisfy the peasants thoroughly. Because people were encouraged to be part of traditional festivities, they surround or follow to watch stilts, land boats, dragon lanterns, etc. Now since the pictures are beautiful, the peasants hope that the figures in the pictures can walk down from the frame, can be touched, or they themselves can go into the pictures and become figures in the pictures. Only in this way can they be satisfied. It was just to satisfy the peasants who had habitual and traditional way of watching shows that we found the new performing methods.[3]

While the external form of this theatre was basically derived from pre-modern Chinese peasants' tradition, the internal spirit was mainly derived from modern Western ideology. For example, the overall slogan of the theatre experiment, "of the peasants, by the peasants, for the peasants,"[4] was modelled on the American Declaration of Independence. On the other hand, the mass education leaders thought, compared to the better educated Western people, Chinese peasants were "ignorant, poor, weak and selfish," therefore the mass educators' mission was to influence the peasants with some modern progressive ideas through the medium of spoken drama.

Because Hsiung's ideological basis was traditional Western humanism, compared to the revolutionaries' led by the Communist Party in China at the same time, his theatre project was but mild reform. He and his colleagues cautiously avoided provoking the peasants' rebellious action. While writing *Cross the River* Hsiung thought about one possible ending in which the peasants beat the ferry owner to death; but he gave up this ending, because he recognized: "In this way, the peasants can be satisfied; but it seems to encourage rebellion. For the order of the present society and as educators, we don't have any reason to do this."[5] Finally he chose the ending in which the villain was taken away by the police. The peasants' rebellion was replaced by the law enforcement from a utopian good government. Similarly, the ending of *Wang Szu* was also based on the assumption of a good government.

Thus, Hsiung's two major principles, to satisfy peasants' habitual way of enjoying performance and not to satisfy their potential for rebellion, made the peasants' "poor theatre" seem radical and provocative but actually pacifist and conservative. While its form seems to have gone far ahead of Western experimental theatres in the 1960s, its content lagged far behind Western playwrights at the turn of the century such as Ibsen and Strindberg. However, these two seemingly incompatible factors were well integrated in the Chinese peasants' theatre experiment supervised by their humanitarian educators. This experiment was highly praised in China in the thirties. Hsiung and his colleagues were so excited by what they had achieved in merging theatre with life that they drew an ambition blue-print for the overall social reform project in which the all-people theatre troupes and the theatre/community-centres should be integrated into the new provincial administrative system. Unfortunately, they did not have time to experiment with it before the whole Ting Hsien experiment was stopped by the Japanese invasion in 1937.

Not until forty years had passed did another surge of poor theatre and environmental theatre appear. Ironically, this surge is diametrically different from the peasants' theatre in both form and content: its form is less "poor" and "environmental" while its content is more revolutionary and provocative.

By the advent of the new Chinese experimental theatre, fragmentary material of Grotowski's theatre and Artaud's theory had been introduced into China. One of the experimental productions was even overtly labelled "poor theatre." In the professional theatre long dominated by Stanislavsky Method and socialist realism, however, it is very difficult to really do poor theatre or environmental theatre. The rather superficial yet most practical problem is the fact that all theatres have prosceniums. Therefore the first two centre-staged productions in Beijing and Shanghai in 1982, *Absolute Signal* (絕對信號 ; written by Kao Hsing-chien 高行健 and Liu Hui-yuan 劉會遠 , directed by Lin Chao-hua 林兆華 , presented by Beijing People's Art Theatre) and *Mother's Song* (母親的歌 ; written by Yin Wei-hui 殷惟慧, directed by Hu Wei-min 胡偉民 , presented by Shanghai Youth Drama Troupe), had to take place in the rehearsal halls, which usually were not open to the public. These were the two earliest attempts to shorten the distance between stage and life formalized by the dogma of socialist realistic theatre, in which an artificial frame was always held from far away and above showing the audience some trimmed truth. These two productions were distinguished mainly by directorial innovations on conventionally written plays. Each was performed in the small theatre-in-the-round. While still keeping the "curtain line" between performers and spectators during the performance without a curtain, it literally lowered the performance from the higher level in the stage, where the dogmatic theatre people had usually held the position to lecture the audience, onto the same level where the spectators sat closely around.

Soon afterwards in 1984, a production labelled "poor theatre" and really involving audience during performance came out. *The Old B Hanging on the Wall* (掛在牆上的老 B)[6] was a resolute experiment on removing the "curtain line" between stage and life. Unsatisfied with the inconsistent experiment of the two previous theatre-in-the-round productions, this experiment started from the beginning of playwriting. It adopted a Pirandellian rehearsal-like opening, and furthermore, opened the predicament to the audience. At first, the spectators were asked to go home because the leading actor was unexpectedly absent; then they were asked whether they would like to see the acting of Old B, a "perpetual understudy" who had broken in from a caricature hanging on the wall and volunteered to fill in. The unusual opening almost forcibly elicited the active participation of the spectators.

There is a decided difference between urban theatregoers in the eighties and the naive peasants in the thirties. The latter's naivety and spontaneity make their participation much more likely than the sophisticated and reserved urban theatregoers whose behaviour patterns are restricted by the modernized or modernizing social modes. Having considered most theatregoers' reserve, the playwright conceived a character in the play as an amateur actress coming from the audience to evoke the expressions of other spectators, and the directors decided to expand this bridge by bringing a chorus of amateurs from factories to further blur the line between professional performers and spectators. This chorus worked well in the workshop-rehearsal stage. Unfortunately, because the regulation of modern division of labour did not allow the workers to appear in theatre every night as peasants were allowed before, these amateurs all withdrew before the play officially opened.

The creators of *The Old B Hanging on the Wall* had a hard time in making this first "poor theatre" production, because the "poorness" was, in many aspects, incongruous with the institutionalized modern theatre system in China. As a matter of fact, one of the reasons why the directors labelled the production "poor theatre" was that it was practically poor. Because of the avant-garde nature of the play which did not seem to get official approval easily, the volunteer team bypassed the censoring committee when they started working on it. Therefore they did not get regular production budget from the national theatre. While the directors, Kung Hsiao-tung 宮曉東 and Wang Hsio-ying 王曉鷹, two new graduates from Central Drama Institute, wanted to take advantages of the poorness for the sake of an exciting experiment, the unofficial nature of the production in a highly disciplined system where all public events should be official encountered many problems, such as the choice of actors, use of long-term space, publicity, etc. The play was never done in any regular theatre but toured in many universities and a few factories in Peking, Shanghai and other cities. To many people's surprise, it worked successfully in the experimental way, especially in university dining halls, gymnasiums, and once in a big university auditorium seating for thousand people, mostly students.

College students not only could identify themselves with the Old B, who has an urgent desire for participation in an environment where he can hardly fulfil it, but also considered participation in this theatre experiment a part of their own life. In other words, students had found a rare public place to realize their desire for active participation while their usual place of socio-political participation was limited in their classrooms.

Soon after *Old B*'s production opened, *Magic Cube* (魔方), another radically experimental play, was created in Shanghai in 1985 by a group of college students. It was also a "poor theatre" production, comprised of a variety-show-like programme of miscellaneous short performing pieces, surrounded closely by student spectators. Professional theatre soon mounted this play. Wang Hsiao-ying, one of the directors of *The Old B Hanging on the Wall*, took *Magic Cube* to Peking and made it a popular hit. Around that time quite a few other plays with similar approach of style appeared in both professional and student amateur theatres.

Compared to the peasants' "poor theatre" in the thirties, the audience participation in the eighties is not that remarkable. For example, unlike *Cross the River* that involved hundreds of peasants including both performers and spectators, *The Old B Hanging on the Wall* was basically a professionals' production that involved physically a limited number of bold spectator. While students are more and more willing to express themselves and to participate in public affairs, the social conventions still hinder audience's physical participation in theatre.

On the other hand, the present theatre system also prevents "poor theatre" experiment from fully blossoming. When the group from the big national theatre—China Youth Art Theatre—toured in universities, students could not help seeing them as guest artists, because all theatres were supposed to be in an elite "arts and literature circle." On campus, the highly demanding education system makes it hardly possible for students to maintain long-standing amateur theatres. Let alone workers' theatres in factories.

Now, the contrast between the peasants' unconscious "poor theatre" and the student-involved conscious "poor theatre" in China is clear. While the peasants' theatre has a more open and radical form, the guiding idea is quite conservative. The students-involved theatre is not as open as the peasants' in form and it does not involve life the way the peasants' theatre did because of the restrain of modern urban conventions, yet the limited participation is motivated by provocative ideas. To compare these two types of "poor theatre" further, some more comparisons with the Western counterparts will prove enlightening.

As opposed to the conventional realistic theatre, the Chinese "poor theatres" in the thirties and in the eighties and their Western counterparts— poor theatre and environmental theatre—all have one thing in common: they have all broken the barrier separating stage and life, and have become social events far beyond mere theatre performances. But the nature and formation of these events are not the same. The most obvious difference is that the Chinese "poor theatres" are basically marked by play productions, because they are initiated by playwrights; whereas the Western poor theatre and environmental theatre are basically marked by theatre groups, because they are initiated by directors/producers. Much of these Western theatre groups' achievement is embodied in the intensive psychophysical work- shop process which leads to the transformation of the group members' body and mental state not only as actors but as human beings. Much of the Chinese "poor theatre" productions' achievement is embodied in the cogni- tive messages which the plays and the participants address. This contrast seems to show that the Western groups are more interested in means whereas the Chinese productions more in end, which apparently contradicts the traditional comparison that Westerners are more goal-oriented and their Eastern counterparts more process-oriented. Why?

Artaud, the predecessor of poor theatre and environmental theatre in the West, was inspired by Balinese performance, which did not emphasize cognitive messages, to create his theatre of cruelty, a kind of highly influential theatre with no well-known productions. Grotowski and Schechner are also impressed by Oriental theatre's long training process and adopt it in their own programmes.

While the Western avant-garde theatre people turn to the East, China has come into a period of modernization. People have been changing their life style in favour of many modern features which seem Western. The long-lasting static life rhythm no longer exists. Even the poor, mostly illiterate peasants in the thirties were not satisfied with the old operas; they wanted to do their own plays immediately without having spent any time on acting training. Their educators certainly wanted to change and uplift them as quickly as possible. In fact, the theatre they devised was a quicker as well as more pleasant way to spread their social messages. They adopted the form of massive traditional festivities, instead of the highly conventionalized operas, just to put in some modern progressive ideas.

As for the "poor theatre" in the eighties, most people involved are so eager to express their ideas for social reform, though somewhat implicitly, that many critics think one of the most important characteristics of these productions is that they evoke thinking rather than feeling. One of *Magic Cube*'s scenes, "Detour" (繞道而行), in which a brave child pushes through a misleading blocking sign across the road while many credulous people take detour, openly encourages independent thinking. They place urgent emphasis on agitating the people, and do not spend much time to cultivate their actor's body movements.

Compared to Grotowski's and Schechner's theatres which emphasize much more the exposure and transformation of human nature through actors' mutual and visceral exploration, the Chinese theatres almost exclusively emphasize social reform. For example, the *Old B*'s characterization was originally similar to Grotowski's notion of the "holy actor":

> If the actor, by setting himself a challenge publicly, challenges others, and through excess, profanation and outrageous sacrilege reveals himself by casting off his everyday mask, he makes it possible for the spectator to undertake a similar process of self-penetration. If he does not exhibit his body, but annihilates it, burns it, frees it from every resistance to any psychic impulse, then he does not sell his body, but sacrifices it. He repeats the atonement; he is close to holiness.[7]

The actor, Kao Hui-pin 高惠彬 , through intensively exploring himself and the Old B, the most identifiable character he had ever played in his over twenty years' career, felt "the author is so cruel" because he could not help stripping all his masks and becoming a "holy actor" in the production. He felt inadequate in acting this way because he lacked the training of a "holy actor"; and he worked extremely hard to make up for the lack. Most spectators, however, neglected this aspect about the inner weakness of Old B himself, but were particularly impressed by the other aspects about the faults in the social system. Generally speaking, in the body and the story, the two basic things of a performance as Schechner emphasizes in his *Environmental Theatre*,[8] most modern Chinese see only the story and its social meanings.

The "poor theatre" in the thirties was itself part of a social reform project. The "poor theatre" in the eighties started as some kind of artistic innovation and philosophical exploration, yet has become a symptom of social reform. Although the main social issues of the two theatre experiments are very different, one helps the society to change the peasants, the other urges the people to accelerate the ongoing change of the society, the sociopolitically oriented nature is the same.

Grotowski said little directly about the sociopolitical connotation of his work in his book and interviews, although his adapted productions were full of implicit sociopolitical concerns such as the proud intellectuals being persecuted while living and exploited after death in the *Constant Prince*, the hopeless labour camp full of horror and pity in *Akropolis*. He finally left for the West, and turned into the paratheatrical, a kind of reclusively communal activity which thoroughly removes the line between art and life and has much less sociopolitical significance than anthropological significance.

Schechner used to be active in the freedom movement and was committed to the participatory democracy.[9] These experiences helped him form his idea of environmental theatre; but the sociopolitically rebellious messages of the movement were much reduced in his later theatre experiments. He did not want to limit, with any explicit message, the possibilities the audience could find, but let people have maximum experience of creativity.[10] Gradually, his theatre experiment has also gone to an anthropological direction, away from directly addressing specific sociopolitical issues as he had done before.

In short, the Chinese society in a vibrant process of modernization makes many theatre people and theatregoers leave the leisurely way of appreciating old theatre, which is detached from daily reality, in favour of the special "poor theatre" or "environmental theatre," which easily associates daily life and rehearses with immediate social issues. The Western society which gradually enters postmodern time makes some theatre people bored of modern civilization, which is full of high-tech, informational noise and various masks, in favour of the poor theatre and environmental theatre, which explore the essence of human beings and try to expand this kind of theatre/ritual exploration as life itself. Both are blurring the line between stage and life, but by comparison, the experiment in China is more like concentration of some general social life into theatre experience as the participants' social or a-social life.

The poorness of Grotowski's theatre is a collective attempt to strip the burden and masks of modern civilization, so that people can get back to the essence of human nature to find a new communal life. Schechner's environmental theatre has the similar attempt. The poorness and environmentalness of the Chinese theatre in the thirties is an attempt to utilize the tradition of festivities to make the theatre for social reform more accessible and enjoyable. The former is obviously the characteristic of the postmodern era and the latter the premodern.

The Chinese "poor theatre" or "environmental theatre" in the eighties is in an ambiguous position in the history. When it attempts to develop some premodern features such as to create some festival atmosphere in audience participation or to establish some semi-professional community theatre groups, the disciplines and organizations of the modern society stand in the way. When it attempts to explore the depth of the performer's psychophysical entity and the essence of human nature in some postmodern way, most people involved cannot keep up. That is why the contemporary Chinese experimental theatre is not as extensive as the peasants' "poor theatre" in a certain area; nor is it as intensive as its Western counterparts in a certain project.

Nevertheless, the contemporary Chinese theatre experimenters' advantage is that there are two significant examples they can learn from, especially the incredibly successful experience of the Ting Hsien peasants' "poor theatre," which was ignored for almost half a century, but is going to shed considerable light on the present experiments. On the other hand, if the premodern poorness can finally help the modern theatre become more flexible, then the postmodern poorness will also work soon; because there is not a clear-cut line between the premodern and postmodern in terms of form, and in addition, more and more Chinese artists are becoming aware of the approaching of the postmodern era. After all, China will be more open; so will its modern theatre, whether by adopting the premodern traditions or by making the postmodern innovations. "Poor theatre" or "environmental theatre" in China will have a greater prospect while it continues to fulfil its sociopolitical missions.

NOTES

1. Hsiung Fu-hsi, *Hsi-chü ta-chung hua chih shih-yen* 戲劇大衆化之實驗 (The Experimentation of the Popularization of Theatre) (Shanghai: Cheng-chung shu-chü 正中書局 , 1937), p. 98.

2. Wu Hsiang-hsiang 吳相湘 , *Yen Yang-ch'u chuan* 晏陽初傳 (The Biography of Y. C. Yen) (Taipei: Shih P'ao ch'u-pan kung-szu 時報出版公司 , 1981), p. 324.

3. Yang Ts'un-pin, "Hsü" 序 (Preface); in *Kuo-tu chi ch'i yen-ch'u* 過渡及其演出 (*Cross the River* and Its Production) (Shanghai: Cheng-chung shu-chü, 1935), p. 14.

4. Ch'en Tuo 陳多 , et al., *Hsien-tai hsi-chü chia Hsiung Fu-hsi* 現代戲劇家熊佛西 (Modern Dramatist Hsiung Fu-hsi) (Beijing: Chung-kuo hsi-chü ch'u-pan-she 中國戲劇出版社 , 1983), p. 139.

5. Ibid., p. 157.

6. Sun Hui-zhu, "The Old B Hanging on the Wall," in *Tulane Drama Review* (Winter 1986), p. 94.

7. Jerzy Grotowski, *Towards a Poor Theatre* (Holstebro: Odin Teatres Forlag, 1968), p. 34.

8. Richard Schechner, *Environmental Theatre* (New York: Hawthorn Books, 1973), p. 172.

9. Schechner, p. 66.

10. Ibid.

10. The Deaths of Cordelia and Tou O:
Morality or Theatricality

Mei-shu Hwang

Readers familiar with Shakespeare's *King Lear* and Kuan Han-ch'ing's 關漢卿 *Tou O yüan* 竇娥冤 may wonder what these two girls' deaths have in common. No. There is no sufficient common ground between these plays to make any meaningful comparison in terms of theme, background, or dramatic structure. It might be ridiculous to bring them together for comparison just because one is a representative work by William Shakespeare and the other by a great Chinese playwright who is called by some people the "Chinese Shakespeare." My simple attempt here is only to use them as examples to see how a playwright's mind may work—what might come to his first consideration when he has to choose between ideas and theatricality.

We will start with *King Lear*'s stage history, which has been summarized by A. C. Bradley as follows:

> Some twenty years after the Restoration, Nahum Tate altered *King Lear* for the stage, giving it a happy ending, and putting Edgar in the place of the King of France as Cordelia's lover. From that time Shakespeare's tragedy in its original form was never seen on the stage for a century and half. Betterton acted Tate's version; Garrick acted it and Dr. Johnson approved it. Kemble acted it, Kean acted it. In 1823 Kean, "stimulated by Hazlitt's remonstrances and Charles Lamb's essays," restored the original tragic ending. At last, in 1838, Macready returned to Shakespeare's text throughout.[1]

Why did Dr. Johnson and critics of that period find Cordelia's death so horrible and unacceptable? Yet why was Shakespeare's original ending becoming favorable again after 1838? This is very interesting for discussion because such a change of taste exists not only in theatre in the West; the same phenomenon is also found in Chinese drama and fiction, and *Tou*

O yüan has suffered a similar fate. But this is not the concern of this short paper. My present interest lies in the questions: Why did Shakespeare let Cordelia die? Is theatricality involved in this decision?

There have been many profound analyses of the death of Cordelia. For instance, Northrop Frye approaches it from a distinction between authentic tragedy and melodrama;[2] Stephen Booth deals with it in relation to the argument about whether Lear dies happily or not, thinking that Cordelia is still alive.[3] Diane Elizabeth Dreher says that to Lear Cordelia represents his "mother's unconditional love" and "'the Death goddess,' like the Valkyrie in German mythology who carry off the dead warrior."[4]

I wonder how many audience in the theatre, who see the play for the first time or even for the second or fifth time, would be able to analyse, or like to analyse it so deeply? It seems to be of little significance to make it clear if Lear's death is a "merciful" release. How many people in the audience would have the illusion that Cordelia might still be alive and how many of them might feel joy with Lear? The simple "fact" on stage is that Cordelia does not rise again. I also wonder if Shakespeare's plays were orginally made for scholars and philosophers to study, or for the common theatre-goers to watch. Though his great plays are rich in meaning for students of literature, directors, and actors to ponder and reponder, there should be some easier ways to approach them by the audience, who can hear the lines once and once only in the theatre at a speed controlled by the actors. Otherwise, his works should only be popular in classrooms in academic institutes, but not so widely staged in theatres all over the world.

King Lear is often considered to be the greatest of Shakespeare's tragedies. However, critics have pointed out that it is not a perfect play in terms of dramaturgy. "The improbabilities in *King Lear* surely far surpass those of the other great tragedies in number and in grossness." For instance, no reason is given why Edgar should write a letter to Edmund while they live in the same house.[5] Young Cordelia can see the hypocrisy of Goneril and Regan. How could it be possible that Lear is not aware of that at all?[6] Perhaps incidents like these could be explained as a special means to emphasize the stupidity of old Lear and old Gloucester. But how should we account for Lear's sudden appearance in Act IV scene vi alone "fantastically dressed with wild flowers"? In Act III scene vi, we see him carried off in sleep by Kent, Gloucester, and the Fool. When Kent reappears in the French camp near Dover, he says to a French gentleman, "Well, sir, I'll bring you to my master Lear, / And leave you to attend him" before he himself leaves for "some dear cause" (IV, iii, 50–51).[7] How could it happen that Lear runs away under such circumstances? It is just as strange that the Fool disappears suddenly forever after Act III scene vi, and is never seen or mentioned again with Lear, or Cordelia, for whose "going into France, … the Fool hath much pined away" (I, iv, 71–72).

From the view-point of justice or morality, the play is as confusing. The characters seem all to believe that there is justice in the world. We hear Lear complain once and again of his daughters' ingratitude and cry for "vengeances of Heaven" (II, iv, 159). If we consider social justice, Edmund is not wrong to growl:

> … Why bastard? Wherefore base?
> When my dimensions are as well compact,
> My mind as generous, and my shape as true,
> As honest madam's issue? Why brand they us
> With base? with baseness? bastardy? base, base?   (I, ii, 6–10)

Even Lear, who thinks he is "a man/More sinn'd against than sinning" (III, ii, 60), says:

> O! I have ta'en
> Too little care of this. Take physic, Pomp;
> Expose thyself to feel what wretches feel,
> That thou mayst shake the superflux to them,
> And show the Heavens more just.   (III, iv, 32–36)

And the Fool's song in Act II scene iv sums up the idea of social injustice and human indifference or ingratitude. He sings:

> Fathers that wear rags
>   Do make their children blind,
> But fathers that bear bags
>   Shall see their children kind.
> Fortune, that arrant whore,
> Ne'er turns the key to th'poor.   (II, iv, 46–51)

All these show that the characters, both good and evil, have in their minds some criteria of justice, which is reinforced by the death penalties to all the evil ones. Goneril kills herself after she poisons Regan; Edmund is killed by Edgar; Duke of Cornwall is stabbed by his own servant; even Oswald, Goneril's faithful steward, dies at Edgar's hands. (He seems not altogether evil. While lamenting his own "untimely death," he asks Edgar to take his purse and deliver the letter to Edmund.) (IV, vi, 43–47)

However, it is difficult to explain Gloucester's blindness with the same moral principle. His loyalty and goodness definitely surpass his foolishness in believing Edmund's words against Edgar. Cordelia's sudden death at the end of the play is the most puzzling in terms of the justice or injustice of God or Nature. Her "proud integrity in the beginning"—like Kent's "utter lack of tact or forbearance" and Edgar's "unsuspecting simplicity"—is "slips, innocent errors, or the excess of their virtues."[8]

Why do the good characters have to suffer such severe punishments which are even more horrible than those the evil have received? If Gloucester's being blinded is a dramatic means to show the Duke of Cornwall's and Regan's evil doing, the price seems so high and so extreme that it seems to destroy the existence of divine justice. In the same light, Lear's death is questionable. As Wilson Knight has pointed out, "Lear is the only tragic-hero in Shakespeare who repents" although his repentance is "not before God, but before a human being, Cordelia."[9] To repent before a human being may take greater courage than to do so before God, and Lear has greatly changed at the time he is going to prison. He no longer cries for revenge as he had so many times before.

Do all these contradictions or ambiguities suggest that human beings are all fools and their world is absurd? Can Gloucester's and Lear's lines represent the theme of the play when they complain?—

Gloucester: As flies to wanton boys, are we to th' Gods;
            They kill us for their sport. (IV, i, 36–37)
Lear: When we are born, we cry that we are come
      To this great stage of fools. (IV, vi, 180–81)

Yet if *King Lear* aims to present the absurdity of human beings, this seems against the overall impression of the logic and ethics of the play, which have been established from the very beginning when Lear tells Cordelia: "Nothing will come of nothing" (I, i, 89) and later to the Fool "nothing can be made out of nothing" (I, iv, 130). In fact, these lines are another way of saying "Whatsoever a man soweth, that also shall he reap" or "Reap as one has sown." Similar ideas are repeated in various ways throughout the play. In short, the world in *King Lear* is a logical one. Even when Lear argues with his daughters about the number of his followers, he tries to reason without reason:

O! Reason not the need; our basest baggars
Are in the poorest thing superfluous:

Allow not nature more than nature needs,
Man's life is cheap as beast's. (II, iv, 262–65)

If Shakespeare is to represent a world of absurdity in *King Lear*, he needs to have more than Cordelia's death and Lear's own foolishness. Though there are some illogical or implausible incidents, as mentioned above, the plot of the play develops along a logical and moral line. Otherwise, Tate and Johnson would not object to the unhappy ending only. Besides, to let Cordelia die for such a purpose is in a sense not absurd but immoral.

Of the theatrical discussions of *King Lear*, what James P. Driscoll says about Cordelia's last appearance is worth special attention. He writes:

> Although Cordelia is hanged, none of the play's imagery encourages us, even indirectly, to envision her suffering overwhelming physical or psychological pain. It is Lear who has been stretched out on the rack of this tough world, has been spoiled by crosses, and has borne the most.... The most terrifying fact the play presents is the irrevocable finality of Cordelia's death, and Lear's response to it forms the most painful event in all Shakespeare.[10]

It is very interesting to notice that Cordelia's suffering, if there is any at the moment, is not shown on stage. Then, in what sense is her death "most terrifying"? How does Lear's response to it form "the most painful event"?

In terms of playwriting and/or the *mise-en-scéne* effect here, it seems to me that Cordelia's death is only a means—and seems the best possible means—to help create a powerful ending of the play: Lear's "aloneness" or "final tragic isolation," to use Howard's words.[11] I can see no better alternatives to energize an equal effect and inspire more pity for both Lear and Cordelia. In *King Lear*, as in many other successful plays by him or other playwrights, Shakespeare keeps a special eye on theatricality. He is an artist, not a moral teacher or preacher.

By carrying Cordelia's body in his arms, Lear can easily catch the audience's attention. He is like an Oedipus holding Jocasta in his own arms and telling the audience directly why and how the queen hanged herself and he blinded himself—instead of putting her body on the *ekkyklema*, with the messenger to report their stories. And Lear's self-introduction, "Howl, howl, howl, O!" (V, iii, 256), is so simple and thus so powerful. Besides, the death of Cordelia provides some surprising effects in plot development as well.

Like Cordelia in *King Lear*, the "life" of Tou O has undergone similar changes: In the Yüan play, she is executed at the end of Act III; in the Ming version *Story of the Gold Lock*, she is not only saved but also reunited with her long absent husband; in the Peking Opera *Snow in June* (六月雪), she is also saved but her husband does not return. In 1980, a new Peking Opera version tried to go back to the Yüan ending. But some people with the mentality of a Tate and Dr. Johnson exercised their power of censorship and "saved" her life again.

As I mentioned earlier, the change of the ending is not my present concern. My interest now is the nature of the three wishes she prays for while she is being beheaded. The wishes are: May Heaven witness for her innocence by (*a*) making all her blood fly up to the piece of white silk hanging over her, (*b*) covering her body with three inches of snow, and (*c*) affecting a drought of three years in the ch'u county.

Is it fair and natural for her to make much a prayer, and for Heaven to grant her all the three wishes—especially the second and the third—if it is a Heaven of justice? To my knowledge, nobody seems to have questioned the fairness till Yao Shu-hua's 姚樹華 "Tou O," which appeared in 1974. Yao makes a farmer complain to Tou O's father:

> Sir, she was a good daughter-in-law. There is no doubt about that. But she has made us suffer a drought of three whole years. Sir, for the last three years, everytime we think of her we could not help hating her.... If it's not because of her, our children would not have died of hunger, and we would not have to live such a worse-than-death life.[12]

And even Tou O herself says to her father:

> O! Father, you said Heaven showed pity on me? No! When I was in prison, I prayed day and night without taking food, but Heaven didn't listen. Why did it listen to my last prayer and grant me all the three wishes?! ... My personal foolishness has killed so many lives. I wish Heaven had never listened to that prayer of mine! I wish I had died silently! Then, I would still have been innocent. But now, my name is stained with blood; I have become a real murderer ... [13]

Such an interpretation of the story of Tou O must not be what Kuan Han-ch'ing had in mind. Though Kuan did not like the Mongolian government, *Tou O yüan* seems more than a simple play of social criticism or a satire against the ruling class. It is true that Kuan's Tou O does "cry injustice, to Earth and Heaven" when she knows that "her soul has soon to leave for Yama's domain," and she "couldn't help grunting against Heaven and Earth." She also cries:

Oh, Heaven, ...
The virtuous suffer poverty and die young,
The evil enjoy wealth, fame, and live long.[14]

Superficially, all these can be taken as the playwright's voice against the injustice of Heaven and/or the government of the time. In a deeper sense, they also show a strong belief in the so-called "Blue Heaven," a traditional symbol of ultimate righteousness or justice. Perhaps it is better to say that Tou O is only wondering why Heaven would not take immediate action to right her wrong. My reason is very simple. If she does not believe in Heaven, she certainly would not pray to it for help. She would not say to the judge right before her death:

You say it is endless to wait for Heaven to act,
And men are not to be pitied.
But Heaven will listen to my prayer.[15]

To me, Kuan's Tou O is not a pure symbol of the traditional Chinese virtue—filial piety. There is no doubt that she courageously sacrifices her own life to protect her mother-in-law. But facing death, she still shows fear, like Sophocles' Antigone, who says to the chorus when she is being sent to death:

Look upon me, friends, and pity me
Turning back at the night's edge to say
Good-by to the sun that shines for me no longer;
Now sleepy Death
Summons me down to Acheron, that cold shore:
There is no bridesong there, nor any music.[16]

Without such fears, Tou O and Antigone would be "flat" characterizations. Their fears do not mean that they have no confidence in what they believe, but show the humanness of their characters. As Antigone believes in Gods, Tou O firmly believes in Heaven. They are two human beings of noble ideals and spiritual conflicts.[17]

Now we have to face another problem—a technical problem of dramatic art. That is: Is not the realization of her first wish a miracle strong enough to prove her innocence? Why did Kuan Han-ch'ing add the snow and drought in the play?

I suspect that the stories of snow and drought must have been well-known during his time as symbols of the virtuous woman. So, for Tou O to pray for the same heavenly proof or miracle, her lines could more easily make the audience identify her with women of great virtue. In other words, a successful use of allusion is a very economical way to stir a sea of imagination in the audience's mind. Besides, the snow and drought are not physically presented and felt in the theatre, but mentioned in a few lines of songs and dialogue. The audience consciously or unconsciously "ignores" their actual potential for damage. Like Shakespeare, Kuan was basically a dramatist, not a logical thinker. He looked for stage effect, not perfect reasoning. Few people seem to have looked at these wishes as Yao Shu-hua does.

In theatre, as soon as the mood of a play, especially of a tragedy, wins the feelings of the audience, emotion will take care of almost everything. Shakespeare and Kuan Han-ch'ing must have known this very well and have certainly made the best use of Cordelia's death and Tou O's prayer for such purposes. They are actually very simple devices and easy to comprehend and, therefore, all the more effective in the theatre. If the great playwrights had analysed their material as carefully and deeply as many critics do and had tried to make the plays pure vehicles for their thoughts and ideas, they would have very likely turned out to be theatrical failures.

NOTES

1. A. C. Bradley, *Shakespearean Tragedy* (New York: Meridian Books, 1955), p. 197.
2. Northrop Frye, *Fools of Time: Studies in Shakespearean Tragedy* (Ontario: University of Toronto Press, 1967), pp. 115ff.
3. Stephen Booth, *King Lear, Macbeth, Indefinition, and Tragedy* (New Haven and London: Yale University Press, 1983), pp. 24–26.
4. Diane Elizabeth Dreher, *Domination and Defiance: Fathers and Daughters in Shakespeare* (Lexington: University Press of Kentucky, 1986), p. 65. For a quick review of the discussions treating the ending of the play, see Chiu Chin-jung's M.A. Thesis "*King Lear*'s Ending" (Taiwan University, 1981).
5. Bradley, p. 207.
6. Harold S. Wilson, *On the Design of Shakespearian Tragedy* (Ontario: University of Toronto Press, 1968), p. 189.
7. All quotations from *King Lear* are from *The Arden Shakespeare*, edited by Harold F. Brooks and others, published by Methuen in London and New York.
8. Harold S. Wilson, p. 190.

9. George Wilson Knight, *Shakespeare's Dramatic Challenge: On the Rise of Shakespeare's Tragic Heroes* (Washington, D.C.: University Press of America, 1981), p. 111.

10. James P. Driscoll, *Identity in Shakespearean Drama* (London and Toronto: Associated University Press, 1983), p. 129.

11. Jean E. Howard, *Shakespeare's Art of Orchestration* (Urbana and Chicago: University of Illinois Press, 1984), p. 131.

12. Yao Shu-hua, "Tou O" 竇娥, in *Wen-chi* 文季, No. 3 (May 1974), p. 251. All English translations from this play and others are mine.

13. Ibid., pp. 246–47.

14. Tsang Chin-shu 臧晉叔 (ed.), *Yüan ch'ü hsüan* 元曲選 (Taipei: Cheng-wen shu-chü 正文書局, 1970), p. 1509.

15. Ibid., p. 1511.

16. Sophocles, *Antigone*, English version by Dudley Fitts and Robert Fitzgerald, in *Drama: An Introductory Anthology*, ed. Otto Reinert (Boston and Toronto: Little, Brown and Company, 1961), p. 20.

17. For further analysis on Kuan's *Tou O yüan* concerning Tou O's characterization and Tou O as a Christ image, see my article "*Tou O yüan* chung ti yüan yü yüan" 竇娥冤中的冤與願, *Chung-wai Literary Monthly* 中外文學, Vol. 13, No. 1 (June 1984), pp. 88–103.

11. Shakespeare and Possibilities of Comparison: Notes on Ideas of Order[*]

Louise S. W. Ho

One distinctive feature of the Middle Ages which seems foreign to us today was its moral certainty. The West, at least, had arrived at a system by which one could define good and evil. By applying Aristotle, Aquinas produced a system which was both consistent and comprehensive. Thus, the Medieval mind achieved a perspicacity which confirmed itself in articulation. This moral certainty extended beyond the Middle Ages into the Renaissance. The former did not end abruptly to be replaced by a "cultural rebirth." It was a continuous process that merged one with the other, as indeed in the case of Shakespeare, where Medieval notions merged with Renaissance questioning of those very notions. This moral certainty was encoded into a world-view of order which extended from the smallest atom to the stars and planets, from the material world to the angels, from plant life to human life, and so on, to the last iota of the created world. God, the creator, the ultimate, the absolute, the primum mobile of all being is the first cause in this system which is expressed through three main analogical headings: correspondences, hierarchies and microcosmic-macrocosmic relationships. What Tillyard called in the 1930s "The Elizabethan World Picture" was not as universally known as he claimed. Allan Sinfield, Jonathan Dollimore, Leonard Tennenhouse, among others, have recently tried to show that the so-called "Elizabethan World Picture" was really a ploy for an ideological justification for the rulers and elite of society. According to them, that ideal picture was neither popularly shared nor true, as disorder was more the fact of those times. While Shakespeare's plays did adhere to, implicitly or explicitly, the Medieval picture of cosmic order, they dramatized worlds far

---

[*]All quotations from Shakespeare are taken from the Arden edition of the plays.

more complex and ambiguous than what that picture defined. Shakespeare used the images, the concepts, the language of that very order, but he presented worlds that did not fit only that order, nor worlds that acquired meaning solely through the perspectives of that order. I shall take up this point later. Now, I should give examples of good and evil as they are defined by the analogical framework mentioned above.

Macbeth opens with a physical violence which is echoed in the metaphysical violence of scenes alternating between unadulterated good and evil. We shift abruptly from one to the other with nothing in between to assuage the shock of contrast. One instance of perfect harmony is embodied by the ideal king Duncan, rewarding his brave generals in a ceremony expressive of hierarchy on earth which reflects a cosmic hierarchy. The imagery of growth and life and fruition is introduced by him thus:

> (*addressing Macbeth*) Welcome hither.
> I have begun to plant thee, and will labour
> To make thee full of growing. Noble Banquo,
> That hast no less deserv'd, nor must be known
> No less to have done so, let me infold thee
> And hold thee to my heart.

Following the imagery introduced by his king, Banquo answers:

> There if I grow,
> The harvest is your own.

The king is seen in the corresponding roles of farmer, gardener, grower, God. Here is the one who controls in a reciprocal relationship with one's subsidiaries, together, they will bring the co-operative action to fruition. God looks over his creation with loving care, so does the farmer his farm and his helpers, so does a king his faithful subjects. The body politic is at one with itself, and the macrocosm relates in the same way with the former and the microcosm of a Macbeth (as he was at that point), a Duncan, a Banquo. As they approach Macbeth's castle, they have no reason to think otherwise than that the music of the spheres is heard, a sweetness which is reflected in the sweetness of nature:

> This guest of summer,
> The temple-haunting martlet, does approve
> By his lov'd mansionry that the heaven's breath
> Smells wooingly here; no jutty, frieze,

Buttress, nor coign of vantage, but this bird
Hath made her pendent bed and procreant cradle.
Where they most breed and haunt, I have observ'd
The air is delicate.

It is thus that Banquo romanticizes the honeymoon of order which quickly turns out to be very short-lived indeed.

Cordelia in *King Lear*, when being asked how she loves her father, she does not make extravagant public protests of love as do her sisters, instead she refers to her contract with the cosmic order of the universe.

Unhappy that I am, I cannot heave
My heart into my mouth. I love your Majesty
According to my bond; no more nor less.

With the word bond, she refers to the bondage (bounden duty) that nature imposes on the relationship between father and child. It is within the laws of nature that she should love her father, and she loves him from the very position she occupies as daughter in the hierarchy of being, neither more nor less. She identifies her particular individuality as it relates to the universal scale. There is individuality, there is volition, she asserts both in terms of a larger whole, that is, in terms of the cosmic order.

Edmund in *King Lear* and Iago in *Othello* are examples of evil as defined within the cosmic order. They give neither credence to nor conceive of any meaning for the world view of cosmic order. They are "existentialists," they live outside the norm of things. They live by creating their own essence, they sever themselves from the fundamental structures of morality. The illegitimate Edmund cunningly plots to rob the estate from his legitimate brother, and appeals to Nature for assistance. "Thou, Nature, art my goddess; to thy law / My services are bound ... Now, gods, stand up for bastards!"

The nature he is appealing to is one of chaos, of lawlessness, of savagery and non-civilization, quite the opposite of the nature that Cordelia invokes. He addresses a world in which individuals achieve their own destiny, albeit by deceit or murder. He, the illegitimate will topple the legitimate heir, and prosper; he sees no value in the raiments of order like ceremony, occasion, propriety, custom (I use these words in their Elizabethan sense). He hears his father lamenting discord among brothers, fathers and children, and that such disorder is reflected among the heavenly bodies. His reaction is that man is his own estate, man is an enclosed individual unto himself.

> This is the excellent foppery of the world, that, when, we are sick in fortune, often
> the surfeits of our own behaviour, we make guilty of our disasters the sun, the moon,
> and stars; as if we were villains on necessity; fools by heavenly compulsion; knaves,
> thieves, and treachers, by spherical predominance; drunkards, liars, and adulterers,
> by an enforc'd obedience of planetary influence;

Wilson Knight, among others, has remarked on the motiveless evil in Iago's deeds. In the West, at any rate, evil is ultimately an act of the will. Satan is, after all, a Western commodity. The fact that there is no weighty reason for his cleverly studied plots makes his evil more clearly a pure act of will.

> Virtue? A fig! 'Tis in ourselves that we are thus or thus. Our bodies are our gardens
> to the which our wills are gardens; ... the power and corrigible authority of this lies
> in our wills.

When we consider Macbeth, the case is not so simple. Is Macbeth really evil or has he made some terrible mistakes? The basis of his evil is his equivocation between good and evil and he lacks the mental fortitude to decide which is which. The language in which Macbeth thinks is the very language of cosmic order. From beginning to end he examines his own actions against a back-drop of cosmic order, even as they oppose that order.

I now revert to my earlier point about the worlds in Shakespeare's plays which lie entirely outside the analogical framework. The Greeks in *Troilus and Cressida* speak the language of that framework; so do the Romans in *Antony and Cleopatra*. Ulysses' speech on hierarchy as an extension of cosmic order (so often quoted out of context) has been held up as an ideal expression of the "Elizabethan World Order." It is quickly contradicted by Ulysses' next psychological ploy in appearing to snub Achilles so as to rouse him to action. There his grandiose exhortation to Greek unity seems happily forgotten. If the inconsistency had to be seen as such, it would have been explained sooner or later. As it is, the audience is left alone to follow the action as it develops. There are more possible world-views than one. In *Antony and Cleopatra*, the Roman world is given its yardstick of order, both in the honouring as well as the dishonouring of that order. However, the play gives no moral framework for the Egyptian side of things. Cleopatra's blatant irresponsibility and skittishness are sui generis; she is the "serpent of old Nile," yet she is the tragic heroine, not a villain. Both she and Antony project a world which cannot be defined or explained; nevertheless, it is one which overshadows the Roman one by its wonderful power and magnificence. In *Richard II*, the dethroning scene is a piece of shocking arbitration. Historically, there has not been, could never be a formal ceremonial dethroning of a king, for that matter, a king of sound Plantagenet descent. (This scene was by and large censored during Elizabeth I's reign.) Richard, the rightful monarch, preordained by God to rule, is a bad king, he is now asked by the usurper, Bollingbroke, to step down in his favour. In a world where de jure positions are supposedly solidly identified with de facto positions, the elaborate presentation on stage of the schizoid splitting one from the other must leave the mind in a complete daze. The analogical framework provides Bollingbroke with no possible means for legitimization whatsoever. Yet, he is the victorious one. He will continue for another three plays, his son will be the ideal king, Henry V. Quite clearly, Shakespeare's drama undermines the very order his plays assume. The tension between the systematic and the undifferentiated lies at the heart of Shakespearean drama. Thus, dramatic tension extends to the very value system in which other "texts," other "codes" are to be determined. Because it is drama, such radical subversion does not suffer the claustrophobia experienced in texts that adhere to writing alone. There is plenty of actual space for subversions of all kinds to play out themselves. Dramatists like Shaw and Ibsen have their didactic moments, they are out to make a point. Shakespeare keeps his points to himself. He does not present one point of view, nor make a commitment to any point of view. Truly, the play is the thing. We call that Shakespeare's anonymity.

Given that the Shakespearean mode is multi-dimensional and multi-referential, in all its texts, is it also multi-tolerant? By that I mean whether or not the Shakespearean play will still be recognizably so, if, say, we were to rewrite Shakespeare by using the Chinese cosmic system as formalized in the Han dynasty as a substitute for the Western Medieval cosmic order. The cosmic framework in both Medieval Europe and Han China were, ultimately, man's attempt to make sense of the world. Both systems sought to impose order on phenomenon to make it meaningful. The Western one provided the means by which existence in all its facets became intelligible as well as moral. The Chinese sought to make sense of chaos in order to survive it.

The system of correspondences is implicit in Taoist writings, for example in the *Ta-tung chen-ching* 大洞眞經 and the *Huang t'ing ching* 黃庭經. Parts of the body correspond with parts of the universe. The body is the microcosm which corresponds to the macrocosm. There is in fact an actual chart of the body which shows these correspondences: "Nei ching t'u" 內經 圖 . In *The Doctrine of the Mean*, which is one of the *Four Books*, man's moral actions are believed to exert physical changes in the natural order. The more important the person the more powerful will his influence be on the natural order. For example, a King's misdeeds will cause more serious disaster than those of our ordinary person. Harmony is achieved when microcosm and macrocosm agree.

In terms of hierarchy, *T'ai chi* gives birth to the *Yin* and the *Yang* which gives birth to the five elements or agents, and these give birth to "myriad things." Thus, one gives birth to two which gives birth to five which gives birth to phenomena.

The Five Elements, the *Yin* and the *Yang*, the trigrams or hexagrams of the *Book of Changes* make up the basic principles for observing phenomena, therefore, phenomena are categorized according to them. The system of the Five Elements are an abstract concept which corresponds to the five planets that are visible to the naked eye. In heaven there are five stars; on earth things take on qualities corresponding to those five stars. There are five tastes, five colours, five seasons, we have five internal organs, five cardinal points and so on. These are eternal and sacred principles discovered by ancient sages. This is why they are held as true even when observation proves otherwise.

The *Yin* and the *Yang* are the polar limits of change. The two terms originated from words describing the light and dark sides of a mountain. The polar limits mark the extremes beyond which change cannot continue. They work like the oscillations of a pendulum. Examples of these extreme states are: hot and cold, light and shade, male and female etc. These states originated from observations of nature like day and night, the full-moon and the crescent, male and female etc.

The *Book of Changes* contain sixty-four hexagrams which are symbolic representations of all the possible states of the universe. Each hexagram is in fact an abstract picture of the universe. Hexagrams must be used in combination with divination. In divination, an initial and a second hexagram are chosen through manipulation of yarrow stalks. The first hexagram represents the present state of affairs, the second one represents the state towards which the present state is moving. The two hexagrams, together with the manipulation of the yarrow stalks, provide the information for the diviner to adjust himself to the cosmic order and thus to benefit from propitious influences. Behind this system is the assumption that the universe moves according to specified order which can be known via these symbolic representations in their manipulations in divination.

Possibilities seem endless. One could compare the two world pictures to see how cultural, ideological, conceptual frameworks match with or clash against each other. The Shakespearean text would be made, at some point, open-ended, thus allowing for a variety of rearrangements of relationships between signifier and signified, with the purpose of enriching them. One could also rewrite Shakespeare by using the imagery and ideas of Chinese cosmology. It should not be impossible to inject the said Chinese images into, for example, Ulysses' speech, to make it still Ulysses, and with a difference. Adaptation of Shakespeare into other genres has not been all that unusual. Examples that come to mind are Verdi's *Otello*, Akira Kurosawa's *The Throne of Blood* (*Macbeth*), Chinese operas of *Othello* and *Macbeth* in the Shakespeare Festival of 1986 held in various parts of China.

Whereas this essay has made no attempt at any comparative study, it hopes to have ferretted out an area which has potentials for such study. Potentials apart, I should like to point to a singularly successful adaptation, and that is Kurosawa's recent film, *Ran* (1985). Kurosawa himself denied any adaptation of *King Lear* in his film. This is beside the point. Neither his public avowal nor private intentions need concern us. There are indeed many points of contact thematically between *Ran* and *King Lear*. Other than that, what is truly striking is the way his script echoes again and again lines from *King Lear*, even after both the characters and their respective speeches have been transposed, modified, or radically changed. At the beginning of the film, Kent and Cordelia are collapsed into one character, the third son Saburo. Later on, Kent re-emerges as Tango, at the same time taking on the figure of Lear's Fool. Tsurumaru is a young lad, blinded by Hidetora (the Lear figure) in exchange for his life. That was in the past when Hidetora burned Tsurumaru's parents' castle and killed them, sparing him after having gouged out his eyes. His attitude to fate and the gods parallels Gloucester's attitude as expressed thus:

As flies to wanton boys are we to th' gods—
They kill us for their sport.

The textual parallels between the film and the play are strangely achieved. Kurosawa grafted the Lear play into his sammurai story, success-fully allowing lines from the play to penetrate all the changes, asserting themselves as well as merging with the given context.

I began by assuming a specific Shakespearean text. I proceeded to show how Shakespeare undermined himself with reference to ideas of cosmic order. I then suggested scrambling of the text with possible injections from a different culture. I end by reasserting a specific Shakespearean text as it re-emerges in *Ran*. Allow me to end by quoting Edmund as he lies dying:

> The wheel is come full circle; I am here.

12. The First Chinese Drama in English Translation

A. Owen Aldridge

English audiences were introduced to Chinese drama in the middle of the eighteenth century when three different versions of the Yüan play *Chao-shih ku-erh* were presented on London stages. These productions represent little in the way of British research concerning Chinese dramatic tradition, however, since all three were renditions of a translation in French of the original play. One of these had passed through three metamorphoses: a translation by a French Jesuit, Joseph Henri Prémare, in a famous compilation by another French Jesuit, Du Halde, published in his *Description ... de la Chine*; an adaptation of Prémare suited to French tastes by Voltaire, in his *L'Orphelin de la Chine*; and, finally, an adaptation of Voltaire's play by an English playwright Arthur Murphy. The two other renditions consisted of a more or less faithful translation of Voltaire and a translation of Prémare's version, the latter the closest to the Chinese original of the three British adaptation.

The first direct translation of a Chinese dramatic work into English took place in 1817, when a pioneer British Sinologist John Francis Davis took another Yüan play from the same collection holding *Chao-shih ku-erh* and rendered it faithfully into his own language. The Chinese title of the play *Laou-seng-urh* by Kuan Han-ch'ing was converted by Davis into *An Heir in His Old Age*. Equally important with this translation itself was an essay affixed to the published version in 1817 entitled "A Brief View of the Chinese Drama," the first formal treatment of the subject in any European language. It is not clear whether this essay is by Davis or some other hand.

After a left-handed compliment to the Jesuit missionaries to China, portraying them as more enlightened and less prejudiced than members of the other orders, the essayist observes that their publications reveal very little of the Chinese taste for lyric poetry or theatrical exhibitions. "We are left," he maintains, "almost wholly in the dark with regard to the nature of this kind of composition, as well as of the actual state of the drama, and indeed of that department of literature in general which is usually known by the name of *belles lettres*." The Jesuits, he suggests, have been overwhelmed by the Chinese reverence for ancient writings and as a result have "so stuffed their communications with excessive panegyric on the beauties of the four King, and the wisdom and virtues of Yao and Shun, as to leave themselves no time to inquire into the modern state of general literature."

For a second time gently rebuking Catholic commentaries, the essayist quotes from Morrison's Chinese grammar a Chinese author whom he credits with sounder views on literature than those possessed by either Père Cibot or Abbé Grozier. This native source compares the progress of Chinese poetry to the gradual growth of a tree: "the ancient *She-king* (the book of Odes) may be likened to the roots; when *Soo-loo* flourished, the buds appeared; in the time of Keen-ngan there was abundance of leaves; but during the dynasty Tang, many reposed under the shade of the tree, and it yielded rich supplies of flowers and fruit." Against the allegations of Cibot and Grozier that the theatres in China are comparable to houses of ill repute, the essayist affirms that dramas are instituted to inculcate virtue. He maintains, moreover, that there is no such thing as a public theatre in China, and that dramatic representations are given either in the homes of the great and wealthy or in the open on the occasion of public festivals. "The Chinese are so passionately fond of scenic representations," he affirms, that in the great houses "no entertainment is ever given without a company of comedians to amuse the guests." The essayist provides a description of the physical features of the Chines stage, the first ever presented in a European publication. Comparing it to a booth at a European fair, he observes that a "Chinese company of players will at any time construct a theatre in the course of a couple of hours; a few bamboos as posts to support a roof of mats, and a floor of boards, raised some six or seven feet from the ground; and a few pieces of painted cotton to cover the three sides, the front being left entirely open, are all that is required for the construction of a Chinese theatre." Reminding his readers that in England the first painted cloths for movable scenes were those of Inigo Jones in 1605, he quotes a passage from Sir Philip Sidney to compare Chinese scenic improvisation with that in Elizabethan England.

In another publication Davis has provided a parallel glance at the English theatre given by a native of China. It appears in a poem of ten stanzas entitled "London" translated by Davis himself. An entire stanza is given over to this unique description of the English stage of the Regency period by a native Chinese.

> Their theatres are closed during the long days;
> It is after dark that the painted scenes are displayed:
> The faces of the actors are handsome to behold,
> And their dresses are composed of silk and satin:
> Their songs resound in unison with stringed and wind instruments,
> And they dance to the inspiring note of drums and flutes:
> It constitutes the perfection of harmonious delight,
> Every one retires with a laughing countenance. [Poeseos sinensis]

The essay accompanying Davis's translation of *Laou-seng-urh* affirms that a Chinese theatrical company usually "consists of eight or ten persons, who are literally the servants or slaves of the master or manager. They travel about from place to place in covered barge, on canals or rivers near to which most great cities are situated; these barges are their habitations, and in these they are instructed in their parts by the master." He adds that females are allowed on the stage, but persons who are free may not be purchased to be used in stage entertainments. He particularly emphasizes the point that many stage performances "would appear to descend into lowness and vulgarity, in the inverse ration of the rank and situation in life of the parties for whose amusement they are exhibited." He may have based this singular opinion upon the nature of theatrical exhibitions witnessed by various travellers to the Middle Kingdom. A naturalized American, André Everard van Bramm, for example, reported in 1797 that a performance he attended in the company of the emperor took place in the midst of the exchanging of gifts and the consuming of food. The performance consisted nearly entirely of acrobatics. A man balanced a ladder with his feet and a boy climbed up and down upon it for nearly a quarter of an hour; after this the acrobat performed the same feat with an enormous vase in which the boy climbed in and out. [I:168] An English traveller, Sir George Staunton, who visited at about the same time, however, was entertained in a temporary theatre in which the drama being presented had many resemblances to those of the English stage. "The piece represented an Emperor of China and his empress living in supreme felicity, when, on a sudden, his subjects revolt, a civil war ensues, battles are fought, and at last the arch-rebel who was a general of cavalry, overcomes his sovereign, kills him with his own hand, and routs the imperial army. The captive empress then appears upon the stage in all the agonies of despair resulting from the loss of her husband, and of her dignity, as well as the apprehension for that of her honour. Whilst she is tearing her hair and rending the skies with her complaints, the conqueror enters, approaches her with respect, addresses her in a gentle tone, soothes her sorrows, and with his compassion talks of love and adoration, and like Richard the Third, with lady Ann in Shakespeare, prevails in less than half an hour, on the Chinese princess to dry up her tears, to forget her deceased consort, and yield to a consoling wooer. The piece concludes with the nuptials, and a grand procession." [272] Regardless of its moral tendencies, this play can hardly be considered as vulgar or obscene.

Van Bramm also had a favourite Chinese play, one which he had several times seen performed, but never in the imperial presence. He says that its Chinese title is *Chon-fou-kan* or *Fidelity Rewarded*. It concerns a mandarin summoned to the court who leaves behind him two wives, an infant child, and a faithful female servant. During his absence, the two wives afflicted with boredom desert the homestead, seeking adventure elsewhere. The servant remains with the child, caring for him as her only mission in life. One day when he has reached the age of thirteen and has fallen asleep from fatigue and undernourishment, she gently strokes him with a leather strap to awaken him, and he bounds up in anger, rebuking her for daring to chastize him when she is not his real mother. She sheds tears over his ingratitude, and they are reconciled. Soon after the mandarin returns and is told that his wives have been reduced to servitude after abandoning him. He shows his gratitude to the faithful servant by promising to marry her, and the son renders homage to his father and to his future stepmother.

Our essayist quotes another European traveller to China, Barrow, who describes the dramatic portrayal of "a woman being condemned to be flayed alive, for the murder of her husband; she appears on the stage not only naked, but completely excoriated." This would seem to be an example of extreme realism attained by a high development of the cosmetic art. The essayist, in keeping with the comparatist flavour of his presentation, points out that similar scenes had been exhibited in England; Adam and Eve had appeared without clothing in mystery plays, and several persons had appeared almost naked in a pastoral play performed before James the First.

In his concluding remarks, the essayist reflects unfavourably on Prémare's translation of *Chao-shih ku-erh*, which he dismisses as "garbled" and "the solitary specimen of this kind of composition in any European language, before that which is now offered to the public." He accuses Prémare of omitting most of the poetry, a legitimate objection that has since been echoed by many Chinese authorities. Since these parts of the play are those which "have been compared with the Greek chorus, and in which sentiment, eloquence, passion, are all expressed," the English critic affirms that Prémare has "left out the very best parts of the play." The essayist says nothing about the merits of Davis's translation, an indication perhaps that Davis and the essayist are the same person. He contents himself with the observation that "the comedy of an 'Heir in his Old Age,' is the simple representation of a story in domestic life—a plain 'unvarnished tale,' in which Chinese manners and Chinese feelings are faithfully delineated and expressed, in a natural manner, and in appropriate language."

Davis's translation is clear, precise and presumably faithful to the original, indeed a long passage which has since been translated by a modern scholar is almost identical with the twentieth-century rendition. The play concerns the domestic problems of an old man, Lew, his wife, his second wife, his daughter, his son-in-law, and his nephew. The latter is an orphan who has inexplicably aroused the animosity of the first wife. Lew in a soliloquy says he had planned to divide his property equally between his nephew and his daughter, but has just learned that his second wife is pregnant and does not know whether the offspring will be a girl or a male heir. The son-in-law tells the daughter that he has married her only in hopes of gaining her inheritance and that these hopes will be frustrated if a son is born to the second wife. He accordingly threatens to have her killed unless she leaves the household, and when she does so he tells Lew that she has run away with another man. Lew assumes that this stroke of ill fortune has descended because of his avarice, and he vows to distribute alms at the temple on the next day. The focus then shifts to the memorial rites for family ancestors. The wife perceives that the daughter worships at the graves of her husband's family, but neglects those of her father's. In the meantime, the nephew at great personal sacrifice tends the graves of his uncle's family. Realizing that the nephew is more dependable than the son-in-law, the wife has a change of heart towards the nephew. The daughter and son-in-law are banished, and the family keys delivered to the nephew. After three years have passed, the daughter and son-in-law return, and the nephew intercedes for them. The second wife and her child also appear. Lew's daughter then explains to her father that her husband had wanted the wife killed, but that she had realized that if anything happened to this wife his posterity would be cut off. She had accordingly concealed the wife in a place of safety and brought up the child. She then implores him not to harbour resentment against herself, his own daughter. "Though you have a dutiful nephew, how can he be compared to your own child?" The father thereupon divides his property among his daughter, nephew and infant son. He concludes with thanksgiving: "When we went to the tombs, at the usual season, to perform the rites, the feelings of affection returned, and jealousy became changed to love. —Thus by pointing out the desolate spot, I taught a bitter lesson to my old wife; —nor did I give away a part of my wealth in vain, for, by the favour of Heaven, I have an heir in my old age!"

Shih Chung-wen in her survey of Yüan drama considers *Laou-seng-urh* only in regard to the theme of filial piety. The action, however, is not really based on the virtue of the nephew, but on the selfishness of the first wife and the wickedness of the son-in-law. Other themes are those of avarice, of the tragic disgrace of not having an heir, of the superiority of a literary life to a mercantile one, of the necessity of continued homage to one's ancestors, of the greater dependability of blood relations to those entering the family through marriage, and of the greater importance of male offspring than female, for "a daughter is born to be of another family." These themes are presented in a sentimental manner. If the play is a comedy as Davis describes it, it is a "comédie larmoyante" rather than a farce of a display of wit.

Indeed two reviews of Davis's translation embodied discussions of whether the play is properly a comedy at all. One was anonymous in the *Quarterly Review* in 1817 and the other by the French Sinologist Abel-Rémusat in the *Journal des Savans* in the following year. The *Quarterly* reviewer notes that the divisions of the drama closely approximate those of most European nations. It has four acts and a *sie-tsze* or prologue, which the reviewer compares to that in Greek drama. The resemblance, he adds, "does not stop here. The lyrical compositions, which in the serious and historical plays are more frequent than in dramas like the one in question, bear a very striking affinity to the chorus of the old Greek tragedy, with all due distance, however, as to taste and genius, and like the chorus too, they are sung with an accompaniment of music." Referring to Davis's observation that these songs are usually obscure, the reviewer expresses the opinion that "they are meant to convey some sage reflection, or some moral truth, bearing on the subject of the dialogue, and that their obscurity is owing to the figurative significance of the symbols." [16:406] The French reviewer,

Abel-Rémusat says nothing about the resemblance of the play to Greek drama beyond indicating that it does not to a great degree violate the classical requirement of the unities. Sceptical of Voltaire's principle that Chinese drama precedes the Greek in antiquity, he maintains that regardless of its age it has never enjoyed a place of honour. He contrasts *Laou-seng-urh* as a comedy with *Chao-shih ku-erh* as a tragedy. Although drawing attention to the sentimental or touching elements in *Laou-seng-urh*, he emphasizes that one scene portraying domestic emotions is "assaisonné de traits vifs et comiques" and another concerning beggars is "egayée par quelques tours de fourberie dont ces sortes de gens ont coutume d'user" [Janvier 1818, 33]. He also observes that Davis has suppressed a small number of passages of gross indecency and insupportable ennui. Furthermore he charges that Davis has omitted almost one-third of the complete work in order to render the drama more rapid and more conforming to the Western way of seeing things. These omissions he criticizes on the ground that the purpose of a translator is to portray the taste and genius of another nation, not to amuse frivolous readers, a point of view that could legitimately be debated in the context of modern theories of translation. [31] Abel-Rémusat designates dramas such as *Chao-shih ku-erh* as light productions and suggests that those who translate them, using a knowledge of demotic Chinese, are slightly inferior to those who work with more conventional materials in European libraries. [29] He, nevertheless, concludes that the play "se distingue par la simplicité du plan, le choix heureux des incidens, l'observation exacte des caractères, quelques situations comiques, et par un style naturel et simple dans la prose, noble et élèvé dans la melopée." He is, therefore, in essential agreement with the English essayist that the play is a simple, unvarnished tale, faithfully portraying Chinese manners and feelings in natural and appropriate language.

13. *The Orphan of the House Chao* in French, English, German and Hong Kong Literature

Adrian Hsia

The Yüan play *The Orphan of the House Chao* (趙氏孤兒), as the full Chinese title *Chao-shih ku-erh ta pao-ch'ou* 趙氏孤兒大報仇 indicates, has revenge and retribution as its central theme. Even though the latter is basically a Buddhist thought in the Chinese play, it is, however, an integral tenet of the established religions East and West: one harvests what one has sowed. When the Yüan play was first introduced to Europe in the incomplete translation of Père Prémare in 1735, which was included in J. B. Du Halde's *Description Géographique, Historique, Chronologique, Politique et Physique de l'Empire de la Chine et de la Tartarie Chinoise*, it caught the attention of several playwrights who adapted the play by changing the content and the theme of the original to suit their own respective world views.

Ch'en Shou-yi 陳受頤 mentioned in his pioneer essay of 1936 on the influence of *The Orphan of the House Chao* in Europe that "there were five European adaptations in the eighteenth-century: two in English, and one in French, German, and Italian, respectively."[1] He may not have known then that there were already two German doctoral theses on the China-motif in German literature, one in 1934 and the other in 1935.[2] Both theses described the use of the motif of the orphan in one German novel and two German plays.[3] Later on one of the plays, a fragment by Goethe titled *Elpenor*, was examined in more detail.[4] In this paper, we shall survey the use of the Chinese orphan-motif in English and French literature briefly and then examined its use in German literature in some detail. Finally, we shall analyze the *Chao-shih ku-erh* written by the Hong Kong playwright Li Chüeh-pen 黎覺奔 in 1964.

Du Halde was the first European to comment on the Yüan play in writing, relying on information given by the translator Prémare. The first concern of the eighteenth-century Europe regarding drama was the handling of the three unities which were, of course, non-existent in the Chinese play. Then Du Halde went on to explain that the Chinese stage does not distinguish between tragedies and comedies which is not entirely true. We know that it is also not true for mid-eighteenth century Europe where the *comédie larmoyante* already existed. For us of the generation of epic drama, it is of interest to note that du Halde already described some of the characteristics of an epic play such as that the Chinese do not strictly distinguish between narrative and dramatic forms, that the actors always introduce themselves and their roles, and last, but not least, the actors may suddenly begin to sing in the middle of a dialogue or they may interrupt the singing to recite a few sentences which were not acceptable according to the rules of that time.[5] Du Halde specified:

> Les Tragédies Chinoises sont entremêlées de chansons dans lesquelles interrompt assez souvent le chant, pour réciter une ou deux phrases du ton de la déclamation ordinaire; nous sommes choqués de ce qu'un Acteur au milieu d'un dialogue se met tout d'un coup à chanter, mais on doit faire attention que, parmi les Chinois, le chant est fait pour exprimer quelque grand mouvement de l'âme, comme la joie, la douleur, la colère, le désespoir; par exemple, un homme qui es indigné contre un scélérat, chante; un autre qui s'anime a la vengeance, chante; un autre qui est prêt de se donner la mort, chante.[6]

All these characteristics of an epic play were considered irregularities and shocking flaws for a drama. Even Voltaire, the sinophile, who thought that China had cultivated the dramatic art three thousand years earlier than Greece, considered "cette pièce est toute barbare en comparaison des bons ouvrages de nos jours."[7] He had to make allowances that the Yüan play was written in the early fourteenth century and insisted that it was superior to any of the French dramas of the same period. Nevertheless, the regular drama as perfected by the French masters of the seventeenth century was the criterion to measure if a nation was civilized or not. Voltaire explained it this way:

> Plus l'Allemagne s'est perfectionnée, et plus nous l'avons vue adopter nos spectacles: le peu de pays ou ils n'étaient pas reçus dans le siècle passé, n'étaient pas mis au rang des pays civilisés.[8]

Therefore, Voltaire had to rewrite the Chinese play according to the rules of classical French drama, starting with a tragedy of three acts in 1753.[9] When it was completed in 1755 and staged in Comédie Française, it had five acts.

Thus according to Voltaire, he advanced the Chinese play from dramatic infancy to maturity.

We know that alternating the dramatic form of the Chinese play according to the three unities was not the sole purpose of Voltaire. We are also aware of his feud with Rousseau regarding "si le rétablissement des sciences et des arts a contribué à épurer les mœurs" in which China became the centre of dispute. Rousseau maintained that all the arts and sciences of China offered no protection against the military prowess of the Tartars. The Chinese were actually corrupted by its civilization and were degenerated into slaves and villains. That was in 1750. Voltaire's *L'Orphelin de la Chine*, his version of the Yüan play, was used to reinstate the ultimate converting power of morality. Perceived with this background, Voltaire's contention that he described the manners of the Chinese and Tartars lacking in the original, becomes comprehensible. He wanted to demonstrate "la supériorité naturelle que donnent la raison et le génie sur la force aveugle et barbare"[10] with his version of the drama. That the Chinese play was written during the Yüan dynasty suggested the Mongols to Voltaire, because they were the first—and his contemporaries the Manchus were the second—Tartars to conquer China. With the Mongols in mind, Genghis Khan became the natural candidate for the role of the Mongolian emperor whom the French philosopher admired.

Voltaire was convinced that he was improving on the original Yüan play. However, he invented a plot which offends against the poetical verisimilitude by the standards of his own times. In Voltaire's play, Genghis Khan is the rejected lover of Idamé, the wife of the mandarin Zamti whom the last Ming emperor entrusted his infant son and implored to save in a most unlikely manner: the Chinese monarch, in chains, cries out in a "sacred language," unknown to the crowd surrounding him, to Zamti who was watching the butchering of royal family in secret to preserve his last and only hope, his son. The plot also implies that Genghis Khan only rose to power because he was rejected as a lover. Both instances are too fantastic. It is not imaginable that a love affair between a Mongolian beggar—i.e., Genghis—and the daughter of a high ranking mandarin was possible, or that none of the soldiers surrounding the royal family understood Chinese or any other sacred language. More, the infant prince is hidden in the royal cemetery all by himself. Later on, after Idamé has exposed her husband's high treason for surrendering their son as the royal orphan, she stealthily leaves the palace and brings the prince to the Korean army which is coming to the rescue of the Ming emperor. The Korean army proclaims the orphan king, however, it is routed by a Mongolian force led by Genghis Khan himself, and Idamé is recaptured. These events all take place in one single day, the same day as the butchering of the royal family. Idamé is brought to Genghis Khan for the second time, who cannot harm her because he is still madly in love with her, and he would not force her to love him. He promises to spare her husband and even the infant prince and adopts her son as his own if she would renounce her marriage. Again Genghis Khan is rejected by Idamé who requests her husband and she be brought together again for a moment, unguarded and unobserved. The Mongol, of course, grants her the boon. Alone with her husband, she proposes suicide as their neighbouring islanders, the Japanese, would do. Her husband cannot kill her, so he intends to kill himself, but Idamé would not permit it. At this moment, Genghis appears with the guards. He professes himself vanquished by their virtues and would rear the orphan of the Ming dynasty as his own son. He appoints Zamti interpreter of the law and asks him to teach reason, justice and morality. Zamti readily acknowledges his new sovereign, forgetting the plea of the last Ming emperor to preserve his last and only hope—his son. Now the son will live, but the hope is dead, for Genghis Khan has conquered the heart of the most loyal mandarin. Henceforth, the conquered are supposed to rule the conqueror. This change is brought out, according to Genghis Khan, alone by the virtues of Idamé.[11]

Voltaire could have changed the title of the play to Genghis Khan, for he is the real hero of the play. Because of his blind love for Idamé, he tolerates everything, including high treason, both of Idamé, the virtuous mother, wife and subject, and Zamti, the virtuous subject, father and husband. Because of his love, Genghis is tolerant, because he is tolerant, he makes the shrewdest move to capture the heart of the conquered Chinese represented by the virtuous couple, the best strategy which can be developed by any conqueror. Thus the intention of Voltaire to demonstrate the natural superiority of reason and genius over blind force and barbarism differs from the message of the play which I read as virtue succumbs to crafty politics in the long run. For Genghis Khan in Voltaire's play has all the qualities of a natural and wise politician. Because of the contradiction between the philosopher's and the dramatist's messages, the play lacks verisimilitude. Genghis is too much romanticized. He is depicted to go to Peking as a beggar and falls in love with a beautiful maiden. He is rejected, leaves Peking to conquer the world and then returns to conquer China. Because he insists on winning the heart of his former lover instead of simply taking her, he becomes a wise ruler and a real conqueror. It smacks too much of a romanticism of the *Arabian Nights*. It also ignores that China is a vast empire where it takes more than a few hours to proclaim a new king and to defeat an army. Voltaire lamented that the Chinese origin lacks "unité de temp et d'action, développements de sentiments, peinture des mœurs éloquence, raison, passion" which he supplies in his version which, because of the added melodramatic elements, appears as a romance in dramatic form.

Despite Voltaire's professed sinophilism, we should not lose sight of the fact that he was addressing an ideal which he thought to have found in ancient Confucian China. This Golden Age, however, ceased to exist before Voltaire's time. As far as the contemporary, politically real China is concerned, Voltaire had a very low opinion of it. To wit, he wrote

> Les Chinois, comme les autres Asiatiques, sont demeurés aux premiers éléments de la poésie, de l'éloquence, de la physique, de l'astronomie, de la peinture, connus par eux si long-temps avant nous. Il leur a été donné de commencer en tout plus tot que les autres peuples, pour ne faire ensuite aucun progrès. Ils ont ressemblé aux anciens Egyptiens, qui, avant d'abord enseigné les Grecs, finirent par n'être pas capables d'être leurs disciples.
>
> Ces Chinois chez qui nous avons voyagé a travers tant de périls, ces peuples de qui nous avons obtenu avec tant de peine la permission de leur apporter l'argent de l'Europe, et de venir les instruire, ne savent pas encore à quel point nous leur sommes supérieurs, ils ne sont pas assez avancés pour oser seulement vouloir nous imiter. Nous avons puisé dans leur histoire des sujets de tragédie, et ils ignorent si nous avons une histoire.[12]

If China was not advanced enough to imitate Europe,[13] then indeed, Voltaire could impose the rules of French drama on a Yüan play and rewrite it to his taste, believing he had created a truer Chinese drama.

Across the Channel, an English adaptation was already published in 1741, fourteen years before Voltaire's, which turned out to be a political drama directed against Robert Walpole, the first Prime Minister in British history.[14] This drama was probably never staged and the author, William Hatchett, was unknown. In 1759, the new adaptation of Arthur Murphy was produced in Theatre Royal in Drury Lane, with the famous actor David Garrick playing the role of Zamti, the mandarin. Murphy was not quite satisfied with Voltaire's play, especially the role of Genghis Khan, who, as the leader of the Mongols, should not be represented as "Le Chevalier Genghis Khan." Voltaire discovered a certain Shakespearean trait in the

Yüan play which he, of course, considered as a weakness. Murphy considered Shakespeare to be "the most wonderful genius that ever existed since the era of Homer." He would like the Shakespearean trait developed which would also be in tune with the roughness of the Mongol emperor. But Murphy could not fathom the dimensions of a world conqueror who Genghis Khan was, he presented him more like a chieftain of a Germanic tribe or the Vikings: He has Zamti, tortured, such a thought never entered the mind of Voltaire's idealized Genghis Khan, and he falls in single combat with the revenging "Orphan of China" who proclaims: "Now let me hence to hail/My people with the sound of peace."[15] He intends to have a monument erected for Zamti who dies after he has witnessed the triumph of the Orphan and is succeeded by his son. So they live happily ever after.

Murphy also differed from Voltaire's play in other fundamental ways. Above all, Voltaire's idealism of virtue conquers all. He paints the characters in different shades of white, while Murphy uses black and white colours, and Genghis Khan was a tyrant pure and simple. However, Arthur Murphy was even not quite happy with his version of the *Orphan of China* which is limited by the plot of the original. Voltaire was a monarchist, his ideal ruler was an enlightened, patriarchal despot like K'ang-hsi, Ch'ien-lung, or even Yung-cheng, he was happy to model his Genghis Khan according to his idealized images of these monarchs. With the constitutional monarchy of Britain, Murphy had no understanding for the absolute loyalty of a subject towards his ruler. But he was not able to change the feudal fealty to a loyalty to a nation or a cause. He merely states in the prologue:

> One dubious character, we own, he draws,
> A patriot zealous in a monarch's cause!
> ....
>   If then, assiduous to obtain his end,
> You find too far the subject's zeal extend;
> If undistinguish'd loyalty prevails
> Where nature shrinks, and strong affection fails,
> On China's tenets charge the fond mistake,
> And spare his error for his virtue's sake.
>   From nobler motives our allegiance springs,
> For Britain knows no Right Divine in Kings.[16]

Since the political message intrinsic in the plot is not shared by the playwright, he cannot take his own play too seriously. The palace intrigue invented by him can be viewed in this vein. Zamti has collected a handful of persons faithful to the former king or emperor in order to start a coup d'état when the Mongols are recovering from their debauchery. A collaborator of Zamti sends away the guards of Genghis to quell the oncoming rebels outside the eastern gate and leads the orphan with a sabre in his hand to the Mongol who is unattended. The revenge is carried out in single combat. The subsequent collapse of the Mongol Empire is indicated. The whole concept is only possible in a romance of the knights of the round table.

Such a judgement is actually in tune with the intention of the playwright who was not only interested in the dramatic tension and potentials of the plot, but also in the exotic setting. This he expresses very clearly and straightforwardly in the Prologue which begins with the following lines:

> Enough of Greece and Rome. The exhausted store
> Of either nation now can charm no more:
> ....
> On eagle wings the poet of to-night
> Soars for fresh virtues to the source of light,
> To China's eastern realms: and boldly bears
> Confucius's morals to Britannia's ears.[17]

Should the viewer or reader still miss the intention of the playwright, a reminder is given that is the Epilogue spoken by Mandane, the wife of Zamti, played by Mrs. Yates:

> You've seen their eastern virtues, patriot passions,
> And now for something of their taste and fashions,
> I long to know it—Do the creatures visit?
> Dear Mrs. Yates, go tell us—Well, how is it?
> First, as to beauty—set your hearts at rest—
> They are all broad foreheads, and pig's eyes at best.
> And then they lead such strange, such formal lives!
> —A little more at home than English wives:
> Lest the poor things should roam and prove untrue,
> They all are crippled in the tiny shoe,
> A hopeful scheme to keep a wife from madding!
> —We pinch our feet, and yet are ever gadding.
> Then they have no cards, no routs, ne'er take their fling,
> And pin money is an unheard-of thing!
> Then how d'ye think they write—you'll ne'er divine—
> From top to bottom down in one straight line. [*Mimics*]

We ladies, when our flames we cannot smother,
Write letters—from one corner to another. [*Mimics*]
   One mode there is in which both climes agree;
I scarce can tell—'mongst friends then let it be—
—The creatures love to cheat as well as we.[18]

One marvels how the Epilogue of a tragedy can be as merry as this. However, Murphy's contemporaries were quite satisfied with his work. Oliver Goldsmith, who felt that Chinese literature did not show any imagination, can be considered to be a typical case. He thought that by Europeanizing the play, Murphy made it "more perfect," it may not be truly Chinese, but it was "entirely poetical." If being poetical means plentifulness of action, then Murphy's drama is indeed poetical, as the plot is concentrated on intrigue, torture and revenge. But, because of these factors, it has also become a conventional action drama painted in black and white. In addition, the Europeanization made the play seem improbable for a more knowledgeable audience who no longer subscribe to this brand of exoticism.

In Germany, the Yüan play did not catch the fancy of the writers until much later. Christoph Martin Wieland, one of the leading writers before Goethe, used the story of the orphan as the personal history of the protagonist Tifan in the novel *Der goldene Spiegel oder die Könige von Scheschian*, published in 1772.[19] Tifan's uncle has all his brothers and their families killed, only Tifan escaped death because Dschengis, the faithful vizier of his father, sacrificed his son for Tifan who ascends to the throne later without a revenge and becomes a model ruler who rules with virtue.[20] About a decade later, Goethe was also attracted by the Chinese orphan. As he belonged to the generation of Rousseau, he could not admit the Chinese source, so he disguised it with Greek names and titled his drama *Elpenor*. Between 1781 and 1783, he worked on it intermittently, but could only complete a little more than one act. In 1798, he sent the fragment to Friedrich Schiller as a classical example of misappropriation of subject matter. Schiller agreed with him that it was the product of a dilettante without knowing that it originated from Goethe. Schiller's confirmation sealed Goethe's lips, he never revealed the source of *Elpenor*. Goethe camouflaged his fragment so well that it took the Goethe scholarship nearly a century to identify the source.[21] In Goethe's play the king Lykus has his brother murdered and his son kidnapped. It is never explained what has happened to this child, but it is hinted that Lykus is rearing him as his own son. Antiope, the wife of the murdered brother, sees Elpenor, supposedly the son of Lykus, and immediately experiences maternal feelings towards him. Lykus gives her Elpenor to rear after she promises to make him her heir. She instills hate into him, making him promise to avenge her unhappy life caused by Lykus. The fragment ends when Elpenor is supposed to return to Lykus. Goethe could not continue the play probably because of the terrible impending revenge which is dramatic enough, but hardly in tune with his humanitarian inclinations. Even in his wildest Storm and Stress years, Goethe never preferred dramatic suspense to the representation of ideals. His heroes, such as Werther and Götz von Berlichingen, prefer their own death to killing others. Even Faust in his wildest moments does not kill intentionally. Since Goethe could not find a way to reconcile revenge with the ideals of humanitarianism, he was unable to complete the fragment. Besides, Goethe had already written other works of a related nature such as *Iphigenie auf Tauris* in which the title heroine, at the risk of her own life, exposes her intrigue—conceived by her brother—to Thoas, King of the Scythians. Like Voltaire's Idamé, Iphigenie converts the barbarian king to humanitarian values through her own virtue. However, here it is not the place to conduct a close examination.

Because of the implicit dramatic suspense and the strong emotions represented, the revenge of the orphan would be suitable for a Storm and Stress drama. However, Voltaire was rather the ridicule than the ideal of the generation of German writers who were profoundly influenced by Rousseau. However, the Chinese orphan at least did catch the attention of a contemporary of Goethe. The complete German adaptation of the Chinese orphan appeared anonymously in 1774 as *Der Chineser oder die Gerechtigkeit des Schicksals.*[22] However, this drama never had a chance to be recognized, for Germany was electrified by Goethe's *Die Leiden des Jungen Werther*, published in the same year. Moreover, *Der Chineser* was written in alexandrine which appeared to the contemporaries, who were waiting for a stormy and passionate language, as stilted and old-fashioned. The most important factor of all, however, was that China had already fallen out of favour. It was considered as the country of artificiality and falsehood. In addition, the drama is about court intrigues in which the citizenry have no part. These, in their turn, could not empathize with the characters like they did with Friedrich Schiller's *Kabale und Liebe*, published in 1784.

The plot of *Der Chineser* is not without its dramatic merits. The older mandarin Hantong is jealous of the present favorite of the emperor who commands the former to give the hand of his daughter Lilifa to the younger one in marriage. Hantong enlists the help of Kambul whom he brought up in his household and later procured for him the position of mandarinate to remove his rival Lanfu. He promises his daughter as reward, since he knows that they are deeply in love with each other. Because of being a virtuous person, Kambul is indecisive. However, Lilifa also beseeches him to think of their happiness. He falsifies a letter in the name of his rival and plays it into the hands of the emperor. The plot is successful, the emperor sends his late favorite a dagger, a piece of rope, and poison who has no choice but to commit suicide. Kambul succeeds his place as the favorite. At this moment, Kambul's dying father reveals to him that he is actually the orphan of the house of "Tschao," and Hantong was the murderer of his father. Kambul now plots revenge. He reveals to Hantong that the orphan of "Tschao" is still alive. At the very moment when the latter begs him to liquidate the orphan, Kambul kills him. At this very moment, Lilifa arrives at the scene. Torn between revenge and love, she kills the fiancée of the murderer, i.e., herself.

The playwright of *Der Chineser* had read Voltaire's version with care. Like the English adaptor Murphy, he disagrees with the French philosopher who claimed that the Chinese original lacked description of Chinese manners. The German playwright thought that the original plot was a typical Oriental story in which the virtue is rewarded and the vice punished. He also regrets that the Chinese play was against the rules of Aristotle. While Voltaire compared it to French drama of a century before, the German said it was like the German plays of thirty years ago. Since Murphy's adaptation also conforms, though stretching the time and place elements, to the three unities, we can be sure that all adaptors measured and improved the Chinese play according to Aristotle's poetics and, with the exception of Voltaire, also to Shakespeare, and all also improved on the described "Chinese way of life": Voltaire by injecting his brand of Confucian ethics, Murphy by showing there is no divine right of kings and that a tyrant must be overthrown, and the German playwright by exposing the so-called Oriental despotism. However, if we compare it with other German political and social dramas of the same period such as Gotthold Ephraim Lessing's *Emilia Galotti* (1771)[23] and Schiller's *Die Räuber* (1782), *Die Verschwörung des Fiesko zu Genoa* (1783), and *Kabale und Liebe* (1784), we cannot find a fundamental difference between Oriental and Occidental despotism. The only difference seems to be that Occidental monarchs sent assassins, while Oriental despots asked their subjects to kill themselves. Nevertheless, in the realm of imagination, Oriental despotism meant the worst kind of all generic absolutisms.

Within three decades, playwrights of three countries had adapted the Yüan play to their own needs. For Voltaire, his ideal absolutism governed by virtue and reason can be found in ancient China even if he had to idealize Genghis Khan in the process, while for Murphy the divine right of kings and virtue can coexist in a fictitious China ruled by the tyrant Genghis Khan. For the German anonymous late-comer, China degenerated into a stereotypical Oriental despotism in which virtue was asphyxiated before it could germinate. In this German play which has a potential, but unexploited Shakespearean plot and poor characterization, we can already anticipate the "sinophobia" of the nineteenth-century thinkers and writers led by Hegel.[24]

The European adaptations of *The Orphan of the House Chao* in eighteenth century was determined by the different perceptions of China of the authors. The individual temperament and preference, but also the collective consciousness which is in its turn formed by the perceived needs of the society, influences the conception of China. Thus this perception acts as a filtering agent, it re-shapes the received stimuli according to the pre-determined modality. The Jesuit missionaries created the first useful modality out of practical needs. If they wanted to succeed to christianize China, they had to know its "state religion." When their modality became known in Europe, the political and social thinkers remodelled it somewhat to fit their concept of a natural religion. The modality is perpetually in a dynamic process of change through the increased accumulation of stimuli and the material and spiritual needs of the European Society. The German philosophers Gottfried Wilhelm Leibniz's and Christian Wolff's enthusiasm for China was even more accentuated than Voltaire's: Leibniz suggested the sending of Chinese missionaries to Europe, and Voltaire was the last of the champions of sinophilism. Materialistic interests superseded idealistic ones. China was gradually re-shaped from an idealistic kingdom of wisdom into a backward country where vices and corruption prospered, especially because it stubbornly resisted any forms of European infiltration so that even Voltaire had harsh words for this distant country. By our analysis of the adaptations of the Yüan drama, we can also follow, to a certain extent, the development of this tendency as manifested in the variations of the same subject matter.

We have to skip time and space to study the adaptation of the same motif in Hong Kong, the confluence of many streams and currents. The Hong Kong playwright Li Chüeh-pen professed that from the European adaptations he read Arthur Murphy's.[25] As a Chinese writing a Chinese historical drama for a Chinese audience, he had to work within a different framework. It seems that one of his first tasks was to convince himself and his colleagues that a historical drama does not have to follow true historical events, that it can be fictitious. It had to be established first that even the recorded historical events were not equally reliable, some were obviously invented in later ages. It would be a worthwhile venture to examine the development of the story of the orphan from recorded historical events, enriched later by invented events which were at most semi-historical, to purely fictitious events which were in turn embellished and expanded by other fictitious events until there were several full-fledged dramas which were believed to be representing historical events by their audiences.[26] The dialectical relation between fiction and history can be illuminated by such an analysis.

From the account rendered by the playwright on the genesis of his play, it seems that he consulted the Yüan play, which we examined above to some extent, last. As a matter of fact, this Hong Kong play[27] bears some resemblance to the Ming play *Pa-yi chi* (Stories of the Eight Righteous Men) as it also records eight main events in eight different episodes or scenes, although only four righteous men are characters of this Hong Kong play, and an epilogue. These scenes are very close to what Bertolt Brecht calls *Bilder*, numbering them consecutively throughout the play, thus in the Hong Kong play Act II begins with Scene 4, Act III with Scene 5 etc. While the division of the play into five acts and an epilogue seems to conform very consciously to a tradition with Act III, the smuggling out of the infant, as the climax, the division of the play into eight or rather nine scenes (the Epilogue constitutes the ninth scene) follows the internal necessity of the play. The playwright did not seem to realize he was innovating the Chinese "spoken drama" imported from the West as opposed to its own indigenous operatic dramas.

Obviously the Hong Kong playwright is not following Brecht and his brand of epical drama, he makes it expressly clear that he wished to have nothing narrated, and everything enacted. It is even doubtful that Mr. Li had already heard of Brecht at that time, since the play was written and performed in 1964. He intended his play to be a theatre of illusion without adhering to the three unities. He did not even create a hero in the traditional sense of the word, but only a number of major characters. The playwright confessed that the most important character, the grandmother of the orphan, was deleted, because the actress playing the part suddenly withdrew from rehearsal owing to personal conflicts. Without her, the play has four model characters of whom two of them play the most important roles as they personify the two traditional Confucian virtues which the play is exemplifying. The first three scenes are devoted to Chao Tun, the grandfather of the orphan, a righteous, conscientious, faithful and fearless mandarin. He personifies the Confucian virtue *chung*, loyalty to the ruling family. His *chung* is so outstanding that the assassin sent by the corrupt mandarin would rather commit suicide than kill him. However, the prince listens to the corrupt mandarin and orders him killed. The result is the massacre of the whole household of over three hundred persons.

The second virtue to be extolled is *yi*, one's loyalty towards one's friends. The herbal doctor Ch'en Yin is a *men-k'e*, meaning literally "a guest of the gate," i.e., a guest who is fed and clothed by his host for years on end. Ch'en Yin is grateful to the family of Chao. When he sees that the corrupt mandarin is massacring the Chao household with a detachment of soldiers at the upper palace, he rushes to warn the son living at the lower palace. However, the son and his wife, a royal princess and eight months with child, refuse to flee. They map out a plan to save the child after the birth. That is in the fourth scene (the first in Act II) of the play. Thereafter Ch'en Yin appears in every single scene. He is the pivotal point of the play centring on the orphan, i.e., from Act II or Scene 4 onwards towards the end. He smuggles the infant out of the palace (Scene 5), he designs another scheme to sacrifice his own son as the corrupt minister is ordering all infants to be killed (Scene 6), he goes to the corrupt minister to denounce his friend, the other righteous person who is sacrificing his own life to carry out the scheme, who is supposedly harbouring the orphan (Scene 7), and when the orphan is grown up he reveals to him his true identity which eventually leads to the execution of the corrupt minister (Scene 8). Then we still have the Epilogue, which is obviously created for the sole benefit of Ch'en Yin. The *yi* of Ch'en Yin has come to the ears of the new ruler who wishes to appoint him an official of his court, Ch'en declines saying he has fulfilled his duty to the orphan, now he has to fulfil his other duty: he must join his friend, the co-conspirator of the plot who sacrificed his own life to save the orphan.

Even though the playwright insists that his play does not have a protagonist or that every character is a protagonist, it is obvious that both the structure and the content of the play highlight Ch'en Yin. Apart from the social position, he is in every way superior to the Minister Chao Tun, his benefactor. *Yü chung* or "stupid loyalty" to the ruler has always been a debatable virtue, especially when the ruler is addicted to personal pleasures at the expense of the lives and properties of the common people. After the republican revolution of 1911, it has become a dead virtue, the nation, regime and the party superseded the dynasty. Even though it is now still a political virtue in China, it has become more volatile with the dynamic political situation. For example, Japan, the national arch-enemy of China for a few decades, is now looked upon with admiration. Moreover, especially in Hong Kong, a British colony, *chung* has become an ambiguous virtue. However, *yi* remains as alive as ever. Moreover, it is a social virtue, it can be found and practised in all social situations and by people of all walks of life, even by persons as different as policemen and gangsters. With *hsiao*, filial piety, only applicable to an ever decreasing number of related generations, *yi* has emerged as the most important virtue, especially in Hong Kong. It seems that the Hong Kong playwright Li Chüeh-pen has subconsciously written a play to extol this Confucian virtue. Also dictated by the prevalent social values, the idea of personal revenge, according to which the orphan should kill the corrupt Minister with his own hands, is changed to justice rendered. However, the most extraordinary feat of Li is the dramatic form of his play which is a combination of epic and illusionary drama, a form which Peking and Shanghai only began to propagate after 1979 by emulating the theory and practice of Bertolt Brecht.[28]

We have analyzed the adaptations of *Chao-shih ku-erh* in different European countries in the course of the eighteenth century, with Goethe's fragment of 1781–1783 being the last of the adaptations. At the present moment, there is no bibliographical data available which would suggest there were other adaptations of a latter date in the Western countries. In comparison, the other Yüan play *Hui lan chi* (The Chalk Circle) took a different route, it aroused interest primarily in the twentieth century.[29] The ways of both Yüan plays suggest the life and re-incarnation of a subject matter or literary motif is determined by the ideological or psychological need of a specific time and place. *Chao-shih ku-erh* had and probably still has a special place in the Hong Kong society. Some version of it is still performed in Taiwan.[30] Relevant data about the same play in the area of the

Chinese mainland are not available at this moment. On the other hand, *Hui lan chi*, in the adaptation of Bertolt Brecht, was performed in China starting in 1985, but as an exotic drama taking place in Grusinia. Art indeed knows no national boundaries, but is determined by the ideological and psychological requirements of given peoples at given periods.

NOTES

1. Ch'en Shou-yi, *"The Chinese Orphan*: A Yüan Play. Its Influence on European Drama of the Eighteenth Century," in *T'ien Hsia*, III, No. 2 (September 1936), p. 89.

2. Ed. Horst von Tscharner published his thesis *China in der deutschen Dichtung* in Berlin in 1934, which he later incorporated in his monograph *China in der deutschen Dichtung bis zur Klassik* (München: Verlag von Ernst Reinhardt, 1939), while Ursula Aurich published her thesis *China im Spiegel der deutschen Literatur des 18 Jahrhunderts* in Berlin in 1935.

3. Ursula Aurich, *China im Spiegel der deutschen Literatur des 18 Jahrhunderts* (Nendeln/Liechtenstein: Kraus Reprint Limited, 1967), pp. 80–90; and Ed. Horst von Tscharner, op. cit., pp. 62–66 and 82f.

4. For a complete re-examination of Goethe's *Elpenor*, see the doctoral thesis of Erich Ying-yen Chung, *Chinesisches Gedankengut in Goethes Werk* (University of Mainz, 1977), especially pp. 195–203.

5. J. B. Du Halde, *Description ... de la Chine* (Paris, 1735), Part III, p. 342.

6. Ibid. Unable to find the translated version of the eighteenth century, I am supplying my own translation:

   "The Chinese tragedies are intermingled with songs during which the singing is often enough interrupted for reciting one or two sentences in a tone of ordinary declamation; we are shocked that an actor suddenly starts to sing in the middle of a dialogue, but one should pay attention that amongst the Chinese, the singing is often done to express certain strong emotional moments such as joy, pain, anger, despair; for example, a man who is angry with a villain, sings, another who is about to take revenge, sings, still another who is ready to commit suicide, sings."

7. *Œuvres complétes de Voltaire* (Paris: Imprimerie de P. Dupont, 1823), Théatre, tome troisiéme, p. 437.

8. Ibid., pp. 436f. The English translation reads as follows: "The more Germany improves, the more of our dramatic representation has it adopted. Those few places where they were not received in the last age are never ranked amongst the civilized nations." In *The Works of Voltaire*, translated by William F. Fleming (New York: The St. Hubert Guild, 1901), Vol. VIII, p. 177.

9.   Leo Jordan studied the three-act version in detail in *Voltaires Orphelin de la Chine in drei Akten*. Gesellschaft für Romanische Literatur, Band 33 (Dresden, 1913).

10. Ibid., p. 436.

11. Ibid., p. 438.

12. Ibid., p. 438. The English translation of Fleming reads as follows (op. cit., p. 179): "The Chinese, as well as the rest of the Asiatics, have stopped at the first elements of poetry, eloquence, natural philosophy, astronomy, and painting; all practiced by them so long before they were known to us. They began in everything much sooner than us, but made no progress afterwards; like the ancient Egyptians, who first taught the Greeks, and became at last so ignorant, as not even to be capable of receiving instruction from them.

     "These people, whom we take so much pains and go so far to visit; from whom, with the utmost difficulty, we have obtained permission to carry the riches of Europe, and to instruct them, do not to this day know how much we are their superiors; they are not even far enough advanced in knowledge to venture to imitate us, and don't so much as know whether we have any history or not."

13. For Voltaire's relationship to China, see Arnold H. Rowbotham, "Voltaire, Sinophile," *PMLA*, Vol. XLVII (1932), pp. 1050–65.

14. For information on William Hatchett's *The Chinese Orphan*, see Ch'en Shou-yi, op. cit., pp. 97ff.

15. Arthur Murphy, *"The Orphan of China*: A Tragedy," in *The British Drama: A Collection of the Most Esteemed Tragedies, Comedies, and Farces in the English Language* (London: Jones & Company, 1824), p. 1413.

16. Ibid., p. 1394.

17. Ibid., p. 1394.

18. Ibid., p. 1414.

19. The review is quoted in part by Ch'en Shou-yi, op. cit., p. 113.

20. Ursula Aurich discussed Wieland's novel to a certain extent in her thesis *China im Spiegel der deutschen Literatur des 18 Jahrhunderts* (Berlin, 1935), pp. 131–35.

21. Cf. the chapter on *Elpenor* in Erich Ying-yen Chung, *Chinesisches Gedankengut in Goethes Werk*, pp. 195–204.

22. Göttingen: Verlag bei Vietorinus Boßiegel, 1774.

23. Lessing's *Nathan der Weise* (1779) also uses an orphan-motif to emphasize humanitarian values.

24. Cf. "Die chinesische Religion oder die Religion des Maßes" and "Die orientalische Welt" by Georg Wilhelm Friedrich Hegel, reprinted in Adrian Hsia (ed.), *Deutsche Denker über China* (Frankfurt: Insel-Verlag, 1985), pp. 141–88. Hegel expanded on the views of Johann Gottfried Herder on China; cf. ibid., pp. 117–34.

25. Li Chüeh-pen, *Chao-shih ku-erh* (Hong Kong: Hua-chiao hsi-chü chu-pan-she, 1970), p. 158.

26. Cf. Mo Chien-p'u, *"Chao-shih ku-erh* k'ao cheng," in ibid., pp. 131–39, and Wu

Yeh-heng, "*Chao-shih ku-erh* nei-jung chi Yüan tsa-chü ts'an-k'ao chih-liao," in ibid., pp. 143–45.

27. At least there is another Hong Kong play written by Kung Te-hsin, titled *Shu*. However, it is not quite clear if it had been published or not. Cf. Li Yüan-hua, "Yü-chu *Chao-shih ku-erh* yen-ch'u ch'eng-kung," in ibid., pp. 140–43.

28. Cf. Adrian Hsia, "Bertolt Brecht in China and His Impact on Chinese Drama: A Preliminary Review," *Comparative Literature Studies*, Vol. 20, No. 3 (1983), pp. 231–45.

29. On the European adaptations of *The Chalk Circle*, cf. Adrian Hsia, "Die Eindeutschung des Kreidekreismotivs," in Ingrid Nohl (ed.), *Ein Theatermann, Theorie und Praxis* (Festschrift für Rolf Badenhausen) (München, 1977), pp. 131–42.

30. Cf. Erich Ying-yen Chung, op. cit., p. 203, note 272.

14. Bret Harte and Mark Twain's *Ah Sin*: Locating China in the Geography of the American West

James Moy

The grounds are so disposed as to disguise and to hide: something, always a body in some way. But also to disguise the act of hiding and to hide the disguise: the crypt hides as it holds. Carved out of nature, sometimes making use of probability or facts, these grounds are not natural.

—Derrida

Whoever sees Mr. Parsloe in this piece sees as good and as natural and consistent a Chinaman as he could see in San Francisco. I think his portrayal of the character reaches perfection…. The Chinaman is going to become a very frequent spectacle all over America, by and by, and a difficult political problem, too. Therefore it seems well enough to let the public study him a little on the stage beforehand.

—Mark Twain

In the nineteenth century, an emerging America struggled desperately for a sense of national identity. Towards this end American writers often contrasted the national ideosyncracies of its most recent immigrant population with those of the more established American community. This was particularly true of the popular theatre of the day which tended to hold representations of the latest immigrant group up for ridicule. The process of comparison had a socializing effect on the incoming immigrant population because its members, viewing the stereotypical representations on stage, could laugh at and deny any connection with the garish characterizations presented in the theatre while affirming their new allegiance to America. Accordingly, the British, the French, the German, the Irish and the Italian, each in turn were subjects for viciously humourous attacks before receding into the background to later emerge as central characters on the American stage.

Self-consciously serious literary attempts of the day, on the other hand, sought to offer democratically even handed, finely drawn, characterizations of both fully assimilated Americans and recently landed foreigners. Rarely did these two opposing tendencies (the popular and the literary) intersect. The focus of this study is one moment in which these two trajectories did intersect to create a space for representations of the Chinese in the geography of America's western states.

As most scholars will readily agree, both Mark Twain (1835–1910) and Bret Harte (1836–1902) are remembered as writers whose works display apparently heartfelt desire for accurate portrayals of life on America's western frontier.[1] In keeping with tendencies in the portrayals of other ethnic groups, the emergence of a play, especially by the likes of Mark Twain and Bret Harte, with a Chinese character in the title role would seem to suggest the assimilation of the Chinese into the mainstream of American life. From the outset it becomes all too obvious that this is not the case. While it is not entirely clear why the appearance of such a Chinese character on the American stage does not follow the pattern of other ethnic immigrant populations, it is hoped that an examination of the tensions which define the space of the Chinese character in the American west will result in a deeper understanding of the position occupied by the Chinese on America's western frontier.

Mark Twain and Bret Harte's *Ah Sin* opened in New York at Daly's Fifth Avenue Theatre on 31 July 1877, after preview performances at the National Theatre in Washington, D.C.[2] The plot is typically melodramatic, working to fulfil the expectations of late nineteenth-century American audiences. Both the *New York Times* and *The World* of 1 August 1877 printed generally favourable reviews of the piece. The *Times* review offered the following summary of the plot:

> It turns upon the rascality of one Broderick who all but murders Bill Plunkett—the champion liar of Calaveras—and then accuses York, a "gentleman miner" of the crime. Just as a committee of lynchers are about to act upon a verdict of guilty, Ah Sin fastens the guilt of the deed upon Broderick by the exhibition of the murderer's coat which Broderick thought he had long since done away with and Plunkett being subsequently brought into court safe and sound, the piece terminates happily.[3]

Significantly, while the title of the play is *Ah Sin*, it is clear from the plot summary that the title character serves not as a lead but merely as a plot advancing device towards the end of the piece. The character Ah Sin enters the text with much fanfare. But his entrance is almost unnoticed because he does so between major sweeps of narrative which establish Plunkett's position and Broderick villainy.[4] Ah Sin, then, at this moment in the text exists merely as a disruption in the narrative, serving as a mechanism for displacing or deflecting any potential serious content. He next appears as an absent presence not acknowledged when he secretly contrives to predetermine the outcome of a poker game in favour of his master.[5] In his first appearance as an active character in the play, Ah Sin agrees to actions which place him on the wrong side of the law.[6] While continually subjected to physical abuse, Ah Sin is treated with contempt as Broderick calls him a "slant eyed son of the yellow jaunders … you jabbering idiot … you moral cancer, you unsolvable political problem."[7]

" But the hands that were played | And the points that he made,
  By that Heathen Chinee,   Were quite frightful to see —

(Courtesy of the University of Wisconsin Libraries)

Clearly a marginal and substandard character, then, this position is reinforced throughout the piece. Miss Tempest describes him almost endearingly as one might describe a pet: "Don't mind him—don't be afraid … Poor Ah Sin is harmless—only a little ignorant and awkward." Mrs. Tempest complains that "When he shakes his head it makes me nervous to hear his dried faculties rattle." Indeed, as a "poor dumb animal, with his tail on top of his head instead of where it ought to be," Mrs. Tempest feels Ah Sin capable of at best mere imitation: "Well upon my word, this mental vacuum is a Chinaman to the marrow in one thing—the monkey faculty of imitating."[8] His lack of comprehension of American ways coupled with his desire to learn through imitation causes Ah Sin to fall victim to much comic business. When Mrs. Tempest drops a plate while setting the table, Ah Sin follows her lead and shatters a whole set of dinnerware.[9] Similarly, his inability to grasp American vernacular produces a comic situation when he is asked to show what he "picked up" while attending the theatre. Instead of singing the song he learned, Ah Sin displays the bric-a-brac he picked up from the floor of the theatre.[10]

Yet despite Judge Tempest's comment that "The imperturbability of these Chinamen is insufferable,"[11] it is not clear that the Chinese sought to be cast in the role of Other. In this play Ah Sin seeks continually to blend in only to find in his voice a strange counterpoint as all eyes in the silent room turn to him as if to question his right to participate.[12] In scenes of general conviviality when all present would shake hands, Ah Sin extends his only to be spurned.[13] Mark Twain proclaimed that "Whoever sees Mr. Parsloe in this piece sees as good and as natural and consistent a Chinaman as he could see in San Francisco. I think his portrayal of the character reaches perfection."[14] Generally speaking, newspaper critics of the day agreed with Mark Twain's assessment. One of these papers, however, called Ah Sin "a contemptible thief and an imperturbable liar."[15] Clearly, then, this constitution of the Chinese as a marginal Other was one created for and enforced by the American public. One whose fears were such that laws suppressing the Chinese were deemed necessary. Ah Sin reminds us "Chinaman evidence no good,"[16] and indeed since 1863 the Chinese had been forbidden the right to testify against whites in courts of law. Even the Burlingame Treaty of 1868 which allowed open emigration denied the Chinese the right of naturalization, to become American citizens. These and other similar laws effectively legislated the Chinese out of existence as legal entities, giving rise to the saying that to have a "Chinaman's chance" was to have no chance at all.[17]

Given the legal status of the Chinese, then, Ah Sin's participation in the play serves as a subversion of the existence, in the legal sense, of the Chinese character, but not one which promises a positive future. Throughout the play, Ah Sin's very presence serves as a subverting or displacing agent as the authors specify in the stage directions: "Ah Sin proceeds with his duties but is always in the way between the lovers at critical places."[18] Narrative actions must "pause" to allow for Ah Sin's entrance as his queue draws physical abuse to the Chinese character.[19]

In addition, it is significant to note that all of Ah Sin's appearances on stage are brief with the character almost always displaced into a peripheral position by the continuation of an interrupted sweep of narrative or driven from the stage altogether. While he is central to the closing tableaux for the end of each act of the play, all of these exciting visual moments are displaced into the space of void between acts. Indeed, it could be said that through Ah Sin the Chinese character seemed to disappear at the very moment of his depiction. Still, Ah Sin is constituted as body, a presence, though admittedly one whose appearances were brief and disruptive. Much is made of the impenetrability of the Chinaman, while York feels threatened by the laundryman's preoccupation with the "universal uncleanliness of the American people" and the Oriental countenance: "His face is as unintelligible as a tea chest."[20]

The inability to understand the Chinese reduced the Ah Sin character to the generalized John Chinaman of Bret Harte's earlier writings: "The expression of the Chinese face in the aggregate is neither cheerful nor happy.... There is an abiding consciousness of degradation, a secret pain or self-humiliation, visible in the lines of the mouth and eye.... They seldom smile, and their laughter is of such an extraordinary and sardonic nature— so purely a mechanical spasm, quite independent of any mirthful attribute—that to this day I am doubtful whether I ever saw a Chinaman laugh."[21] Harte described the typical Chinese face: "His complexion, which extended all over his head except where his long pig tail grew, was like a very nice piece of glazed brown paper-muslin. His eyes were black and bright, and his eyelids set at an angle of 15 [degrees]; his nose straight and delicately formed, his mouth small, and his teeth white and clean."[22] Later, Harte claims that despite the surface cleanliness, the Chinese "always exhaled that singular medicated odor—half opium, half ginger—which we recognized as the common 'Chinese smell.'"[23]

With "mechanical spasms" for laughter, a "Chinese smell," eyes at a fifteen degree angle, and "brown paper muslin skin," a generalized Chinese character such as Ah Sin became little more than an assemblage of fetishized fragments, comprising the most obvious aspects of difference. Accordingly, while provided with a presence on the stage, the Ah Sin character existed as an absence made complete by the addition of aspects which validated the Chinese character's marginality and foreignness. Visually, Ah Sin was constituted as an absent body within a loose fitting shapeless tunic which served to neutralize any potential male threat, or power. Wearing a conical hat, Ah Sin's hair was braided into a long queue to provide him with a "tail on top of his head instead of where it ought to be." In his essay entitled "John Chinaman," Harte describes the slippers worn beneath puffy pantaloons which were also a standard part of the Chinese character's dress: "To look at a Chinese slipper, one might imagine it impossible to shape the original foot to anything less cumbrous and roomy."[24] In action, he always displayed the "monkey faculty of imitating."[25]

Not all of Ah Sin's actions were mere imitation. Through close interrogation of the text, it becomes clear that his actions or inaction employed a radically different strategy. Rather than a character defined by his constructive activities and role within the play, Ah Sin serves as an absence suspended in tension, defined not by his actions but by his obliquely constituted parts. Rather than providing action, Ah Sin serves as an agent subversive to consistent narrative action. And even at the end of the piece when he produces the telling evidence, he ironically cannot testify himself but only serve as bearer of the information which in silence speaks more loudly than he can.

Devoid of a significant physical presence, the stage was filled by fetishized impressions of aspects of the Chinese without regard for the actual substance of body. Fragments ultimately stood in for the Chinese character which was absent from America's East coast. If the American audiences of the day had difficulty reading the face of the displaced/displacing Chinese character the task was made even more confusing by the use of a white player in the role of Ah Sin. Still, like Mark Twain, major newspaper critics praised Parsloe's portrayal: "Mr. Parsloe's Chinaman could be scarcely excelled in truthfulness to nature and freedom from caricature." The critic of *The World* felt the performance flawed but good: "Mr. Parsloe's Ah Sin is a creation. He happily steers clear between delineation of the comicality of the character and the burlesquing of it. His make-up is good, except that he looks too pale for a Chinaman, and his ambling walk is a trifle exaggerated, but he avoids turning the stupidity of Ah Sin into the fun-making silliness of the low comedians."[26] Indeed, it becomes clear that through Parsloe's portrayal of Ah Sin the Chinese character was not only doubly displaced but perhaps even erased from the map of American experience at the very moment of his depiction.

Clearly, neither Mark Twain nor Bret Harte had bargained for such a

MR. C. T. PARSLOE

AS

"AH SIN!"

(Courtesy of the University of Wisconsin Libraries)

subversive type of portrayal, but their play was likely doomed the moment the decision was made to collaborate on a project geared to the mass theatre audience. Stepping out of their normal roles as purveyors of contrived literary vernacular texts for a coterie readership, they achieved a new space at the intersection of the popular and the literary. But they failed to realize that the change in medium would radically impact on the way in which they could offer their characters:

> ... the plan is always to get some meaning across to keep the masses *within reason*; an imperative to produce meaning that takes the form of the constantly repeated imperative to moralise information: to better inform, to better socialise, to raise the cultural level of the masses, etc. Nonsense: the masses scandalously resist this ... they want spectacle ... they idolise the play of signs and stereotypes, they idolise any content so long as it resolves itself into a spectacular sequence. What they reject is the "dialectic" of meaning.[27]

Because audience market ultimately drives all emanations of the masses, it could be said that Mark Twain and Bret Harte's attempt at a representative portrayal of the Chinese was subverted by economic imperatives. Indeed, while Ah Sin cannot provide action in this play, it becomes amply clear that monetary exchange is its driving force. It is central to betting in dog fights and the innumerable poker games enacted throughout the play.[28] Among his few assertive actions in the play, Ah Sin overcomes his scruples regarding complicity in illegal actions when offered sufficient monetary return. Finding illegal activity lucrative, he later considers criminal action as a means of income over his "*wahsee washee*" business.[29] By play's end Ah Sin has accumulated over $11,000 and one-half interest in a gold mine, almost all achieved through shady dealings. In this regard, Miss Plunkett is perhaps the best spokesman for the eastern point of view regarding California: "This Californy's the land for me. I reckon there's no end of gold here, and fellows with loads of cash. Becky Simpson hadn't been in California a week till she married a hundred thousand dollars, with considerable of a man thrown in."[30] On another plane, the fetishization of the significance of money and its influence on the action of the play is a reflection of both Mark Twain and Bret Harte's expressed purpose in the writing of the play, the desire to make some money fast.[31] Their attempt, then, to transcend the conventions of the Chinese stereotype ultimately inscribes itself within the very conventions it sought to transcend, leaving the Chinese character suspended, unresolved, erased, but subject to the needs of economics.

Attempts to locate the Chinese within this space of absence (created by erasure) remain blocked by the self-reflexive nature of the masses and their entertainments. The reviewer for *The World* aptly noted that "The language used [in *Ah Sin*] is distinctly American ... and the incidents—the Heathen Chinese himself included—are American everyone."[32] Clearly, in America the only space in which the Chinese could comfortably reside was in the Imaginary. As constituted within the American legal system of the nineteenth century, a good Chinaman came to be defined as one who made no impact whatsoever, or as Ah Sin announced "Me not done nothing, me good Chinaman."[33] Mark Twain "pitied the friendless Mongol," and upon reflection offered a solution: "I wondered what was passing behind his sad face, and what distant scenes his vacant eye was dreaming of ... Money shall be raised—you shall go back to China—you shall see your friends again."[34] Indeed, finally aware of his position in the imaginary geography of the American west, the fictional Ah Sin character expresses his desire to absent himself, claiming that all he really wants is to "... catchee plenty golde, mally Ilish girl, go back to China ..."[35] This was precisely what many American politicians wanted the Chinese to do.

This rupture at the very site of representation, however, preserves an afterimage, a trace of the emergent image now voided of its contents, but maintained through power of the desire which engendered it. Existing within an ideologically enforced space of absence which demands to be filled, the trace provides sites for political manipulation, and the free play of the Imaginary. The dialectic movement between this absented image and the desire to see the Chinese, creates the self perpetuating place for the production of Orientalism.[36] In collaborating in the production of *Ah Sin* for the theatre, Mark Twain and Bret Harte had fallen into this place, a trap.

NOTES

1. For a summary treatment of Twain and Harte's careers see Margaret Duckett, *Mark Twain and Bret Harte* (Norman: University of Oklahoma Press, 1964).
2. Ibid., pp. 143–58.
3. *New York Times*, 1 August 1877, p. 5.
4. Mark Twain and Bret Harte, *Ah Sin*, ed. Frederick Anderson (San Francisco: Book Club of California, 1961), pp. 10–11. Hereafter referred to as *Ah Sin*. It should be noted that the manuscript of *Ah Sin* is in the Clifton Waller Barrett Library of

American Literature at the University of Virginia.

5. *Ah Sin*, pp. 19–22.

6. *Ah Sin*, pp. 24–26.

7. *Ah Sin*, pp. 10–11, 87.

8. *Ah Sin*, pp. 52–53.

9. *Ah Sin*, p. 52. In volume II (p. 130) of *Roughing It* (New York: Harper & Brothers, 1899), Mark Twain elaborates: "They do not need to be taught a thing twice, as a general thing. They are imitative. If a Chinaman were to see his master break up a center table, in a passion, and kindle a fire with it, that Chinaman would be likely to resort to the furniture for fuel forever afterward."

10. *Ah Sin*, p. 68.

11. *Ah Sin*, p. 33.

12. *Ah Sin*, pp. 83–84. The situation which Ah Sin finds himself in is remarkably similar to an encounter experienced by Bret Harte when he visited a Chinese theatre in San Francisco: "It was noticeable, however, that my unrestrained laughter had a discordant effect, and that triangular eyes sometimes turned ominously toward the 'Fanqui devil'; but as I retired discreetly before the play was finished, there were no serious results." Bret Harte, "John Chinaman," in *Writings of Bret Harte*, Standard Library Edition (Boston: Houghton Mifflin, 1896), 14:221.

13. *Ah Sin*, p. 86.

14. *The World: New York*, 1 August 1877, p. 5.

15. Ibid.

16. *Ah Sin*, pp. 69, 88.

17. For a summary treatment of this increasingly anti-Chinese legislation see Elmer Clarence Sandmeyer, *The Anti-Chinese Movement in California* (Urbana: University of Illinois Press, 1973).

18. *Ah Sin*, p. 54.

19. *Ah Sin*, pp. 78–79.

20. *Ah Sin*, p. 29.

21. Bret Harte, "John Chinaman," in *Writings of Bret Harte*, 14:220.

22. Bret Harte, "Wan Lee, The Pagan," in *Writings of Bret Harte*, 2:264.

23. Bret Harte, "See Yup," in *Writings of Bret Harte*, 16:144.

24. Bret Harte, "John Chinaman," in *Writings of Bret Harte*, 14:221.

25. *Ah Sin*, pp. 52–53.

26. *New York Times*, 1 August 1877, p. 5 and *The World: New York*, 1 August 1877, p. 5.

27. Jean Baudrillard, *In the Shadow of the Silent Majorities*, trans. Paul Foss, Paul Patton and John Johnston (New York: Semiotext(e), 1983), pp. 9–10.

28. The poker card player illustrations included with this essay come from a piece first published by Bret Harte in 1870. They provide an interesting visual intertext to nineteenth-century perceptions of the Chinese. Variously entitled "That Heathen

Chinee" and "Plain Language from Truthful James," the wily Ah Sin character in the piece wins at poker by cheating. It is curious that seven years later, Mark Twain and Bret Harte would remove this assertive activity from the play. Clearly, the Chinese presence on the American frontier was beginning to develop into an economic threat. Bret Harte, "Plain Language from Truthful James," in *Writings of Bret Harte*, 12:129–31.

29. *Ah Sin*, pp. 41, 50, 68.
30. *Ah Sin*, pp. 38–39.
31. Margaret Duckett, *Mark Twain and Bret Harte* (Norman: University of Oklahoma Press, 1964), pp. 119–58.
32. *The World: New York*, 1 August 1877, p. 5.
33. *Ah Sin*, pp. 32–33.
34. Mark Twain, "John Chinaman in New York," in *Sketches* (New York: Harper & Brothers, 1922), p. 278.
35. *Ah Sin*, p. 11.
36. Edward W. Said, *Orientalism* (New York: Random House, Inc., Vintage ed., 1979); Edward W. Said, "Orientalism Reconsidered," in *Literature, Politics & Theory: Papers from the Essex Conference 1976–84*, eds. Francis Barker, Peter Hulme, Margaret Iversen and Diana Loxley (London: Methuen, 1986), pp. 210–29; and *Reflections on Orientalism: Edward Said, Roger Bresnahan, Surjit Dulai, Edward Graham, and Donald Lammers*, ed. Warren I. Cohen (East Lansing: Michigan State University, Asian Studies Center, 1983).

Contributors

ALDRIDGE, A. OWEN, editor of *Comparative Literature Studies* and Professor Emeritus, Department of Comparative Literature at the University of Illinois at Urbana-Champaign.

CHANG, HAN-LIANG (張漢良) teaches English and Comparative Literature at National Taiwan University. He is the author of *Hsien-tai shih lun-heng* (Essays on Modern Chinese Poetry) and *Pi-chiao wen-hsüeh* (Theory and Practice of Comparative Literature).

FONG, GILBERT C. F. (方梓勳) received his Ph.D. in East Asian Studies from the University of Toronto, Canada, and taught at York University, Canada. He is now teaching in the Department of Translation at The Chinese University of Hong Kong.

HO, LOUISE S. W. (何少韻) is a poetess and teaches Shakespeare and Modern Poetry in the Department of English, The Chinese University of Hong Kong.

HSIA, ADRIAN (夏瑞春) is professor in the Department of German Language and Literature at McGill University, Canada.

HWANG, MEI-SHU (黃美序) is professor in the Department of Western Language and Literature at Tamkang University, Taiwan; he is the editor of *Tamkang Review*.

LAI, SHENG-CHUAN (賴聲川) received his Ph.D. in theatre studies from the University of California at Berkeley, and is the head of the Department of Drama and Theatre at the National Academy of Performing Arts, Taiwan.

Luk, Yun-tong (陸潤棠) is senior lecturer in the Department of English, The Chinese University of Hong Kong. He is the author of a book, *Film and Literature*.

Moy, James, former editor of *Theatre Journal*, is associate professor in the Department of Drama and Theatre at University of Wisconsin at Madison.

Sato, Toshihiko is professor of Languages and Literature in the Department of Languages and Literature at Virginia State University.

Sun, William Huizhu (孫惠柱) is a Ph.D. candidate in the Department of Drama and Theatre at the New York University; originally from Shanghai Institute of Drama, he is a playwright and critic.

Tam, Kwok-kan (譚國根) received his Ph.D. in Comparative Literature from the University of Illinois, and is teaching in the Department of English at The Chinese University of Hong Kong.

Wang, C. H. (王靖獻) is professor of Chinese and Comparative Literature at the University of Washington, Seattle. He is the author of *The Bell and the Drum: Shih-ching as Formulaic Poetry in an Oral Tradition*; *Ch' uan t' ung ti yü hsien-tai ti* (The Classical and the Modern); and *From Ritual to Allegory*.

Wei, Shu-chu (魏淑珠) teaches Chinese and Comparative Literature at Whitman College, Oregon; she is a Ph.D. candidate in Comparative Literature at the University of Massachusetts at Amherst.

Yung, Sai-shing (容世誠) is a Ph.D. candidate in the Department of Far Eastern Languages and Literature at Princeton University.